MW00713242

The Definitive Guide to iReport™

Giulio Toffoli

The Definitive Guide to iReport™

Copyright © 2007 by JasperSoft Corporation

All rights reserved. No part of this work may be reproduced or transmitted in any form or by any means, electronic or mechanical, including photocopying, recording, or by any information storage or retrieval system, without the prior written permission of the copyright owner and the publisher.

ISBN-13 (paperback): 978-1-59059-928-0

ISBN-13 (electronic): 978-1-4302-0523-4

Printed and bound in the United States of America (POD)

Trademarked names may appear in this book. Rather than use a trademark symbol with every occurrence of a trademarked name, we use the names only in an editorial fashion and to the benefit of the trademark owner, with no intention of infringement of the trademark.

JasperSoft, the JasperSoft logo, JasperAnalysis, JasperServer, JasperETL, JasperReports, JasperStudio, iReport, and Jasper4 products are trademarks and/or registered trademarks of JasperSoft Corporation in the United States and in jurisdictions throughout the world. All other company and product names are or may be trade names or trademarks of their respective owners.

Lead Editor: Steve Anglin
Editorial Board: Steve Anglin, Ewan Buckingham, Gary Cornell, Jonathan Gennick,
 Jason Gilmore, Jonathan Hassell, Chris Mills, Matthew Moodie, Jeffrey Pepper,
 Ben Renow-Clarke, Dominic Shakeshaft, Matt Wade, Tom Welsh
Project Manager: Kylie Johnston
Copy Editor: Ami Knox
Assistant Production Director: Kari Brooks-Copony
Production Editor: Laura Esterman
Compositor: Molly Sharp
Proofreader: Elizabeth Berry
Indexer: Brenda Miller
Artist: April Milne
Cover Designer: Kurt Krames
Manufacturing Director: Tom Debolski

Distributed to the book trade worldwide by Springer-Verlag New York, Inc., 233 Spring Street, 6th Floor, New York, NY 10013. Phone 1-800-SPRINGER, fax 201-348-4505, e-mail orders-ny@springer-sbm.com, or visit http://www.springeronline.com.

For information on translations, please contact Apress directly at 2855 Telegraph Avenue, Suite 600, Berkeley, CA 94705. Phone 510-549-5930, fax 510-549-5939, e-mail info@apress.com, or visit http://www.apress.com.

The information in this book is distributed on an "as is" basis, without warranty. Although every precaution has been taken in the preparation of this work, neither the author(s) nor Apress shall have any liability to any person or entity with respect to any loss or damage caused or alleged to be caused directly or indirectly by the information contained in this work.

The source code for this book is available to readers at http://www.apress.com in the Source Code/Download section.

To my wonderful wife, Caterina

Contents at a Glance

Contents

Foreword

In the early days of JasperReports™ development, users had to manually edit report template files, and the only visual tool to help them see what they were doing was the built-in report design preview tool.

Of course, JasperReports, as a content-rendering library, was, and still is, mainly a developer tool that provides reporting functionality to Java™ applications that need it. Developers are used to working with source code files and XML, so not having a visual tool at the time did not prevent them from downloading JasperReports and using it right away.

But as things moved forward and JasperReports provided new features to its users, it soon became apparent there was a need for more advanced tools that would simplify report design work and make it more enjoyable.

I started to work on such a tool myself at the time and realized that the complexity of the project and the effort required would probably distract me from what I was doing on JasperReports. I decided to not take up this challenge of creating a visual designer for JasperReports and continued to concentrate on the report engine.

Fortunately, Giulio Toffoli came to the rescue, and within a relatively short time he was able to put together a very useful and intuitive visual designer for creating and testing report templates. This was a major boost to the JasperReports community in general, and the iReport™ designer quickly became the most popular GUI tool for JasperReports.

Since then, things have moved along swiftly, with Giulio making sure that iReport continues to evolve and keeps pace with JasperReports, always being up-to-date and supporting the newest features that were added to the reporting engine.

Things got even better back in 2005, when the iReport project joined the JasperReports project and both became core components in what we now know as the JasperSoft® Business Intelligence Suite. This suite is a comprehensive set of tools for integrated reporting, analysis, and data integration. In addition to JasperReports and iReport, the suite includes JasperServer™, a high-performance business intelligence and report server; JasperAnalysis™, an OLAP engine; and JasperETL™, a ready-to-run data integration platform.

The JasperSoft Business Intelligence Suite began as a complete open source reporting and BI solution. Today, JasperSoft offers both open source and professional versions of the suite. The professional version includes JasperStudio™, the professional edition of iReport.

Nowadays, iReport is not only a simple visual report designer. It is a complete and integrated reporting tool that offers various services including report preview in all JasperReports export formats, data connectivity, wizards, and support for visually designing charts and crosstabs. It is also the report designer for JasperServer and Jasper4Salesforce™, with which it interacts through one of its easy-to-use plug-in modules.

Not only has Giulio done a great job creating iReport and making it the popular and very useful tool it is today, but he has also done an amazing job documenting it. This book is a complete reference to all iReport functionality and features and helps you get a quick start with reporting, even without being familiar with the JasperReports engine. With iReport and its documentation, Giulio helped making JasperReports useful to a wider audience, not only to Java developers. I hope you'll enjoy this book as much as I have enjoyed working with Giulio all these years.

Teodor Danciu
Founder and architect of JasperReports, JasperSoft

About the Author

GIULIO TOFFOLI is a senior software engineer at JasperSoft Corporation, where he serves as the iReport project leader. He has been developing Java applications since 1999 and founded the iReport project in 2001. During this time, Giulio has enjoyed designing complex software architectures and implementing custom software solutions with a focus on desktop and multi-tiered, web-based, client-server applications using Java (J2EE/JEE) and open source technologies. Giulio has a degree in computer science from the University of Bologna and currently resides in Italy.

Acknowledgments

iReport contains code and ideas from many people. Though I run the risk of forgetting somebody, I would like to thank the following people for their contribution to this project: Teodor Danciu, Alexander, Andre Legendre, Craig B. Spengler, David Walters, Egon R. Pereira, ErtanO, G. Raghavan, Heiko Wenzel, Kees Kuip, Octavio Luna, Peter Henderson, Vinod Kumar Singh, Wade Chandler, Erica Pastorello, and all reviewers. A special thanks goes to Kristen Kelleher from JasperSoft and all the Apress guys for the amazing job done for the latest release of this book.

Introduction

iReport is an open source program that can create complex reports which can use every kind of Java application through the JasperReports library. It is written in 100% pure Java and is distributed with source code according to the GNU General Public License. JasperStudio is the professional edition of iReport; it is essentially the same application, but is commercially supported by JasperSoft Corporation and released as part of the JasperSoft Business Intelligence Suite, a comprehensive set of tools for integrated reporting, analysis, and data integration. In addition to JasperStudio, the suite is comprised of JasperServer, a high-performance business intelligence and report server; JasperAnalysis, an OLAP engine to drill down and slice and dice data; and JasperETL, a ready-to-run data integration platform providing data extract-transform-load (ETL) capabilities.

Through an intuitive and rich graphic interface, iReport lets you rapidly create any kind of report very easily. iReport enables engineers who are just learning this technology to access all the functions of JasperReports as well as helping skilled users to save a lot of time during the development of very elaborate reports.

This guide refers to the 2.0.0 version of iReport, but a great portion of this information is directly applicable to earlier versions; my commitment is to keep this guide as up-to-date as possible with future iReport versions.

Features of iReport

The following list describes some of the most important features of iReport:

- 100% support of JasperReports XML tags.
- WYSIWYG editor for the creation of reports. It has complete tools for drawing rectangles, lines, ellipses, text fields, labels, charts, subreports, and bar codes.
- Built-in editor with syntax highlighting for writing expressions.
- Support for Unicode and non-Latin languages (Russian, Chinese, Japanese, Korean, etc.).
- Browser for document structure.
- Integrated report compiler, filler, and exporter.
- Support for all databases accessible by JDBC.
- Virtual support for all kinds of datasources.
- Wizard for creating reports automatically.
- Support for subreports.
- Backup feature of source files.
- Support for document templates.
- TrueType fonts support.
- Support for localization.
- Extensibility through plug-ins.

- Integrated support for scriptlets.
- Support for charts.
- Management of a library of standard objects (e.g., numbers of pages).
- Drag-and-drop functionality.
- Unlimited undo/redo.
- Wizard for creating crosstabs.
- Styles library.
- Docking system.

The iReport team is composed of many skilled and experienced programmers who come from every part of the world. They work daily to add new functionalities and fix bugs.

iReport Community

The iReport web site is at http://ireport.sourceforge.net. If you need help with iReport, there is a discussion forum in English: http://www.jasperforge.org/index.php?option=com_joomlaboard&Itemid=215&func=showcat&catid=9. This is the place where you can send requests for help and technical questions about the use of the program, as well as post comments and discuss implementation choices or propose new functionalities. There is no guarantee for a prompt reply, but requests are usually satisfied within a few days' time. This service is free. If you need information concerning commercial support, you can write to sales@jaspersoft.com.

Please report bugs at the following address: http://jasperforge.org/sf/tracker/do/listArtifacts/projects.ireport/tracker.bugs.

In the project site, there is a system to send requests for enhancement (RFE). There is also the ability to suggest patches and integrative code.

All members of the iReport team keep in serious consideration all suggestions, criticism, and advice coming from iReport and JasperStudio users.

Downloading the Code

The source code for this book is available to readers at http://www.apress.com in the Downloads section of this book's home page. Please feel free to visit the Apress web site and download all the code there. You can also check for errata and find related titles from Apress.

CHAPTER 1

■ ■ ■

Getting Started

In this chapter, you'll see what the requirements are for using iReport, the way to obtain the binary distribution and the sources, and how to compile and install it.

Requirements

iReport needs Sun Java 2 SDK 1.5 or newer; in order to compile report scriptlets, it is necessary to install the complete distribution of Java 2 (Java SE Development Kit, or JDK), not only a runtime environment (Java Runtime Environment, or JRE). If you want to compile iReport sources, you should install Jakarta Ant version 1.6 or newer.

As for hardware, like all Java programs, iReport eats a lot of RAM, and so it is necessary to have at least 256MB of memory and about 20MB of free space on disk.

Downloading iReport

It is possible to download iReport from the iReport project page on SourceForge where you can always find the last released iReport distribution (`http://sourceforge.net/projects/ireport`). Four different distributions are available:

`iReport-x.x.x.zip`: This is the official binary distribution in ZIP format.

`iReport-x.x.x.tgz`: This is the official binary distribution in TAR GZ format.

`iReport-x-x-x-src.zip`: This is the official distribution of sources in ZIP format.

`iReport-x.x.x-windows-installer.exe`: This is the official Win32 installer.

`x.x.x` represents the version number of iReport. Every distribution contains all needed libraries from third parties necessary to use the program and additional files, such as templates and base documentation in HTML format.

Accessing Source Code

If you want a more up-to-date version of sources, you can directly access the SVN repository. In this case, it is necessary to have an SVN client (my favorite is Tortoise SVN). If you don't have one, you need to create an account on `http://jasperforge.org/sf/projects/ireport` in order to access the repository.

■**Caution** iReport source code is no longer available on SourceForge CVS server.

The URL of the SVN repository of iReport is `http://scm.jasperforge.org/svn/repos/ireport/trunk/iReport2`.

Compiling iReport

The distribution with sources contains a `build.xml` file that is used by Jakarta Ant to compile and start iReport and/or to create different distributions of the program.

Download `iReport-x.x.x-src.zip`, unzip it into the directory of your choice, for example, `c:\devel` (or `/usr/devel` on a Unix system). Open a command prompt or a shell, go to the directory where the archive was uncompressed, go to the iReport directory, and enter

```
C:\devel\iReport-2.0.0>ant iReport
```

The sources, which stay in the `src` directory, will be compiled into the `classes` folder, and iReport will start immediately.

Setting Up the Start and Base Configuration

If you preferred downloading the binary version of iReport, uncompress the downloaded archive into the directory of your choice, for example, `c:\devel` (or `/usr/devel` on a Unix system). Open a command prompt or a shell, go to the directory where the archive was uncompressed, go to the iReport directory, and enter

```
C:\devel\iReport-2.0.0>iReport.bat
```

or on Unix:

```
$ ./iReport.sh
```

(In this case, it should be preceded by a `chmod +x` if the file is not executable.)

The Windows Installer and iReport.exe

Starting from version 1.2.3, iReport provides a Windows installer created using NSIS, the popular tool from Nullsoft (`http://nsis.sourceforge.net/Main_Page`).

To install iReport, double-click `iReport-x.x.x-windows-installer.exe` to bring up the screen shown in Figure 1-1.

Click Next, review the license agreement as shown in Figure 1-2, and click I Agree if you accept the terms.

Figure 1-1. *iReport Setup Wizard—Step 1*

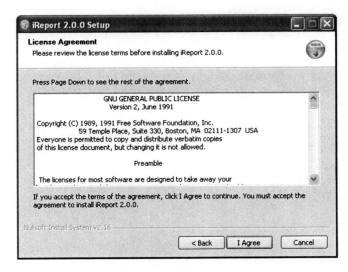

Figure 1-2. *iReport Setup Wizard—Step 2*

iReport can be installed with and without the source code, as shown in Figure 1-3. If you want to install the sources too, you can follow the instructions about how to compile iReport as discussed earlier in the section "Compiling iReport."

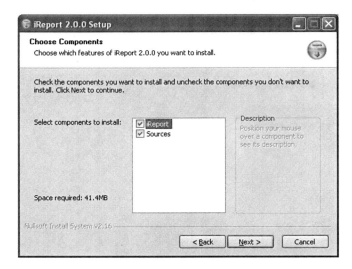

Figure 1-3. *iReport Setup Wizard—Step 3*

At the end of the installation process, you get a new menu item in the program files menu (for instance, on a Windows system, Start ➤ All Programs ➤ JasperSoft ➤ iReport-*x.x.x*).

You can have more than one version of iReport installed on your machine at the same time, but all these versions will share the same configuration files.

The installer creates a shortcut to launch iReport, linking the shortcut to iReport.exe (present in the program home directory); this Win32 binary version is really a wrapper created using JSmooth (http://jsmooth.sourceforge.net/). From iReport 1.2.5 on, the executable created by JSmooth is able to automatically load all JAR files located in the lib directory.

■**Caution** If you experience some problems like ClassNotFound exceptions using iReport.exe, try using iReport.bat instead.

First iReport Execution

On the first execution, iReport will create a directory named .ireport in the user's home directory. Here the personal settings and the configuration of the program are saved. If it is not possible to create this folder, this could cause undesirable effects in the program, and it may not be possible to save the configuration files. In this case, it could be necessary to create the directory manually.

■**Note** Before proceeding to the program configuration, it is necessary to copy the tools.jar file, normally present in the lib directory of Sun JDK, into the iReport lib directory. The absence of this file can produce some exceptions during the compilation of a report (carried out by using classes contained in this Java library). On Mac OS X, the tools.jar file does not exist, but there is a classes.jar file, which contains the required classes to compile.

The iReport initial configuration consists of setting up the programs to run for viewing the produced documents according to their file formats, selecting the language to use, and indicating where to store compiled files. Other configuration settings will be explained subsequently. In order to proceed to the configuration, run iReport and select Options ➤ Settings to bring up the window shown in Figure 1-4.

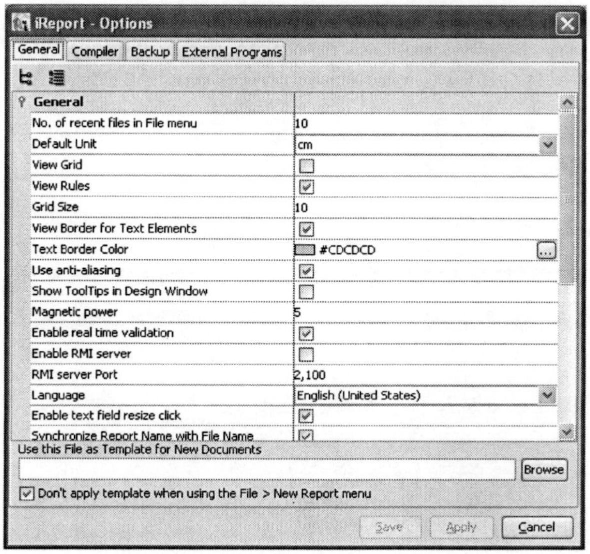

Figure 1-4. *Options window—General options*

Select the language you prefer and go to the Compiler tab, shown in Figure 1-5.

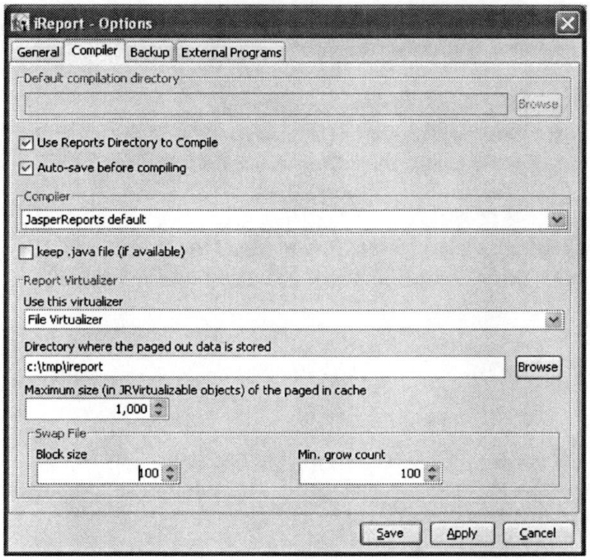

Figure 1-5. *Options window—Compiler options*

In the Compiler tab, you can set where iReport stores JASPER files that are compiled. By default, iReport uses the current directory as the destination for compiled files. Often it is useful to specify a particular directory for saving compiled files; this directory is usually the same one in which the source of the report is located. In this case, check the Use the reports directory for compiles check box.

In this tab, you can also set a specific compiler to use. JasperReports provides different ways to compile your report. The current JasperReports default compiler is the JDT Compiler. If you use the Java compiler (javac), you need to have the tools.jar file in your classpath (you can find this file in your JDK).

I suggest you use the default compiler (JDT). Using this compiler, iReport will be able to point you to errors using clickable items in the Problems tab (see Figure 1-6).

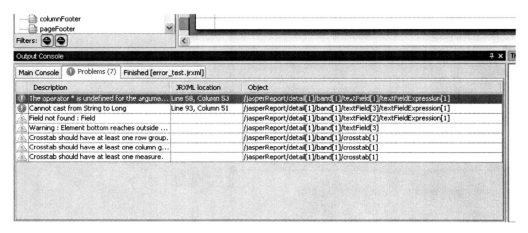

Figure 1-6. *Clickable errors produced using the JDT compiler*

If Groovy is used as the language for expression, a special compiler is used instead of the one specified.

See Chapter 19 for details on the other options present in the Compiler tab.

Complete the configuration by going to the External Programs tab and specifying the external programs to use with different output formats of reports and the editor to use for modifying XML source (see Figure 1-7).

Restart iReport to set all chosen options.

Test the configuration by creating a new blank report (select File ➤ New Document) and confirming all features proposed for the new report. Then click the Run button on the toolbar, shown here:

If everything is OK, you will be prompted to save the report in a JRXML file, and a corresponding JASPER file will be created and a preview of a blank page will appear. This means that iReport has been installed and configured correctly.

Figure 1-7. *Options window—External Programs options*

Creating a JDBC Connection

The most common datasource for filling a report is typically a relational database. Next, you will see how to set up a JDBC connection in iReport. Select Data ➤ Connections/Datasources and click the New button in the window with the connections list. A new window will appear for the configuration of the new connection (see Figure 1-8). Select Database JDBC connection and click Next. In the new frame, shown in Figure 1-9, enter the connection name (e.g., "My new connection") and select the right JDBC driver. iReport recognizes the URL syntax of many JDBC drivers. You can automatically create the URL by entering the server address and database name in the corresponding boxes and clicking the Wizard button. To complete the connection configuration, enter the username and password for access to the database. If you want to save the password, select the Save password check box.

Figure 1-8. *Creating a JDBC connection*

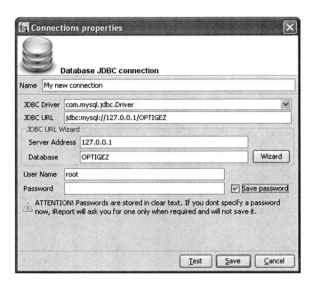

Figure 1-9. *Specifying the properties for a JDBC connection*

Test the connection by clicking the Test button. It is better to test the connections before saving and using them.

iReport is shipped with only the JDBC driver for the MySQL database and the HSQL database engine (HSQLDB). If during the test there is a ClassNotFound error, it is possible that there is no JAR archive (or ZIP) in the classpath that contains the selected database driver. Without closing iReport, copy the JDBC driver into the lib directory and retry; the new JAR will be automatically located and loaded by iReport. In Chapter 9, I will explain extensively all the configuration modalities of the datasources.

At the end of the test, click the Save button to store the new connection.

In this way, you have created a new datasource, so you have to tell iReport to use it as a predefined datasource. Select Data ➤ Connections/Data Sources and then specify the new datasource. The new connection will be automatically considered the active connection.

In general, to set the active connection, you can use the drop-down list in the main iReport toolbar (see Figure 1-10).

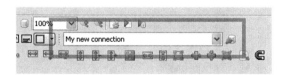

Figure 1-10. *Specifying a JDBC connection*

Another way is by selecting Data ➤ Set Active Connection to bring up the dialog box shown in Figure 1-11.

Figure 1-11. *List of the available datasources*

Then select your connection from the list and click the OK button. From now on iReport will use this connection for every operation that needs access to the database (in particular the acquisition of the fields selected through SQL queries and prints creation).

Creating Your First Report

Now that you have installed and configured iReport, and prepared a JDBC connection to the database, you will proceed to create a simple report using the *Report Wizard*.

For it and for many other following examples, you will use HSQLDB, a small relational database written in Java and supplied with a JDBC driver. To be able to use it, copy the hsqldb.jar file into the lib directory (this file is the database driver, and it is already present in all the iReport distributions from version 0.3.2). In order to know more about this small jewel, please visit the HSQLDB project site at this address: http://hsqldb.sourceforge.net.

In order to set up the database connection used in this example, use the parameters listed in Table 1-1.

Table 1-1. *Connection Parameters*

Properties	Value
Name	Northwind
JDBC Driver	org.hsqldb.jdbcDriver
JDBC URL	jdbc:hsqldb:c:/devel/northwind/northwind
Username	sa
Password	

When the password is blank, as in this case, remember to select the Save password check box when configuring the connection.

Select File ➤ Report Wizard. This loads a tool for the step-by-step creation of a report, starting with a query insertion (see Figure 1-12).

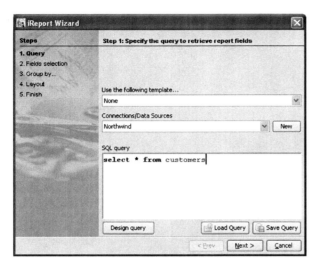

Figure 1-12. *Report Wizard—query insertion*

In the text area, insert a SQL query in order to select data that will go to fill your report, for example:

```
select * from customers order by country
```

and click Next. The clause "order by" is important to the following choice of the grouping (I will discuss the details a little later). iReport will read the fields of the customers table, and it will present them in the next screen of the Report Wizard, as shown in Figure 1-13.

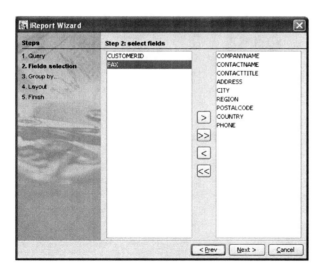

Figure 1-13. *Report Wizard—report fields selection*

Select the fields you wish to include and click Next. Now that you have selected the fields to put in the report, you will be prompted to choose what fields you wish to group by, if any (see Figure 1-14).

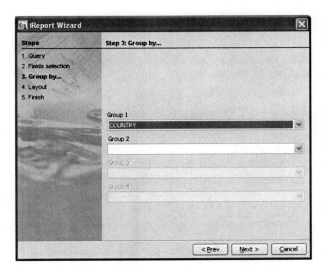

Figure 1-14. *Report Wizard—groupings*

Using the wizard, it is possible to create up to four groups. Others can be defined afterwards. (In fact, it is possible to set up an arbitrary number of groupings.)

For this first report, define a simple grouping on the COUNTRY field, as shown in Figure 1-14.

The next step of the wizard allows you to select the print *template*, which is a model that can be used as the base for the creation of the report (see Figure 1-15). With iReport, some very simple templates are supplied, and you will see how to create some new ones. For the moment, it is enough to know that there are two types of templates: the *tabular* templates, in which every record occupies one line like in a table; and the *columnar* templates, in which the fields of the report are displayed in columns.

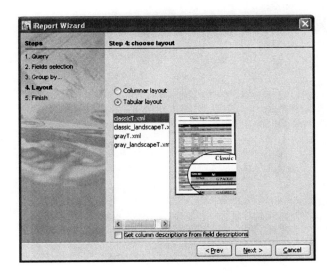

Figure 1-15. *Report Wizard—choosing a template*

For your first report, select a tabular template, preferably the classicT one (here, "T" stands for tabular).

After you have chosen the template, click Next. The last screen of the wizard will appear, and it will tell you the outcome of the operation. Click Finish to create the report, which will appear in the iReport central area, ready for execution, as shown in Figure 1-16.

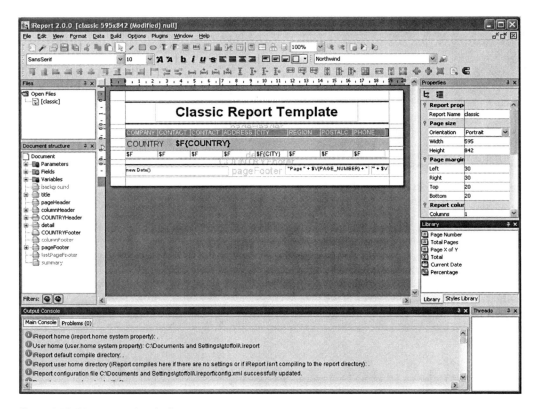

Figure 1-16. *iReport main window*

Before being able to execute the final print, you will have to save the report source created through the wizard and compile it. These operations can be done all at once by clicking the Run report using a connection button, shown here, that is on the toolbar:

After you click the Run report using a connection button, you will be asked for the name under which to save the file. Save the file with the name report1.jrxml. In the *console*, which is in the part below the main window, some messages will appear. They will tell you about what is happening: the report will be compiled, created, and finally *exported* (see Figure 1-17).

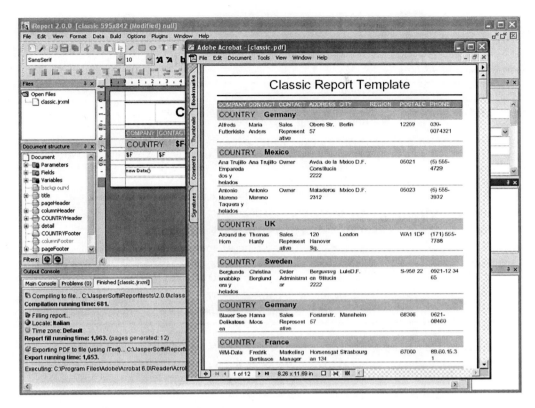

Figure 1-17. *Your first report in PDF format*

At the end of the operation, if everything is OK, the report will be shown in the default program for opening PDF files. The PDF format is the predefined format of export.

Specifying Startup Command-Line Options

It is possible to specify some startup parameters on the command line. These parameters are not case sensitive. They can be truncated so long as they remain unambiguous. For example, the option -ireport-home can be specified as -i because no other option starts with the letter "i," and therefore the command-line interpreter will successfully interpret -i as the truncation of the -ireport-home option.

The Boolean options can be specified using both the contracted form -option and the extensive form -option=true or -option=false according to necessity.

It is possible to obtain the options list by entering

```
iReport.bat -?
```

or

```
./iReport.sh -?
```

Table 1-2 explains the different available options. It refers to the iReport 2.0.0 version, and it may not be complete regarding successive versions.

Table 1-2. *Command-Line Options*

Option	Description
-beanClass *<className>*	Shows the specified class in the Bean Datasource tab (in the query editor window).
-config-file *<fileName>*	Specifies the file name for loading an alternate configuration. The file is never changed from iReport, which will save an eventual modified configuration in the canonical directory, that is, the user home /.ireport.
-embedded	Avoids application exit when the main window is closed.
-ireport-home *<dir>*	Specifies the program directory.
-no-splash	Avoids showing the splash window at startup.
-temp-dir *<dir>*	Specifies the directory where temporary files will be saved.
-user-home *<dir>*	Specifies the user home. The predefined directory is the one stored into the user.home system property.
-version	Outputs the version immediately.
-webstart	Specifies that iReport will use a Java Web Start–friendly class loader.

If Ant is used, it is not possible to specify these options directly from the command line, but it will be necessary to modify the build.xml file by adding the <arg> tags useful to the Java task that runs iReport.

CHAPTER 2

■■■

Basic Notions of JasperReports

The heart of iReport is an open source library named *JasperReports* (JR), developed and maintained by Teodor Danciu, of JasperSoft Corporation. It is the most widely distributed and powerful free software library for report creation available today.

In this chapter, I will illustrate JasperReports' base concepts for a better understanding of how iReport works.

The JasperReports API, the XML syntax for report definition, and all the details for using the library in your own programs are documented very well in *The Definitive Guide to JasperReports* by Teodor Daniciu, Lucian Chirita, Sanda Zaharia, and Ionut Nedelcu (Apress, 2007). Other information and examples are directly available on the official site at http://jasperreports.sourceforge.net.

Unlike iReport, which is distributed according to the GPL license, JasperReports is issued with the LGPL license, which is less restrictive. This means that JasperReports can be freely used on commercial programs without buying very expensive software licenses and without remaining trapped in the complicated net of open source licenses. This is fundamental when reports created with iReport have to be used in a commercial product; in fact, programs only need the JasperReports library to produce print reports, which works as something like a runtime.

Without the right commercial license (available upon request), iReport can be used only as a development tool, and it cannot be part of a program that is not distributed with the GPL license.

Understanding the Report Life Cycle

The report life cycle is very similar to that of a Java class. In Java, this is described by a source file, that is, a file with a .java extension, written according to its language rules. The source is compiled through the *compiler*, creating a *class* file with a .class extension. When the class is used, it is loaded into memory and instanced by the Java interpreter; during execution, the attributes will be emphasized.

Similarly, a report is described by a source file, in XML format, as defined by the DTD (jasperreport.dtd version 1.3.4 is listed in Appendix B). As of library version 0.5.3, the official extension of these source files has become .jrxml (i.e., *JasperReports XML*), replacing the generic .xml extension. These source files are compiled to create a *JASPER* file (with the .jasper extension), which is a kind of predefined report, exactly like a class file is (or represents) for an instance of an object in Java. The JASPER file is loaded in a runtime by your application. It is joined to records coming from a datasource in order to create a print, which can be *exported* in the desired format (e.g., PDF or XLS).

Therefore, it is possible to define two distinct action groups: those that have to be executed during the development phase (design and planning of the report, and compilation of a JASPER file source), and those that have to be executed in a runtime (loading of the file and production of the print).

JRXML Sources and Jasper Files

The report layout definition is contained in a text file in the form of an XML document defined by jasperreport.dtd. This source file is defined by a series of sections, some of them concerning the report's physical characteristics, such as the dimension of the page, the positioning of the fields, and the height of the bands; and some of them concerning the logical characteristics, such as the declaration of the parameters and variables, and the definition of a query for the data selection.

Simplifying a lot, it is possible to outline the sections of a JRXML source, as follows:

```
Report main characteristics
Property (0,+)
Import (0,+)
Global font (0,+)
Parameters (0,+)
Query [SQL//HQL/XPATH/..] (0,1)
Fields (0,+)
Variables (0,+)
Groups (0,+)
     Group header
          Group header elements (0,+)
     Group footer
          Group footer elements (0,+)
Predefined bands
     Predefined bands elements
```

Listing 2-1 shows an example of a JRXML file.

Listing 2-1. *A Simple JRXML File Example*

```xml
<?xml version="1.0" encoding="ISO-8859-1"  ?>
<!-- Created with iReport - A designer for JasperReports -->
<!DOCTYPE jasperReport PUBLIC "//JasperReports//DTD Report Design//EN" ➥
"http://jasperreports.sourceforge.net/dtds/jasperreport.dtd">
<jasperReport
        name="untitled_report_1"
        columnCount="2"
        printOrder="Vertical"
        orientation="Portrait"
        pageWidth="595"
        pageHeight="842"
        columnWidth="266"
        columnSpacing="0"
        leftMargin="30"
        rightMargin="30"
        topMargin="20"
        bottomMargin="20"
        whenNoDataType="NoPages"
        isTitleNewPage="false"
        isSummaryNewPage="false">
    <property name="ireport.scriptlethandling" value="2" />
    <queryString><![CDATA[select * from customers]]></queryString>
    <field name="CUSTOMERID" class="java.lang.String"/>
    <field name="COMPANYNAME" class="java.lang.String"/>
        <background>
            <band height="0"  isSplitAllowed="true" >
            </band>
        </background>
```

```xml
<title>
    <band height="46"  isSplitAllowed="true" >
        <staticText>
            <reportElement
                mode="Opaque"
                x="145"
                y="6"
                width="245"
                height="34"
                forecolor="#000000"
                backcolor="#FFFFFF"
                key="element-1"
                stretchType="NoStretch"
                positionType="FixRelativeToTop"
                isPrintRepeatedValues="true"
                isRemoveLineWhenBlank="false"
                isPrintInFirstWholeBand="false"
                isPrintWhenDetailOverflows="false"/>
            <textElement textAlignment="Center" verticalAlignment="Top"
                    rotation="None" lineSpacing="Single">
                <font fontName="Arial" pdfFontName="Helvetica" size="24"
                    isBold="false" isItalic="false" isUnderline="false"
                    isPdfEmbedded ="false" pdfEncoding ="Cp1252"
                    isStrikeThrough="false" />
            </textElement>
        <text><![CDATA[This is the title]]></text>
        </staticText>
    </band>
</title>
<pageHeader>
    <band height="0"  isSplitAllowed="true" >
    </band>
</pageHeader>
<columnHeader>
    <band height="0"  isSplitAllowed="true" >
    </band>
</columnHeader>
<detail>
    <band height="19"  isSplitAllowed="true" >
        <textField isStretchWithOverflow="false" pattern=""
                isBlankWhenNull="false" evaluationTime="Now"
                hyperlinkType="None" >
            <reportElement
                mode="Opaque"
                x="1"
                y="1"
                width="264"
                height="18"
                forecolor="#000000"
                backcolor="#FFFFFF"
                key="element-2"
                stretchType="NoStretch"
                positionType="FixRelativeToTop"
                isPrintRepeatedValues="true"
                isRemoveLineWhenBlank="false"
                isPrintInFirstWholeBand="false"
                isPrintWhenDetailOverflows="false"/>
```

```
                        <textElement textAlignment="Left" verticalAlignment="Top"
                                rotation="None" lineSpacing="Single">
                            <font fontName="Arial" pdfFontName="Helvetica" size="10"
                                isBold="false" isItalic="false" isUnderline="false"
                                isPdfEmbedded ="false" pdfEncoding ="Cp1252"
                                isStrikeThrough="false" />
                        </textElement>
                    <textFieldExpression
                        class="java.lang.String">
                            <![CDATA[$F{COMPANYNAME}]]></textFieldExpression>
                    </textField>
                </band>
            </detail>
            <columnFooter>
                <band height="0"  isSplitAllowed="true" >
                </band>
            </columnFooter>
            <pageFooter>
                <band height="0"  isSplitAllowed="true" >
                </band>
            </pageFooter>
            <summary>
                <band height="0"  isSplitAllowed="true" >
                </band>
            </summary>
</jasperReport>
```

Figure 2-1 shows the print result from the example in Listing 2-1. In reality, the code of this listing, produced with iReport, is much more long-winded than necessary. This is because iReport does not produce optimized code (e.g., omitting attributes with predefined default values).

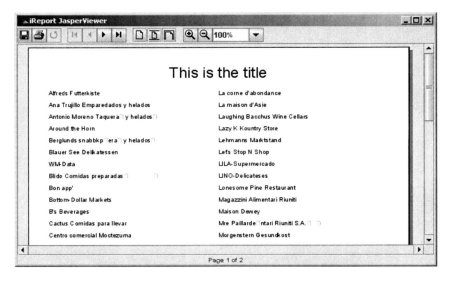

Figure 2-1. *Print resulting from Listing 2-1*

Reducing the XML code, however, would not change the report's final result or execution speed.

During compilation (done through some JasperReports classes) of the JRXML file, the XML is parsed and loaded in a JRBaseReport object. JRBaseReport is a rich data structure that allows you to represent the exact XML contents in memory. All of the parsed expressions are loaded, and the Java class source is produced. This source, which extends the JRCalculator, is compiled by means of a normal Java compiler, and the class created on disk is loaded as a byte buffer. Starting from the initial JRBaseReport, a JasperReport class is instanced (it extends the JRBaseReport class), and the JRCalculator class byte buffer, previously loaded, is stored in a compileData field of this new class. The JasperReport class that you have obtained is serialized into the JASPER file, which is then ready for loading at any given time.

The JasperReports speed is due to all of the report's formulas being compiled into Java native bytecode and the report structure verified during compilation, not runtime.

Datasources and Print Formats

Without the possibility of filling a report through some dynamically supplied data, the most sophisticated and appealing report would be useless.

JasperReports allows you to specify fill data for the print in two different ways: through parameters and datasources, which are presented by means of a generic interface named JRDataSource, as shown in Figure 2-2.

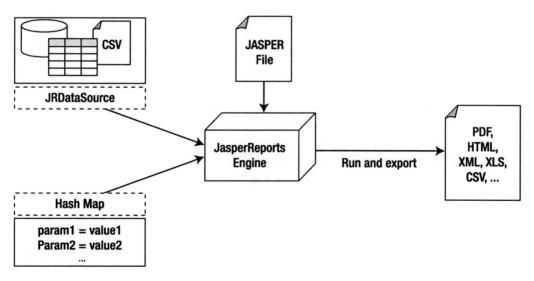

Figure 2-2. *Datasources and parameters in the creation flux of a report*

Chapter 9 is dedicated to datasources, where it is explained how they can be used in iReport and how it is possible to define custom datasources (in case those supplied with JasperReports are not right for your requirements). The JRDataSource allows a set of records that are organized in tables (rows and columns) to be read.

Instead of using an explicit datasource to fill in a report, JasperReports is able to do so through a JDBC connection (already instanced and opened) to whichever relational database you wish to run a SQL query on (which is specified in the report).

If the data (passed through a datasource) is not sufficient, or if it is necessary to specify particular values to condition its execution, it is possible to produce some name/value couples to "transmit" to the print motor. These couples are named *parameters*, and they have to be "declared" in advance in the report. Through the fillManager, it is possible to join a JASPER file and a datasource in a JasperPrint object. This object is a metaprint that can create a real print after having been *exported* in the desired format through appropriate classes that implement the JRExporter interface.

JasperReports puts at your disposal different predefined *exporters* like those for creating files in such formats as PDF, XLS, CVS, XML, and HTML. Through the JRViewer class, it is possible to view the report directly on the screen and to print it.

Compatibility Between Versions

When a new version of JasperReports is distributed, usually some classes change. These modified classes typically define the report structure. So in order to avoid conflicts among reports that are compiled with libraries of different versions, JasperReports associates a SerialVersion (in reality it is inherited from the JasperReport class) with every compiled JASPER file, which identifies the exact library version used for the compilation. If you execute a print loading a JASPER file that has a SerialVersion different from the one supported by your chosen library, an error will occur (at least for reports compiled with a version of JR prior to 1.1.0). The error may be similar to the following:

```
java.io.InvalidClassException:
    net.sf.jasperreports.engine.base.JRBaseReport;
    local class incompatible: stream classdesc serialVersionUID = 406,
    local class serialVersionUID = 600
net.sf.jasperreports.engine.JRException: Error loading object from InputStream
Caused by: java.io.InvalidClassException:
    net.sf.jasperreports.engine.base.JRBaseReport;
    local class incompatible: stream classdesc serialVersionUID = 406,
    local class serialVersionUID = 600
```

However, the "old" report sources can be compiled with newer library versions than those the sources were first compiled with: this is because the newer versions usually introduce only new tags that are not compulsory, without modifying the XML's general structure.

The migration from one JasperReports version to another one is substantially painless, and it can quickly be executed thanks to the iReport plug-in named *massive compiler*, which allows you to carry out a massive compilation of all reports within a directory structure, keeping a safety copy of the already existing JASPER files. (I will talk more about the *massive compiler* in Chapter 17.)

■**Caution** Starting from JasperReports 1.1.0, you are no longer required to recompile the reports to use them with a newer version of the library.

Report Expressions

All of the formulas in JasperReports are defined through *expressions*. An expression is a Java instruction that has an object as a result.

Following are some examples of expressions:

- `"This is an expression"`
- `new Boolean(true)`
- `new Integer(3)`
- `(($P{MyParam}.equals("S")) ? "Yes" : "No")`

These expression examples are nonvalid:

- `3 + 2 * 5`
- `true`
- `(($P{MyParam} == 1) ? "Yes" : "No")`

In particular, the first and the second expressions are not valid because they are of a primitive type (int in the first case and boolean in the second case). The third expression is not valid because it assumes that the MyParam parameter is a primitive type and that it can be compared through the == operator with an int, but this is not true. (I will explain the $P{...} syntax shortly.)

The expression return type is determined by the context. For example, if the expression is used to determine the moment when an element has to be printed, the return type will be Boolean. Similarly, if you write the expression that underlines a numerical field, the return type will be an Integer or a Double.

Within the expression, you can refer to the parameters, variables, and fields, which are defined in the report using the syntax summarized in Table 2-1.

Table 2-1. *Syntax for Referring to Report Objects*

Syntax	Description
$F{*name_field*}	Specifies the *name_field* field ("F" means field)
$V{*name_variable*}	Specifies the *name_variable* variable
$P{*name_parameter*}	Specifies the *name_parameter* parameter
$P!{*name_parameter*}	A special syntax used in the report SQL query to indicate that the parameter does not have to be treated as a value to transfer to a prepared statement, but that it represents a little piece of the query

Fields, variables, and parameters always represent objects (they can assume the null value) and their type is specified at the moment of their declaration. After JasperReports version 0.6.2, a new type $R{*name_resource*} syntax was introduced. It is used for the localization of strings (I will talk about these more in Chapter 10, which is dedicated to the subject of internationalization).

Often an expression can be insufficient for defining the return object. For example, if you want to print a number in Roman numerals or give back the name of the weekday in a particular data, it is possible to transfer the elaborations to an external class method, which is declared as static, as follows:

```
MyFormatter.toRomanNumber( $F{MyInteger}.intValue() )
```

toRomanNumber is a MyFormatter class static method, which takes an int as a unique item (the conversion from Integer to int is done by means of the intValue() method) and gives back the Roman version of a number in a string.

This technique can be used for many aims, for example, to extrapolate the text of a CLOB field or to add a value into a HashMap parameter. This operation cannot be executed by means of a simple expression.

Using Groovy As a Language for Expressions

Starting from JasperReports 0.6.6, Java is no longer the only language available to write expressions. In fact, this version introduced a way to use languages different from Java; JasperReports supports new expressions written using the Groovy language.

Groovy is a full language for the Java 2 Platform: this means that inside the Groovy language you can use all classes and JARs available for Java.

Table 2-2 compares some typical JasperReports expressions written in Java and in Groovy.

Table 2-2. *Groovy and Java Samples*

Expression	Java	Groovy
Field	$F{*field_name*}	$F{*field_name*}
Sum of two double fields	new Double($F{*f1*}.doubleValue() + $F{*f2*}.doubleValue())	$F{*f1*} + $F{*f2*}
Comparison of numbers	new Boolean($F{*f*}.intValue() == 1)	$F{*f*} == 1
Comparison of strings	new Boolean($F{*f*} != null && $F{*f*}.equals("test"))	$F{*f*} == "test"

The following is a correct Groovy expression:

```
new JREmptyDataSource($F{num_of_void_records})
```

JREmptyDataSource is a class of JasperReports to generate on the fly a set of empty records (without all fields set to null). You can see how you can instance this class (a pure Java class) in Groovy without any problem.

Groovy opens the doors of JasperReports to all people who don't know Java.

A Simple Program Using JasperReports

I finish this introduction to JasperReports by presenting an example of a simple program (Listing 2-2) that shows how to produce a PDF file from a JASPER file using a special datasource named JREmptyDataSource. JREmptyDataSource is a kind of empty datasource. The test.jasper file, which the example refers to, is the compiled version of Listing 2-1.

Listing 2-2. *JasperTest.java*

```
import net.sf.jasperreports.engine.*;
import net.sf.jasperreports.engine.export.*;
import java.util.*;

public class JasperTest
{
```

```java
public static void main(String[] args)
{
    String fileName = "/devel/examples/test.jasper";
    String outFileName = "/devel/examples/test.pdf";
    HashMap hm = new HashMap();

    try
    {
        JasperPrint print = JasperFillManager.fillReport(
                fileName,
                hm,
                new JREmptyDataSource());

        JRExporter exporter =
                new net.sf.jasperreports.engine.export.JRPdfExporter();

        exporter.setParameter(
                    JRExporterParameter.OUTPUT_FILE_NAME,
                    outFileName);
        exporter.setParameter(
                    JRExporterParameter.JASPER_PRINT,print);

        exporter.exportReport();
        System.out.println("Created file: " + outFileName);
    }
    catch (JRException e)
    {
        e.printStackTrace();
        System.exit(1);
    }
    catch (Exception e)
    {
        e.printStackTrace();
        System.exit(1);
    }
}
}
```

■ ■ ■

Report Structure

In this chapter, you will learn about report structure; you will see which parts compose a report and how they behave in comparison with data to print.

Document Sections (Bands) Overview

A report is defined by means of a *type* page. This is divided into different horizontal portions named *bands*. When the report is joined with the data generating the print, these sections are printed many times according to their function (and according to the rules that the report author has set up). For instance, the page header is repeated at the beginning of every page, while the detail band is repeated for every single record.

The type page is divided into nine predefined bands to which new groups are added (see Figure 3-1). In addition, iReport manages a heading band (group header) and a recapitulation band (group footer) for every group.

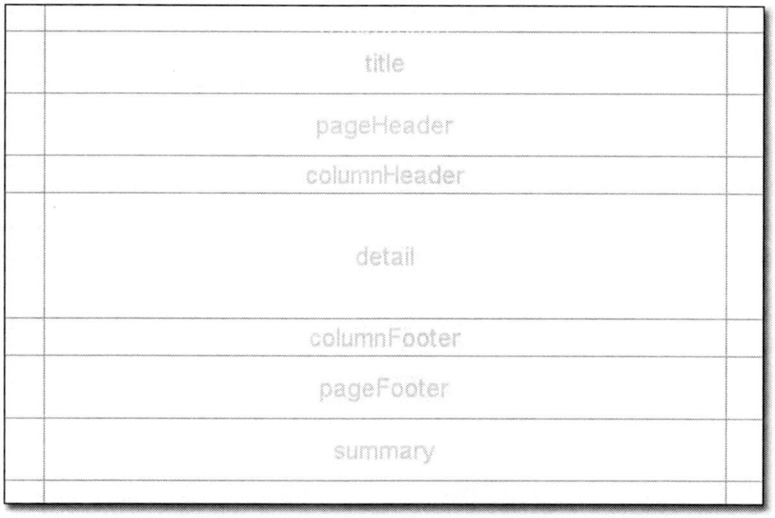

| title |
| pageHeader |
| columnHeader |
| detail |
| columnFooter |
| pageFooter |
| summary |

Figure 3-1. *Predefined bands of a document. (The background and the last page footer bands are not shown.)*

A band is always as wide as the page width (right and left margins excluded). However, its height, even if it is established during the design phase, can vary during the print creation according to the contained elements; it can "lengthen" toward the bottom of a page in an arbitrary way. This typically occurs when bands contain subreports or text fields that have to adapt to the content vertically. Generally, the height specified by the user should be considered "the minimal height" of the band. Not all bands can be stretched dynamically according to the content, in particular the column footer, page footer, and last page footer bands.

The sum of all band heights (except for the background) has to always be less than or equal to the page height minus the top and bottom margins.

The following text briefly outlines each of the predefined bands plus the bands for groups.

Title

The *title* band is the first visible band. It is created only once and can be printed on a separate page. Regarding the allowed dimensions, it is not possible during design time to exceed the report page height (top and bottom margins are included). If the title is printed on a separate page, this band height is not included in the calculation of the total sum of all band heights, which has to be less than or equal to the page height, as mentioned previously.

Page Header

The *page header* band allows you to define a page header. The height specified during the design phase usually does not change during the creation process (except for the insertion of vertically resizable components, such as text fields that contain long text and subreports). The page header appears on all printed pages in the same position defined during the design phase. Title and summary bands do not include the page header when printed on a separate page.

Column Header

The *column header* band is printed at the beginning of each detail column. (The column concept will be explained in the "Columns" section later in this chapter.) Usually, labels containing the column names of a tabular report are inserted in this band.

Group Header

A report can contain zero or more group bands, which permit the collection of detail records in real groups. A *group header* is always accompanied by a *group footer* (both can be independently visible or not). Different properties are associated with a group. They determine its behavior from the graphic point of view. It is possible to always force a group header on a new page or in a new column and to print this band on all pages if the bands below it overflow the single page (as a page header, but at group level). It is possible to fix a minimum height required to print a group header: if it exceeds this height, the group header band will be printed on a new page (please note that a value too large for this property can create an infinite loop during printing). (I will discuss groups in greater detail in Chapter 7.)

Detail

A *detail* band corresponds to every record that is read by the datasource that feeds the report. In all probability, most of the print elements will be put here.

Group Footer

The *group footer* band completes a group. Usually it contains fields to view subtotals or separation graphic elements, such as lines.

Column Footer

The *column footer* band appears at the end of every column. Its dimensions are not resizable at run time (not even if it contains resizable elements such as subreports or text fields with a variable number of text lines).

Page Footer

The *page footer* band appears on every page where there is a page header. Like the column footer, it is not resizable at run time.

Last Page Footer

If you want to make the last page footer different from the other footers, it is possible to use the special *last page footer* band. If the band height is 0, it is completely ignored, and the layout established for the common page will also be used for the last page. This band first appeared in JasperReports version 0.6.2.

Summary

The *summary* band allows you to insert fields concerning total calculations, means, or whatever you want to insert at the end of the report. In other systems, this band is often named "report footer."

Background

The *background* band appeared for the first time in JasperReports version 0.4.6. It was introduced after insistent requests from many users who wanted to be able to create watermarks and similar effects (such as a frame around the whole page). It can have a maximum height equal to the page height.

Specifying Report Properties

Now that you have seen the individual parts that comprise a report, you will proceed to creating a new one. Click the following button:

or select New Document from the File menu to open the Report properties dialog box (see Figure 3-2). Here you will fill in the report properties. This window is recallable anytime by selecting Report properties from the Edit menu.

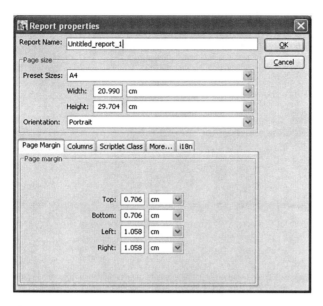

Figure 3-2. *Report properties*

You can also select the Document node in the document structure panel to view the report properties in the property sheet panel.

The first property is the report name. It is a logical name, independent from the source file's name, and is used only by the JasperReports library (e.g., to name the produced Java file, a report is compiled).

The page dimensions are probably the report's most important properties. A list of standard measures is presented. The unit of measurement used by iReport and JasperReports is the *pixel* (which has a resolution of 75 dpi, or dots per inch). However, it is possible to specify report dimensions using units of measurement that are more common, such as centimeters, millimeters, or inches.

Table 3-1 lists the standard measures and their dimensions in pixels. Because the dimensions management is based on pixels, some rough adjustments can take place when viewing the same data using different units of measurement.

Table 3-1. *Standard Print Formats*

Page Type	Dimensions in Pixels
LETTER	612×792
NOTE	540×720
LEGAL	612×1008
A0	2380×3368
A1	1684×2380
A2	1190×1684
A3	842×1190
A4	595×842
A5	421×595
A6	297×421

Page Type	Dimensions in Pixels
A7	210×297
A8	148×210
A9	105×148
A10	74×105
B0	2836×4008
B1	2004×2836
B2	1418×2004
B3	1002×1418
B4	709×1002
B5	501×709
ARCH_E	2592×3456
ARCH_D	1728×2592
ARCH_C	1296×1728
ARCH_B	864×1296
ARCH_A	648×864
FLSA	612×936
FLSE	612×936
HALFLETTER	396×612
11X17	792×1224
LEDGER	1224×792

By modifying width and height, it is possible to create a report of whatever size you like. The page orientation options, Landscape or Portrait, in reality are not meaningful, because the page dimensions are characterized by width and height independent of the sheet orientation. However, this property can be used by certain report exporters.

The page margin dimensions are set by means of the four options on the Page Margin tab.

The remaining options in the Report properties dialog box warrant more detailed discussion. First, I want to talk a bit about the concept of columns before discussing the options available on the Columns tab. Then I will show you the advanced options available through the Scriptlet Class, More, and i18n tabs.

Columns

As you have seen, a report is divided into horizontal sections: bands.

The page, one or more of which make up a report, presents bands that are independent from the data (such as the title or the page footers) and other bands that are printed only if there are one or more data records to print (such as the group headers and the detail band). These last sections can be divided into vertical columns in order to take advantage of the available space on the page.

In this context, the concept of a column can be easily confused with that of a *field*. In fact, a column does not concern the record fields, but it does concern the detail band. This means that if you have a record with ten fields and you desire a table view, ten columns are not needed. However, the elements will have to be placed correctly to have a table effect. Ten columns will result when long record lists (that are horizontally very narrow) are printed.

To illustrate how to set up columns in your reports, following are two examples. The first demonstrates how to set up the values for a single-column report on an A4 sheet. Take a look at

Figure 3-3, which shows the Columns tab in the Report properties dialog box with settings for a single-column report.

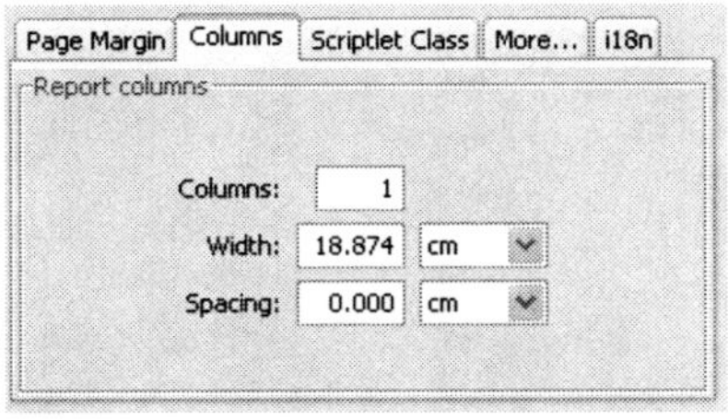

Figure 3-3. *Settings for a single column report*

The number of columns is 1, and its width is equal to the entire page, except for the margins. The space between columns is not meaningful in this case, so it is left at zero, the default.

Figure 3-4 shows how the page settings from Figure 3-3 will appear in the document pane.

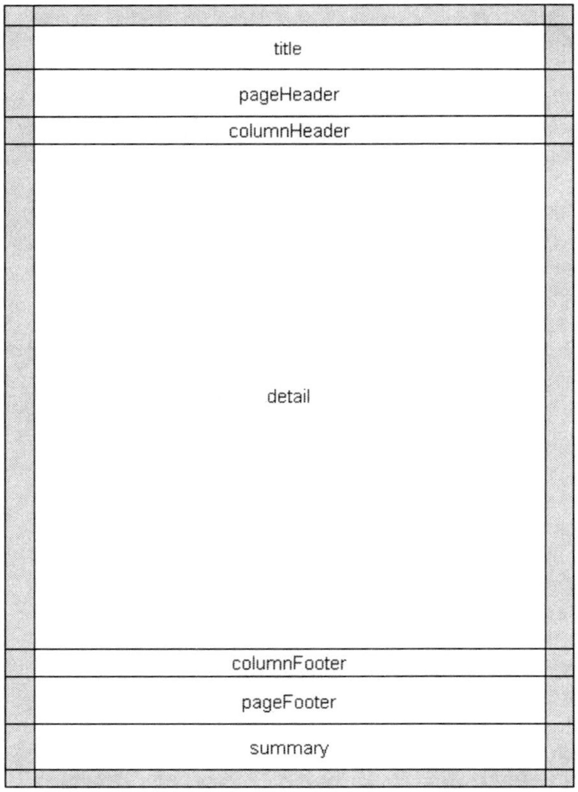

Figure 3-4. *Structure of a single-column report*

As you can see in Figure 3-5, most of the page is not used. If multiple columns are used, this report would look better. Figure 3-6 shows the dimensions used for a two-column report.

Figure 3-5. *Result of a single-column print*

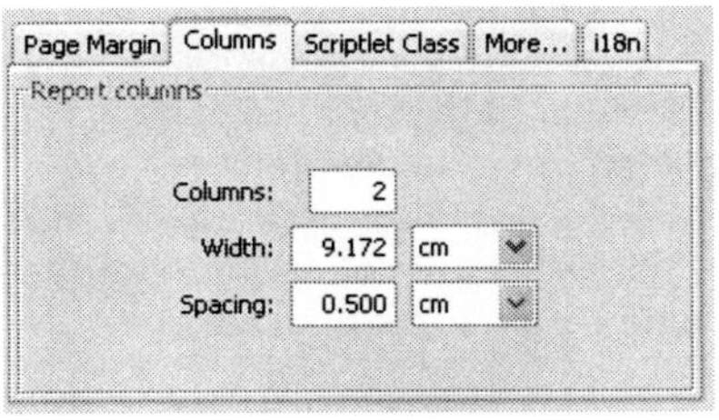

Figure 3-6. *Settings for a two-column report*

In this case, in the Columns field you enter 2 to specify the number of columns you want. iReport will automatically calculate the maximum column width according to the margins and to the page width. If you want to increase the space between the columns, just increase the value of the Spacing field.

Figure 3-7 shows a the layout of a report with three columns separated by some blank space.

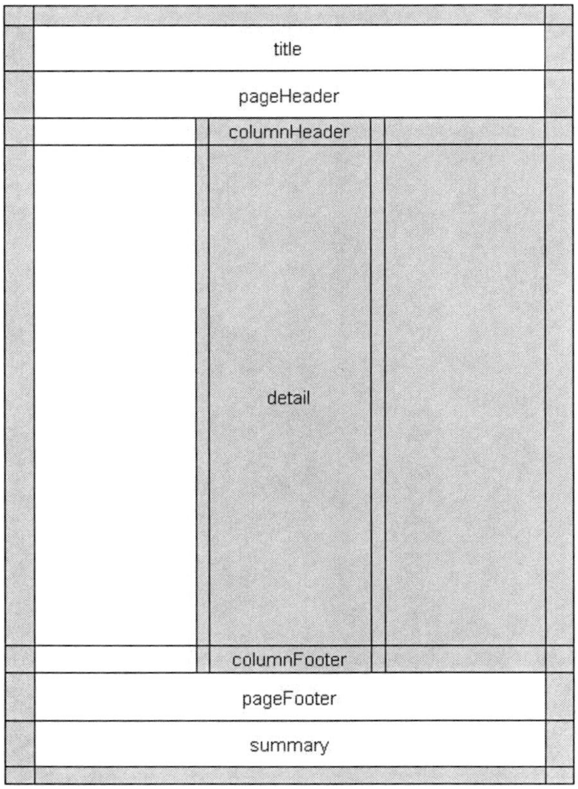

Figure 3-7. *Structure of a three-column report*

Multiple columns, as shown in Figure 3-8, are commonly used for prints of very long lists (for example, a phone directory). Functionally, it is important to remember that when you have more than one column, the width of the detail band and of linked bands is reduced to the width of the columns.

The sum of the margins, column widths, and space between columns has to be less than or equal to the page width. If this condition is not met, the compilation can result in error.

In Figures 3-5 and 3-7, the useful page areas for setting the report elements (fields, images, etc.) are highlighted in white. The parts that you cannot use, such as margins and columns following the first one (which have to be considered as though they were a continuation of the first) are highlighted in gray.

2 columns

Alfreds Futterkiste	La corne d'abondance
Ana Trujillo Emparedados y helados	La maison d'Asie
Antonio Moreno Taquera y helados	Laughing Bacchus Wine Cellars
Around the Horn	Lazy K Kountry Store
Berglunds snabbkpera y helados	Lehmanns Marktstand
Blauer See Delikatessen	Let's Stop N Shop
WM-Data	LILA-Supermercado
Blido Comidas preparadas	LINO-Delicateses
Bon app'	Lonesome Pine Restaurant
Bottom-Dollar Markets	Magazzini Alimentari Riuniti
B's Beverages	Maison Dewey
Cactus Comidas para llevar	Mre Paillardentari Riuniti S.A.
Centro comercial Moctezuma	Morgenstern Gesundkost
Chop-suey Chinese	North/South
Comrcio Mineirooctezuma	Ocano Atintico Ltda.uniti S.A.
Consolidated Holdings	Old World Delicatessen
Drachenblut Delikatessen	Ottilies Kseladensenuniti S.A.
Du monde entier	Paris spcialitssenuniti S.A.
Eastern Connection	Periclos Comidas cisicasti S.A.
Ernst Handel	Piccolo und mehr
Familia Arquibaldo	Princesa Isabel Vinhos
FISSA Fabrica Inter. Salchichas S.A.	Que Delciabel Vinhosasti S.A.
Folies gourmandes	Queen Cozinha
Folk och f HBesr. Salchichas S.A.	QUICK-Stop
Frankenversand	Rancho grande
France restauration	Rattlesnake Canyon Grocery
Franchi S.p.A.	Reggiani Caseifici
Furia Bacalhau e Frutos do Mar	Ricardo Adocicados
Galera del gastrnomo do Mar S.A.	Richter Supermarkt
Godos Cocina Tpicamo do Mar S.A.	Romero y tomillo
Gourmet Lanchonetes	Sant GourmetlotGroceryi S.A.
Great Lakes Food Market	Save-a-lot Markets
GROSELLA-Restaurante	Seven Seas Imports
Hanari Carnes	Simons bistro
HILARION-Abastos	Spcialits du mondeoceryi S.A.
Hungry Coyote Import Store	Split Rail Beer & Ale
Hungry Owl All-Night Grocers	Suprmes dlices Aleceryi S.A.
Island Trading	WM-Data
Kniglich Essenight Grocersr S.A.	WM-Data

Figure 3-8. *Result of a two-column print*

Advanced Options

Up to now you have seen only basic characteristics concerning the layout. Here you will see some advanced options. You will get the chance to examine some of these more thoroughly in the following chapters; the rest you will fully understand and take full advantage of only after having acquired familiarity with the use of JasperReports.

Scriptlet Class Tab Options

A *scriptlet* is a Java class whose methods are executed according to specific events during report creation, such as the beginning of a new page or the end of a group. For those who are familiar with visual tools such as MS Access or MS Excel, a scriptlet can be compared to a *module*, in which some procedures associated with particular events or functions recallable in other report contexts (for example, the expression of a text field) are inserted. (Chapter 11 is dedicated to the scriptlet.)

In the Scriptlet Class tab of the Report properties dialog box (see Figure 3-9), it is possible to specify an external scriptlet (a Java class) or activate iReport's internal scriptlet support.

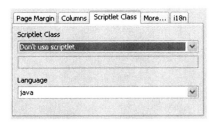

Figure 3-9. *Setting of the scriptlet class and language*

If you do not want to use a scriptlet, select the Don't use scriptlet class option in the Scriptlet class combo box or leave the text field blank where the class name is usually entered.

In the Scriptlet Class tab, you can also choose the language that will be used for expressions (at the time of writing, only Java and Groovy are supported). Please note that the language is not related to the scriptlet class.

More Tab Options

In the More tab (see Figure 3-10), it is possible to specify some print instructions. Let's briefly look at each of the options available on this tab.

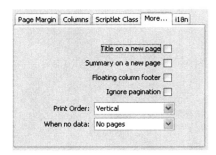

Figure 3-10. *More tab options*

Title on a new page Option

The Title on a new page option specifies that the title band is to be printed on a new page, which forces a *page break* at the end of the title band. As an example, take a look at Figure 3-11, which shows a simple report.

In the editor, the report is always the same: the title band is always on top.

Figure 3-12 shows the print result using default settings.

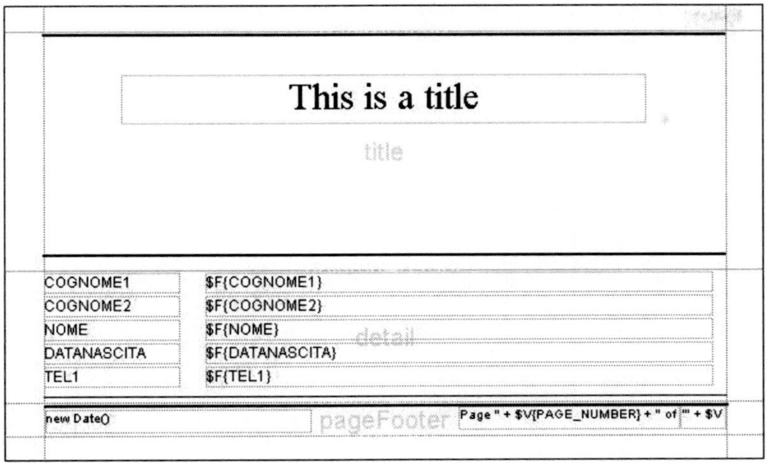

Figure 3-11. *Structure of a columnar simple report*

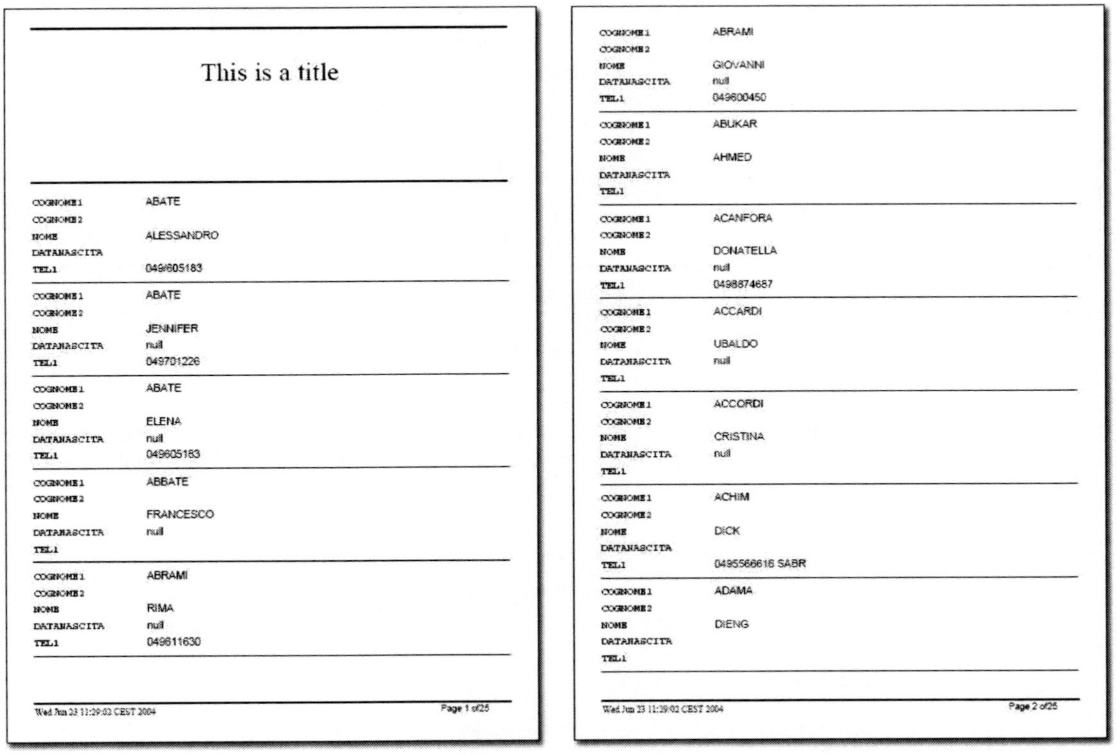

Figure 3-12. *Default print of the title band*

Figure 3-13 shows the print result with the Title on a new page option set to true. As you can see, no one other band is printed on the title page, not even the page header or page footer. However, this page is still counted in the total pages numeration.

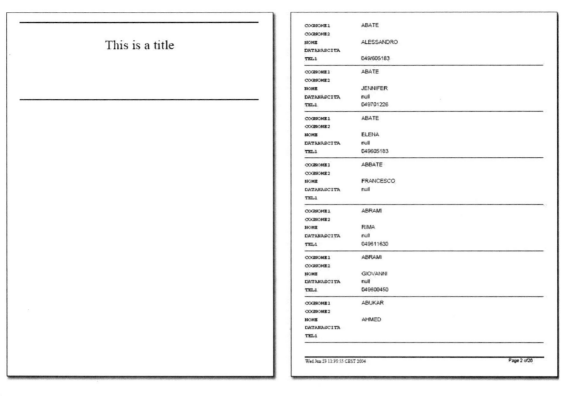

Figure 3-13. *Printing with the title band on a new page*

Summary on a new page Option

This option is similar to the previous option except that the summary band is printed as the last page. Now, if you need to print this band on a new page, the new page will only contain the summary band.

Floating column footer Option

This option allows you to force the printing of the column footer band immediately after the last detail band (or group footer) and not at the end of the column. This option is used, for example, when you want to create tables using the report elements (see the JasperReports `tables.jrxml` example for more details).

Print order Option

The Print order option determines how the print data is organized on the page when using multiple columns. The default setting is Vertical, that is, the records are printed one after the other, passing to a new column only when the previous column has reached the end of the page (like what happens in a newspaper or a phone book). Horizontal print order prints the different records horizontally across the page, occupying all of the available columns before passing to a new line. Refer to Figures 3-14 and 3-15 for examples of vertical and horizontal print order.

Vertical print order

COMPANYNAME	COMPANYNAME	COMPANYNAME
Alfreds Futterkiste	Kniglich Essenight Grocers	The Big Cheese
Ana Trujillo Emparedados y	LILA-Supermercado	The Cracker Box
Antonio Moreno Taquera y	LINO-Delicateses	Toms Spezialitten
Around the Horn	La corne d'abondance	Tortuga Restaurante
B's Beverages	La maison d'Asie	Tradio Hipermercados
Berglunds snabbkpera y	Laughing Bacchus Wine	Trail's Head Gourmet
Blauer See Delikatessen	Lazy K Kountry Store	Vaffeljernet
Blido Comidas preparadas	Lehmanns Marktstand	Victuailles en stock
Bon app'	Let's Stop N Shop	Vins et alcools Chevalier
Bottom-Dollar Markets	Lonesome Pine Restaurant	WM-Data
Cactus Comidas para llevar	Magazzini Alimentari Riuniti	WM-Data
Centro comercial Moctezuma	Maison Dewey	WM-Data
Chop-suey Chinese	Morgenstern Gesundkost	Wartian Herkku
Comrcio Mineirooctezuma	Mre Paillardentari Riuniti S.	Wellington Importadora
Consolidated Holdings	North/South	White Clover Markets
Die Wandernde Kuh	Ocano Atlntico Ltda.uniti S.	Wilman Kala
Drachenblut Delikatessen	Old World Delicatessen	Wolski Zajazd
Du monde entier	Ottilies Kseladensenuniti S.	
Eastern Connection	Paris spcialitssenuniti S.	
Ernst Handel	Pericles Comidas clsicasti S	

Figure 3-14. *Printing with a vertical order*

Horizontal print order

COMPANYNAME	COMPANYNAME	COMPANYNAME
Alfreds Futterkiste	Ana Trujillo Emparedados y	Antonio Moreno Taquera y
Around the Horn	B's Beverages	Berglunds snabbkpera y
Blauer See Delikatessen	Blido Comidas preparadas	Bon app'
Bottom-Dollar Markets	Cactus Comidas para llevar	Centro comercial Moctezuma
Chop-suey Chinese	Comrcio Mineirooctezuma	Consolidated Holdings
Die Wandernde Kuh	Drachenblut Delikatessen	Du monde entier
Eastern Connection	Ernst Handel	FISSA Fabrica Inter.
Familia Arquibaldo	Folies gourmandes	Folk och f HBesr.
France restauration	Franchi S.p.A.	Frankenversand
Furia Bacalhau e Frutos do	GROSELLA-Restaurante	Galera del gastrnomo do
Godos Cocina Tpicamo do	Gourmet Lanchonetes	Great Lakes Food Market
HILARION-Abastos	Hanari Carnes	Hungry Coyote Import Store
Hungry Owl All-Night Grocers	Island Trading	Kniglich Essenight Grocers
LILA-Supermercado	LINO-Delicateses	La corne d'abondance
La maison d'Asie	Laughing Bacchus Wine	Lazy K Kountry Store
Lehmanns Marktstand	Let's Stop N Shop	Lonesome Pine Restaurant
Magazzini Alimentari Riuniti	Maison Dewey	Morgenstern Gesundkost
Mre Paillardentari Riuniti S.	North/South	Ocano Atlntico Ltda.uniti S.
Old World Delicatessen	Ottilies Kseladensenuniti S.	Paris spcialitssenuniti S.
Pericles Comidas clsicasti S.	Piccolo und mehr	Princes Isabel

Figure 3-15. *Printing with a horizontal order*

The output in these two figures should clarify the concept of print order. As you can see, the names are printed in alphabetical order. In Figure 3-14, they are printed in vertical order (filling in the first column and then passing to the following column), and in Figure 3-15, they are printed in horizontal order (filling all columns horizontally before passing to the following line).

When no data Option

When an empty data set is supplied as the print number (or the SQL query associated to the report gives back no records), an empty file is created (or a stream of zero byte length is given back). This default behavior can be modified by specifying what to do in the case of absence of data (that is, "when no data"). Table 3-2 summarizes the possible values and their meaning.

Table 3-2. *Print Types in Absence of Data*

Option	Description
NoPages	This is the default; the final result is an empty buffer.
BlankPage	This gives back an empty page.
AllSectionsNoDetails	This gives back a page composed of all the bands except for the detail band.

i18n Tab Options

The following sections define the options that can be set on the i18n tab, shown in Figure 3-16.

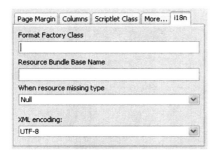

Figure 3-16. *i18n tab*

Format Factory Class

A *format factory class* is a class that implements the interface net.sf.jasperreports.engine.util.FormatFactory. You can set a custom implementation of that class, which will be used to define the default formatter for numbers and dates.

Resource Bundle Base Name

The Resource Bundle Base Name is a parameter used when you want to internationalize a report. The *Resource Bundle* is the set of files that contain the translated text of the labels, sentences, and expressions used within a report in each defined language. A language corresponds to a specific file.

The *base name* represents the prefix through which you can find the file with the correct translation. In order to reconstruct the file name required for a particular language, some language/country initials (e.g., _it_IT for Italian-Italy) and the .properties extension are added to this prefix. (I will explain internationalization in greater detail in Chapter 10.)

If a resource is not available, you can specify what to do by choosing an option from the combo box labeled "When resource missing type." The available options are listed in Table 3-3.

Table 3-3. *When resource missing type Options*

Option	Description
Null	Prints the "Null" string (it's the default option)
Empty	Prints nothing
Key	Prints the missing key name
Error	Throws an exception stopping the fill process

Character Encodings of the XML Source Files

The default format for saving source files is UTF-8. However, if you want to use some characters that need particular encoding in the XML, it is necessary to specify the correct charset.

UTF-8 manages all accented letters and the euro. Other common charsets are listed in the XML encoding combo box (ISO-8859-1 is widely used in Europe).

CHAPTER 4

■ ■ ■

Report Elements

In this chapter, I will explain *elements*, the main objects that can be inserted into a report, and survey their characteristics.

By "element," I mean graphic object, such as a text box or a rectangle. Unlike what happens in a word processing program, in iReport the concept of paragraph or table does not exist; everything is created by means of elements, which can contain text, create tables when they are opportunely aligned, and so on. This approach is what is adopted by the majority of report tools.

The following basic elements are offered by the JasperReports library:

- Line
- Rectangle
- Ellipse
- Static Text
- Text Field (or simply Field)
- Image
- Subreport
- Crosstab
- Chart
- Frame

Through the combination of these elements, it is possible to produce every kind of report.

In addition to the basic elements just listed, iReport provides an additional special element based on the Image element: the Barcode element.

Each kind of element has some common properties, such as height, width, position, and band to which it belongs, while other properties are specific to the type of element (for example, font or, in the case of a rectangle, thickness of the border). It is possible to group the elements into two macrocategories: the graphic elements (Line, Rectangle, Ellipse, Image) and the text field elements (Static Text and Text Field). Subreports represent separate kinds of elements, and because of the complexity of their use, I will touch briefly on them later in the chapter, dealing with them in more detail in Chapter 8. Similarly, I will reserve coverage of Crosstab elements for Chapter 15.

The elements are inserted into bands. In particular, every element is associated with a band, no exceptions. If an element is not completely contained within the band that it is part of, the report compiler will return a message that informs you about the incorrect position of the element; the report will be compiled in any case, and in the worst case, the "out-of-band" element will not be printed.

Inserting and Selecting Elements in a Report

In order to add an element to a report, select one of the tools present on the toolbar (see Figure 4-1).

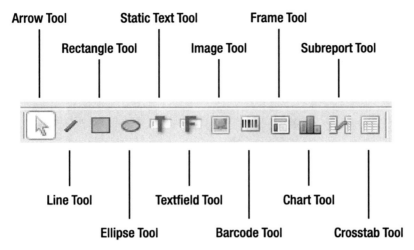

Figure 4-1. *Tools for element creation*

The Arrow tool is used for doing all the most important operations on the elements (selecting, etc.), and its activation switches off another active tool.

When you have chosen the element to insert, click the band where you want to insert the element and draw a rectangle by dragging the mouse downward to the right. When you release the mouse button, a new element will be created, and it will be selected automatically. The new element will also appear in the document structure panel on the right of the iReport desktop, as shown in Figure 4-2.

When dragging an element, iReport suggests places to align it based on the elements already in the design pane. You can turn this feature on or off by activating or deactivating the Magnetic tool:

Double-clicking an element, right-clicking an element and selecting Properties from the context menu, or selecting Edit ➤ Element Properties opens the element properties window (see Figure 4-3).

This window is organized in several tabs. The Common tab contains the properties common to every kind of element, whereas the other tabs are specific to each kind of element.

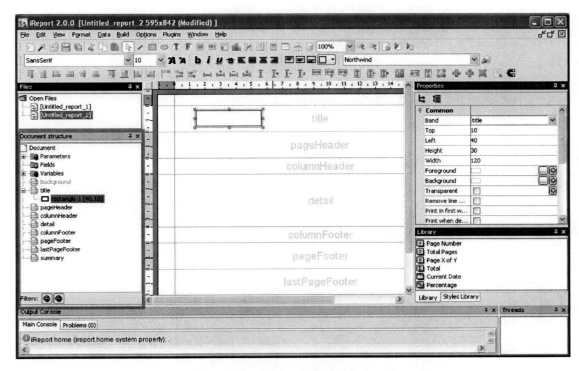

Figure 4-2. *The elements tree, or document structure panel (highlighted on the left)*

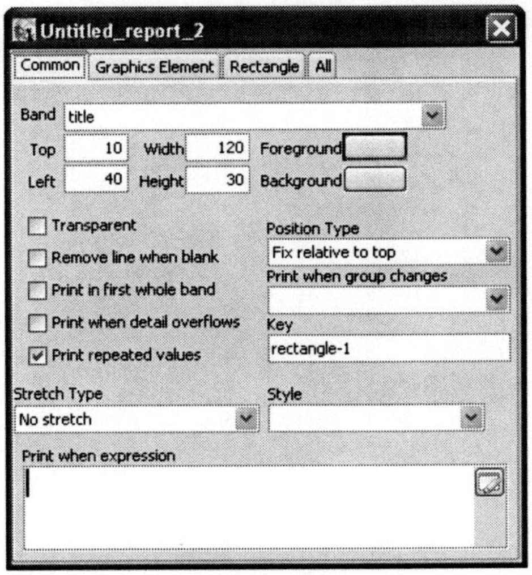

Figure 4-3. *Element properties window*

Starting with iReport 1.2.1, you can access some, but not all, of the element properties from the element properties sheet, shown in Figure 4-4. Figure 4-5 shows where you would find the element properties sheet in the main window.

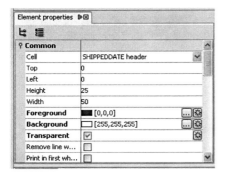

Figure 4-4. *Element properties sheet*

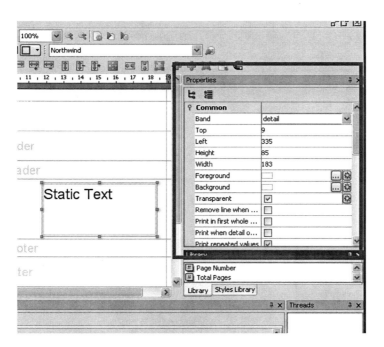

Figure 4-5. *Position of the properties sheet in the main window*

The most important difference between using the element properties window and the element properties sheet is that with the properties sheet you can reset a value to its default using the Reset button (see Figure 4-6). Of course, the Reset button is present only when the property can have a null value, in which case a default value will be used by the report engine. Null values for element properties are important when using a style (see Chapter 5).

Figure 4-6. *The element attribute Reset button*

It is possible to select more than one element at the same time by using the Arrow tool and drawing a rectangle that contains, even only in part, the elements to select. The selection area is highlighted with a pink rectangle.

Alternatively, you can select more than one element at the same time by keeping the Shift key pressed while clicking with the mouse over all elements you want selected.

An element that is not selected appears without any particular selection frame (see Figure 4-7). The first element of a selection is highlighted with an orange frame with blue corners (which appear as dark gray in Figure 4-8), while the secondary elements are highlighted with a frame having gray corners (which appear as light gray in Figure 4-9).

Figure 4-7. *No selected element*

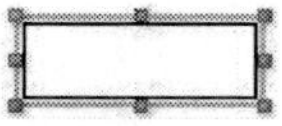

Figure 4-8. *Primary selection*

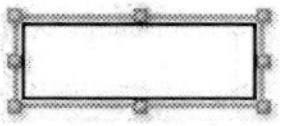

Figure 4-9. *Secondary selection*

The first element of a multiple selection is the primary element of the selection.

In order to resize an element, it is necessary to move the mouse cursor over one of the corners or over one of the selected element sides: click and drag the mouse in order to arrange its dimensions as you wish. For a more careful resize, you can specify the element dimensions directly in the element properties window. If more than one element is selected at the same time, the resize of one element results in the resize of all the other elements.

Moreover, it could be useful to enlarge the report by using the Zoom tool, which you will find on the toolbar (see Figure 4-10).

Figure 4-10. *Zoom tool*

It is possible to select a zoom percentage from the combo box, as shown in Figure 4-10, or to enter directly the zoom value you wish (expressed as a percentage and without the final % character).

Positioning and Elements Order

An element is moved by using the mouse: by clicking the element, it is selected, and it is possible for you to drag it to your desired position. In order to be able to obtain a greater precision in the movement, use the arrow keys to move the element 1 pixel at a time; similarly, using the arrow keys while pressing the Shift key will move the element 10 pixels.

If you prefer to prevent accidental movement of elements, it could be useful to disable elements dragging through the mouse by selecting Options ➤ Disable elements mouse move.

The menu command View ➤ Show grid activates a grid that can be used as a reference for the positioning of the different elements (see Figure 4-11). It is also possible to put into action automatic positioning of elements relative to the grid by selecting Options ➤ Snap to grid.

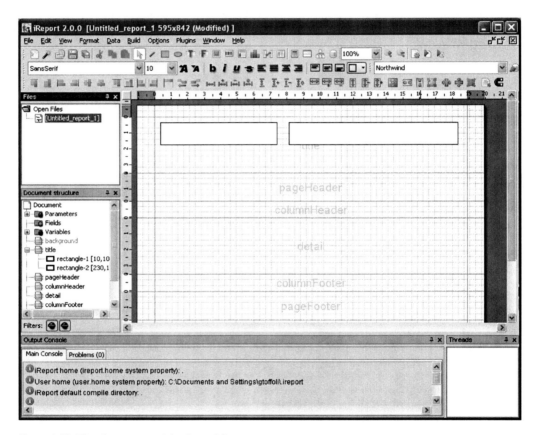

Figure 4-11. *The elements positioning grid*

When the number of elements to organize in the report increases, several tools are available to help you organize those elements; these can be recalled both from the Format menu and from the context menu viewable by selecting the element you are interested in and right-clicking it. Most of these functionalities need a selection of more than one element. In this case, the primary element of the selection is taken as the reference for the operation to perform. Table 4-1 summarizes the formatting functionalities.

Table 4-1. *Formatting Functionalities*

Operation	Description	Requires Multiple Elements?
Align left	Aligns the left sides to that of the primary element	✓
Align right	Aligns the right sides to that of the primary element	✓
Align top	Aligns the top sides (or the upper part) to that of the primary element	✓
Align bottom	Aligns the bottom sides to that of the primary element	✓
Align vertical axis	Centers horizontally the selected elements according to the primary element	✓
Align horizontal axis	Centers vertically the selected elements according to the primary element	✓
Align to band top	Sets the top value at 0	
Align to band bottom	Positions the elements at the bottom as much as possible according to the band to which they belong	
Same width	Sets the selected elements' width equal to that of the primary element	✓
Same width (max)	Sets the selected elements' width equal to that of the widest element	✓
Same width (min)	Sets the selected elements' width equal to that of the most narrow element	✓
Same height	Sets the selected elements' height equal to that of the primary element	✓
Same height (max)	Sets the selected elements' height equal to that of the highest element	✓
Same height (min)	Sets the selected elements' height equal to that of the lowest element	✓
Same size	Sets the selected elements' dimension to that of the primary element	✓
Center horizontally (band based)	Positions horizontally the selected elements in the center of the band	
Center vertically (band based)	Positions vertically the selected elements in the center of the band	
Center in band	Puts the elements in the center of the band	
Center in background	Puts the elements in the center of the page in the background	
Join sides left	Joins horizontally the elements by moving them to the left	✓
Join sides right	Joins horizontally the elements by moving them to the right	✓
HS ➤ Make equal	Distributes equally the horizontal space among elements	✓
HS ➤ Increase	Increases by 5 pixels the horizontal space among elements (by moving them to the right)	✓
HS ➤ Decrease	Decreases by 5 pixels the horizontal space among elements (by moving them to the left)	✓
HS ➤ Remove	Removes the horizontal space among elements by moving them to the left	✓

The elements can be overlapped; it is possible to bring elements to the front or to send them back by using the formatting functions Bring to front and Send to back. The z-order (that is, the position from the depth point of view) is determined by the order in which the elements are inserted into the report. The disposition can be viewed in the elements tree, where the elements are viewed in every band from the lowest to the highest.

As I have already said, an element is always linked to the band it belongs to. If the element is partly or completely out of its band, it will be highlighted with a red frame (only for text elements) in order to indicate that the position is not valid. For other kinds of elements, the incorrect position is highlighted in the elements tree or during the selecting phase, as indicated by red corners in the frame (see Figure 4-12).

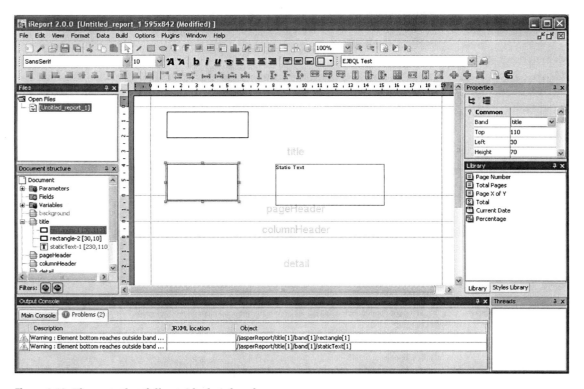

Figure 4-12. *Elements that fall outside their bands*

> **Note** If an element partly covers one other element, the corners are highlighted in green, while an element that completely hides another element has the corners highlighted in pink.

Moving an element from a band to another, iReport automatically changes the Band setting for the element. To specify a different band, use the first combo box present in the element properties window (see Figure 4-13).

Figure 4-13. *Element Band setting*

If two or more elements are selected, only the common properties are visualized. If the values of these properties are different, they will appear blank (usually the field is shown empty). Specifying a value for a particular property applies that value to all selected elements.

Managing Elements with the Elements Tree

The elements tree, shown in Figure 4-14, allows you to localize and select report elements easily and with precision.

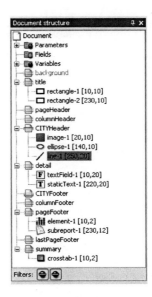

Figure 4-14. *The elements tree*

The report is outlined with a tree structure: the main nodes are the bands (represented by the symbol of a page with a little blue or orange strip); under each band are its elements, represented by their various symbols, names, and coordinates; also they are also organized by hierarchy under the band node.

Double-clicking an element opens the properties window of the selected object. Also, as mentioned previously, a context menu is associated with elements (viewable by selecting at least one element and right-clicking it): beyond the usual functions of copy and paste, there are two particular functions, move up and move down, by means of which you can modify the z-order of an element in the specific band.

If a band node is selected, the properties sheet (normally located on the right side of the main window) will present the properties for that band (see Figure 4-15).

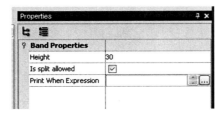

Figure 4-15. *Band properties window*

The meaning of the various band characteristics is explained in Chapter 7.

Basic Element Attributes

All the elements have a set of common attributes presented in the Common tab in the element properties window (as shown earlier in Figure 4-3). These attributes concern information about element positioning on the page: the following list describes the different attributes available.

▨**Note** Coordinates and dimensions are always expressed in pixels in relation to a 72-pixel-per-inch resolution.

Band: This is the band that the element belongs to. All the elements have one, and their position is always linked to it. The positioning of a particular element always has to be made in the specified band.

Top: This is the distance of the top-left corner of the element from the top of the band the element belongs to.

Left: This is the distance of the top-right corner of the element from the left margin of the band.

Width: This is the element width.

Height: This is the element height; in reality, this indicates a minimum value that can increase during the print creation according to the value of the other attributes.

Figure 4-16 shows how the position of an element is relative to the band to which the element belongs to. The band width always equals that of the document page (minus the left and right margin); however, band height can change depending on the type of band and the elements it contains.

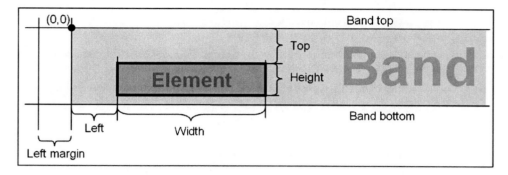

Figure 4-16. *Element positioning*

Foreground: This is the color with which the text elements are printed and the lines and the element corners are drawn.

Background: This is the color with which the element background is filled.

Transparent: If this option is selected, it makes the element transparent; the transparency involves the parts that should be filled with the background.

■**Caution** Not all export formats support the transparency attribute.

Remove line when blank: This option takes away the vertical space occupied by an object, if it is not visible; the element visibility is determined by the value of the expression contained in the Print when expression attribute. Think of the page as a grid where the elements are placed, with a line being the space the element occupies. Figure 4-17 highlights the element A line; in order to really remove this line, all the elements that share a portion of the line have to be null (that is, they will not be printed).

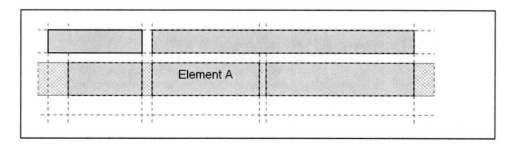

Figure 4-17. *Element A line*

Print in first whole band: This option ensures that an element is printed in the next page (or column) if the band overflows the page (or the column); this type of guarantee is useful when the Print repeated values attribute is not active.

Print when detail overflows: This option prints the element in the following page or column, if the band is not all printable in the present page or column.

Print repeated values: This option determines whether to print the element when its value is equal to that which is used in the previous record.

Position Type: This option determines how the top coordinates have to be considered in the case that the band is changed. The three possible values are as follows:

- *Fix relative to top*: This is the predefined position type; the coordinate values never change.
- *Float*: The element is progressively pushed toward the bottom by the previous elements that increase their height.
- *Fix relative to bottom*: The distance of the element from the bottom of the band remains constant; usually this is used for lines that separate records.

Print when group changes: In this combo box, all report groups are presented. If one of them is selected, the element will be printed only when the expression associated with the group changes—that is, when a new break of the selected group is created.

Key: This is the element name, which has to be unique in the report (iReport proposes it automatically), and it is used by the programs that need to modify the field properties at runtime.

Stretch Type: This attribute defines how to vary the element height during print elaboration; the three possible values are as follows:

- *No stretch*: This is the predefined stretch type, and it dictates that the element height should remain as is.
- *Relative to band height*: The element height is increased proportionally to the increasing size of the band; this is useful for vertical lines that simulate table borders.
- *Relative to tallest object*: The element modifies its height according to the deformation of the nearest element: this option is also used with the *element group*, which is an element group mechanism not managed by iReport.

Print when expression: This is a Java expression like those described in Chapter 2, and it must return a Boolean object; besides being associated with elements, this expression is also associated with the bands. If the expression returns true, the element is hidden. A null value implicitly identifies an expression like new Boolean(true), which will print the element unconditionally.

Graphic Element Attributes

The graphic elements are drawing objects such as the Line and the Rectangle elements; they do not show data generally, but they are used to make reports more readable and agreeable from an aesthetic point of view. All kinds of elements share the Graphics element tab in the element properties window (see Figure 4-18).

Figure 4-18. *Graphics element tab options*

Following is a brief description of the options available in this tab:

Pen: This is the thickness with which you draw lines and frames; the possible values are as follows:

- *None*: The thickness is null, which inhibits the drawing of lines and frames.
- *Thin*: Lines and frames will be drawn using the thinnest available line.
- *1Point*: Lines and frames will be 1 pixel thick.
- *2Point*: Lines and frames will be 2 pixels thick.
- *4Point*: Lines and frames will be 4 pixels thick.
- *Dotted*: Lines and frames will be drawn with a series of dots.

Fill: This is the modality used to fill the background; the only admitted value is Solid, which is the complete filling.

Now that you know the attributes governing graphic elements, let's turn to a brief overview of each of the types of graphic elements available. Recall that in the element properties window, attributes are grouped in tabs, which can vary depending on the element type.

Line

In JasperReports, a line is defined by a rectangle of which the line represents the diagonal (see Figure 4-19).

Figure 4-19. *Top-down Line element*

The line is drawn using the Foreground setting as its color and the Pen setting for its thickness. The Line tab, specific to this element, features one more option:

Line Direction: This indicates which of the two rectangle diagonals represents the line; the possible values are Top-down (see Figure 4-20) and Bottom-up.

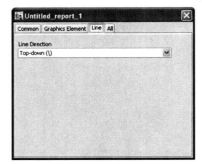

Figure 4-20. *Line direction*

Rectangle

The Rectangle element is usually used to draw frames around other elements. Its border is drawn with the color specified with the Foreground setting and a thickness specified by the Pen setting. The background is filled with the color specified with the Background setting if the element has not been defined as transparent.

In JasperReports, it is possible to have a rectangle with rounded corners (see Figure 4-21). The rounded corners are defined by means of the Radius attribute (on the Rectangle tab, shown in Figure 4-22), which represents the curvature with which you draw the corners, expressed in pixels.

Figure 4-21. *Rectangle element with rounded corners*

Figure 4-22. *Rectangle radius option*

Ellipse

The Ellipse element is the only one that has no attributes specific to it. An ellipse is drawn into a rectangle that is built up on the four sides that are tangent to it (see Figure 4-23). The border is drawn with the color specified with the Foreground setting and a thickness specified with the Pen setting. The background is filled with the Background color setting if the element has not been defined as transparent.

Figure 4-23. *Ellipse element*

Image

The Image element is the most complex of the graphic elements (see Figure 4-24). It can be used to insert raster images (such as GIF, PNG, and JPEG images) into the report, but it can also be used as a *canvas* object, a kind of box where you can draw: the Image element is used, for example, to draw charts and barcodes. Charts are complex enough to deserve their own chapter; I cover them in Chapter 13.

Figure 4-24. *Image element*

Figure 4-25 shows the element properties for an Image element, with the Image tab selected.

Figure 4-25. *Image element properties window*

It is possible to use your own rendering class by using the net.sf.jasperreports.engine. JRRenderable interface. A hypertext link can be associated with an Image element (via the Hyper Link tab). You will see more of the Hyper Link tab at the end of this chapter in the section "Adding Hyperlinks to Elements."

The image characteristics are set up in the Image tab:

Image Expression: This is a Java expression. Its result is an object defined by the Image Expression Class attribute; depending on the return type, the way the image is loaded changes.

Image Expression Class: This is the expression return type.

Table 4-2 summarizes the values that you can specify for the Image Expression Class setting and how the Image Expression result is interpreted.

Table 4-2. *Expression Types to Localize an Image*

Type	Interpretation
java.lang.String	A string is interpreted like a file name; JasperReports will try to interpret the string like an absolute path. If no file is found, it will try to load a resource from the classpath with the specified name. Examples of correct expressions: "c:\\devel\\ireport\\myImage.jpg" "it/businesslogic/ireport/icons/logo.gif"
java.io.File	This specifies a File object to load as an image. Example of a correct expression: new java.io.File("c:\\myImage.jpg")
java.net.URL	This specifies the java.net.URL object. It is useful when you have to export the report in HTML format. Example of a correct expression: new java.net.URL("http://127.0.0.1/test.jpg")
java.io.InputStream	This specifies a java.io.InputStream object that is ready for reading. In this case, you do not consider that the image exists and that it is in a file; in particular, you could read the image from a database and return the inputStream for reading. Example of a correct expression: MyUtil.getInputStream(${MyField})
java.awt.Image	This specifies a java.awt.Image object; it is probably the simplest object to return when an image has to be created dynamically. Example of a correct expression: MyUtil.createChart()
JRRenderable	This specifies an object that uses the net.sf.jasperreports.engine. JRRenderable interface.

In the examples presented in Table 4-2, MyUtil represents an invented class. If you want to use an external class by calling a static method to run particular elaborations, it is necessary to use it with the package it belongs to (for example, it.businesslogic.ireport.util.MyUtil) or to specify its package in the import (through the menu command Edit ➤ Import directives in the report). The methods explained in the examples are static, but when I talk about variables in Chapter 6, you will see how to instance a class at the beginning of the print and how to use it in expressions.

By using fields, variables, and parameters in the image expression, you can load or produce images in a parametric way (as it would happen, for example, for the detail of an illustrated catalog where every product is associated with an image).

Let's take a look at the remaining options in the Image tab:

Scale Image: This defines how the image has to adapt to the element's dimension; the possible values are three:

- *Clip*: The image dimension is not changed (see Figure 4-26).
- *Fill frame*: The image is adapted to the element's dimension (becoming deformed) (see Figure 4-27).
- *Retain shape*: The image is adapted to the element's dimension by keeping the original proportions (see Figure 4-28).

Figure 4-26. *Scaling with the Clip option*

Figure 4-27. *Scaling with the Fill frame option*

Figure 4-28. *Scaling with the Retain shape option*

On error type: This defines what to do if the image loading fails:

- *Error*: This is the default value, which throws a Java exception, stopping the filling process.
- *Blank*: The image is not printed and a blank space will be placed in the report instead.
- *Icon*: An icon is printed instead of the original image.

Vertical Alignment: This attribute defines the image vertical alignment according to the element area. The possible values are as follows:

- *Top*: The image is aligned at the top.
- *Middle*: The image is positioned in the middle vertically according to the element area.
- *Bottom*: The image is aligned at the bottom.

Horizontal Alignment: This attribute defines the image horizontal alignment according to the element area. The possible values are as follows:

- *Left:* The image is aligned to the left.
- *Center:* The image is positioned in the center horizontally according to the element area.
- *Right:* The image is aligned to the right.

Is Lazy: This avoids loading of the image at fill time. The image will instead be loaded when the report will exported, which is useful when an image is loaded from an URL.

Using cache: This option keeps the image in memory in order to use it again if the element is printed anew; the image is kept in cache only if Image Expression Class is set to Java.lang.String.

Evaluation Time: This defines during which creation phase the image expression has to be processed. In fact, the evaluation of an expression can be done when the report engine "encounters" the element during the creation of the report, or it can also be postponed in some particular cases, for example, if you want to calculate a subtotal. The evaluation time is a very interesting functionality, and it is well explained in *The Definitive Guide to JasperReports* by Teodor Daniciu, Lucian Chirita, Sanda Zaharia, and Ionut Nedelcu (Apress, 2007). The possible values are as follows:

- *Now:* Evaluate the expression immediately.
- *Report:* Evaluate the expression at the end of the report.
- *Page:* Evaluate the expression at the end of the page.
- *Column:* Evaluate the expression at the end of this column.
- *Group:* Evaluate the expression of the group that is specified in Evaluation Group setting.
- *Band:* Evaluate this expression after the evaluation of the current band (used to evaluate expressions that deal with subreport return values).

Evaluation Group: See the preceding Group value description for the Evaluation Time setting.

For Image elements (and for text elements), it is possible to visualize a frame or to define a particular *padding* for the four sides, which is space between the element border and its content. Borders and padding are specified in the Border tab (see Figure 4-29), and these are properties that have been included since JasperReports 0.6.3.

You can select the type and color of the border to draw for every side of the element. The border types are as follows:

- *None:* Thickness null (that is, the border doesn't print)
- *Thin:* Line of minimum thickness
- *1 Point:* Thickness of 1 pixel
- *2 Point:* Thickness of 2 pixels
- *4 Point:* Thickness of 4 pixels
- *Dotted:* Dotted line of minimum thickness

A simple preview of the graphic effect produced by the selected border appears in the center of the Border tab.

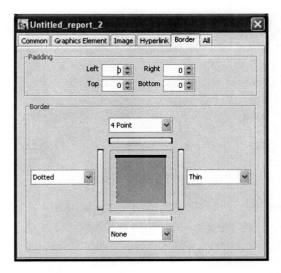

Figure 4-29. *The Border tab options are common to Image and Text elements.*

Text Element Attributes

Like the graphic elements, the elements that allow you to view text have a common properties tab: the Font tab (see Figure 4-30).

Figure 4-30. *The Font tab is common to all text elements.*

In the Font tab, you set the properties of the text shown in the element—not only the font (dimension and type of the character), but also text alignment, eventual rotation, and line space. Here's a look at each of the options for this tab:

Report Font: This is the name of a preset font, from which will be taken all the character properties. The preset fonts are defined at report level, and it is possible to manage them by selecting Format ➤ Fonts.

Line Spacing: This is the interline (spacing between lines) value. The possible values are as follows:

- *Single*: Single interline (predefined value)
- *1-1-2*: Interline of one line and a half
- *Double*: Double interline

Horizontally Align: This is the horizontal alignment of the text according to the element.

Vertically Align: This is the vertical alignment of the text according to the element.

Rotation: This specifies how the text has to be printed. The possible values are as follows (see Figure 4-31 for an illustration of these rotational effects):

- *None*: The text is printed normally from left to right and from top to bottom.
- *Left*: The text is rotated of 90 degrees counterclockwise; it is printed from bottom to top, and the horizontal and vertical alignments follow the text rotation (for example, the bottom vertical alignment will print the text along the right side of the rectangle that delimits the element area).
- *Right*: The text is rotated 90 degrees clockwise from top to bottom, and the horizontal and vertical alignments are set according to the text rotation.
- *Upside down*: The text is rotated 180 degrees clockwise.

Figure 4-31. *The rotation effects*

The other characteristics of the Font tab are explained in Chapter 5, which is completely dedicated to fonts and styles.

Text element properties can be modified also by using the text toolbar (see Figure 4-32).

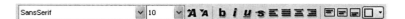

Figure 4-32. *Toolbar for modifying text fields*

Static Text

The Static Text element is used to show nondynamic text in reports (see Figure 4-33). The only parameter that distinguishes this element from a generic text element is the Static Text tab (see Figure 4-34), where the text to view is specified; it is a normal string, not an expression, and so it is not necessary to enclose it in double quotes for respecting the conventions of the Java syntax.

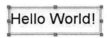

Figure 4-33. *Static Text element*

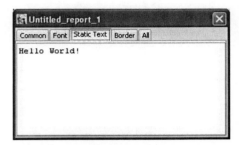

Figure 4-34. *Static Text tab*

Text Field

A text field allows you to print the value of a Java expression (see Figure 4-35). The simplest case is the printing of a string (`java.lang.String`) coming from an expression like this:

```
"Hello World!"
```

Figure 4-35. *Text Field element*

In this case, the result is exactly the same as a static field, except created with a little bit more work, because the string of the example is an expression of constant value; in reality, the use of a Java expression to define a text field's content allows you to have a high level of control on the generated text. JasperReports does not directly associate the data to print to particular text elements (as happens with different tools of the report where the text element represents implicitly the value of a database field); the values of the different fields of the records that are made available by the datasource are stored in objects named *fields*, and they are called in the expressions by means of the syntax explained in Chapter 2.

As with Image elements, a hypertext link can also be associated with text fields, and it is defined by the Hyper Link tab (which I will discuss in the "Adding Hyperlinks to Elements" section later in this chapter).

Figure 4-36 shows the Text Field tab options. Following is a brief description of each of these options.

Figure 4-36. *Text Field tab options*

Text Field Expression Class: This specifies the return type of the field expression. The possible values are many: they include all the Java objects that comprehend the SQL types and some classes for the management of dates. Table 4-3 lists all the selectable types. Note the `java.lang.Object` type: this can be used if none of the other types are applicable to the associated data.

Table 4-3. *Expression Types for a Text Field*

java.lang.Object	java.lang.Float
java.lang.Boolean	java.lang.Integer
java.lang.Byte	java.io.InputStream
java.util.Date	java.lang.Long
java.sql.Timestamp	java.lang.Short
java.sql.Time	java.math.BigDecimal
java.lang.Double	java.lang.String

Evaluation Time: This determines in which phase of report creation the text field expression has to be elaborated (see the information on the Evaluation Time option in the "Image" section earlier for details on this attribute).

Evaluation Group: This is the group to which the evaluation time is referred if it is set to Group.

Stretch with overflow: When this option is selected, it allows the text field to adapt vertically to the content, if the element is not sufficient to contain all the text lines.

Blank when null: This allows you to avoid the text "null" printing when the field expression returns a null object.

Text Field Expression: This is the expression that produces the value to print; it has to return an object of the same type declared in *Text Field Expression Class*.

Pattern: This specifies a string to use with a Format class that is right for the type specified in the Text Field Expression Class setting.

JasperReports is able to format dates and numbers; the following tables provide some parameters and examples of patterns of data and numbers. Table 4-4 shows letters you can use to specify properties of dates.

Table 4-4. *Letters to Create Patterns for Dates*

Letter	Date Components	Examples
G	Era designator	AD
y	Year	1996, 96
M	Month in year	July, Jul, 07
w	Week in year	27
W	Week in month	2
D	Day in year	189
d	Day in month	10
F	Day of week in month	2
E	Day in week	Tuesday, Tue
a	Am/pm marker	PM
H	Hour in day (0–23)	0
k	Hour in day (1–24)	24
K	Hour in am/pm (0–11)	0
h	Hour in am/pm (1–12)	12
m	Minute in hour	30
s	Second in minute	55
S	Millisecond	978
z	Time zone	Pacific Standard Time, PST, GMT–08:00
Z	Time zone	–0800

Table 4-5 shows some examples of formatting of dates and timestamps.

Table 4-5. *Example Patterns for Dates*

Dates and Time Pattern	Result
`"yyyy.MM.dd G 'at' HH:mm:ss z"`	2001.07.04 AD at 12:08:56 PDT
`"EEE, MMM d, ''yy"`	Wed, Jul 4, '01
`"h:mm a"`	12:08 PM
`"hh 'o''clock' a, zzzz"`	12 o'clock PM, Pacific Daylight Time
`"K:mm a, z"`	0:08 PM, PDT
`"yyyyy.MMMMM.dd GGG hh:mm aaa"`	02001.July.04 AD 12:08 PM
`"EEE, d MMM yyyy HH:mm:ss Z"`	Wed, 4 Jul 2001 12:08:56 –0700
`"yyMMddHHmmssZ"`	010704120856–0700

Table 4-6 shows symbols you can use to create patterns for numbers.

Table 4-6. *Symbols to Create Patterns for Numbers*

Symbol	Location	Localized?	Meaning
0	Number	Yes	Digit.
#	Number	Yes	Digit, zero shows as absent.
.	Number	Yes	Decimal separator or monetary decimal separator.
-	Number	Yes	Minus sign.
,	Number	Yes	Grouping separator.
E	Number	Yes	Separates mantissa and exponent in scientific notation. *Need not be quoted in prefix or suffix.*
;	Subpattern boundary	Yes	Separates positive and negative subpatterns.
%	Prefix or suffix	Yes	Multiplies by 100 and shows result as percentage.
\u2030	Prefix or suffix	Yes	Multiplies by 1000 and shows as per mille.
¤ (\u00A4)	Prefix or suffix	No	Currency sign, replaced by currency symbol. If doubled, replaced by international currency symbol. If present in a pattern, the monetary decimal separator is used instead of the decimal separator.
'	Prefix or suffix	No	Used to quote special characters in a prefix or suffix, for example, `"'#'#"` formats 123 as "#123". To create a single quote itself, use two in a row: `"# o''clock"`.

Table 4-7 provides some examples of the formatting of numbers.

Table 4-7. *Example Patterns for Numbers*

Dates and Time Pattern	Result
"#,##0.00"	1.234,56
"#,##0.00;(#,##0.00)"	1.234,56 (−1.234.56)

Thanks to the Create button (highlighted in Figure 4-37), it is possible to open an editor for the pattern and use it to simplify formatting of numbers, dates, currency, and so forth.

Figure 4-37. *Create button in the Text Field tab*

■**Tip** It is possible to transform a Static Text element into a Text Field element by selecting it and pressing the F3 key. If a text field element is selected, pressing F2 brings up a window in which you can easily change the text field expression (without using the element properties window).

A Brief Look at Subreports

The Subreport element is one that is able to contain another report that is created starting from a JASPER file and fed by a datasource that is specified in the subreport properties (see Figure 4-38).

Figure 4-38. *Subreport element*

This section briefly describes the characteristics of subreports. However, because of the complexity of this subject, I will explain subreports in depth in another chapter (Chapter 8).

Subreport properties span two tabs: Subreport (Figure 4-39) and Subreport (Other) (Figure 4-40). All these properties are not available in the element properties sheet.

Figure 4-39. *Subreport tab options*

Figure 4-40. *Subreport (Other) tab options*

Parameters Map Expression: This identifies an expression that is valuated at runtime. The expression must return a java.util.Map; this map contains some coupled names/objects that will be passed to the subreport in order to serve as values for its parameters.

Connection/Data Source Expression: This identifies the expression that will return at runtime a JDBC connection or a JRDataSource used to fill in the subreport.

Using cache: This specifies whether to keep in memory the data structures of the specified subreport in order to speed up subsequent reloading of the data structures.

Subreport Expression Class: This is the class type of the subreport expression; there are several options, each of which defines a different way to load the JasperReports data used to fill the subreport.

Subreport Expression: This identifies the expression that will return at runtime a subreport expression class object. According to the return type, the expression is valuated in order to recover a JASPER object to be used to produce the subreport.

Subreport parameters: This table allows you to define some couplet names/expressions that are useful for dynamically setting values for the subreport parameters by using calculated expressions.

Subreport return values: This table allows you to define how to store in local variables values calculated or processed in the subreport (such as totals and record count).

If you need to pass a set of parameters defined in the master report, you can save some time by clicking the Copy from Master button in the Subreport (Other) tab.

Working with Frames

A Frame element is one that can contain other elements and draw border reports around them, as shown in Figure 4-41.

Figure 4-41. *Frame element*

Since a frame is a container of other elements, in the document structure panel the frame is represented with a node, inside of which you will find the elements it contains (see Figure 4-42).

Figure 4-42. *Frame content*

To add an element to a frame, do one of the following:

- Draw the element directly inside the frame.
- Create or select one or more elements you want to put inside the frame, cut them, select the Frame element, and paste in the cut elements.

Special Elements

Besides the primitive elements provided by JasperReports, iReport supplies another element with custom properties and rendered using an Image element: the Barcode element, which I will discuss first. After that, I will discuss the Page Break element; although it is provided by JasperReports, I consider it a special element since it is managed differently from all the other elements in iReport.

Barcode Element Attributes

Barcode elements allow you to create and print dynamically a value in the form of a barcode (see Figure 4-43). Figure 4-44 shows the Barcode tab, where you edit the properties of a barcode.

Figure 4-43. *Barcode element*

Figure 4-44. *Barcode tab options*

Following are the options available through the Barcode tab:

Type: This specifies the type of barcode that you want printed. The possible values are listed in Table 4-8.

Table 4-8. *Barcode Types*

2of7	EAN128	ShipmentIdentificationNumber
3of9	EAN13	SSCC18
Bookland	GlobalTradeItemNumber	Std2of5
Codabar	Int2of5	Std2of5
Code128	Int2of5	UCC128
Code128A	Monarch	UPCA
Code128B	NW7	USD3
Code128C	PDF417	USD4
Code39	SCC14ShippingCode	USPS

Checksum: This specifies whether the code of control of the barcode has to be printed; this modality is supported by only some types of barcode.

Show Text: This specifies whether the text represented by the barcode has to be printed.

Barcode Expression: This is the expression valuated at runtime that expresses the value to represent by means of the barcode; the return type has to be a string.

Bar Width: This is the width in pixels of a single bar in the barcode (use 0 for the default width). This is NOT the width of the barcode image.

Bar Height: This is the height in pixels of the bars in the barcode (use 0 for the default height). This is NOT the height of the barcode image.

Application Identifier: This is the expression valuated at runtime to define the application identifier used in the UCC128 barcode type.

Evaluation Time and *Evaluation Group*: These have the same meaning as corresponding options in the Image tab options (refer to the "Image" section earlier in the chapter).

All the other options (Scale Barcode Image, On error type, Horizontal Alignment, and Vertical Alignment) are inherited by the Image element, from which the Barcode element derives.

Inserting Page and Column Breaks

Page and column breaks are used to force the report engine to make a jump to the next page or column (see Figure 4-45). A column break in a single column report has the same effect as a page break.

Figure 4-45. *Page and column breaks*

Break elements are available starting from JasperReports 1.3.0, and unlike the other elements, there is no button on the toolbar to create this kind of object. Instead, you insert breaks by selecting Edit ➤ Insert page/column break.

A break can be managed like other elements, so it can be moved, resized, and so on, but the only information really used by the report engine is the vertical position. For this reason, iReport tries to override the values for dimension and left position specified by the user.

The type of break can be defined from the element properties sheet or using the element properties window.

Adding Hyperlinks to Elements

Image, Text Field, and Chart elements can be used both as *anchors* into a document and as hypertext links to external sources or other local anchor. An anchor is a kind of label that identifies a specific position in the document.

These hypertext links and anchors are defined by means of the Hyper Link tab, shown in Figure 4-46. This tab is divided in two parts. In the upper part is a text area through which it is possible to specify the expression that will be the name of the anchor. This name can be referenced by other links. If you plan to export your report as a PDF document, you can use the bookmark level to populate the bookmark tree, making the final document navigation much easier. This feature is supported starting from JasperReports version 1.0.0. To make an anchor available in the bookmark, simply choose a bookmark level greater than 1. The use of a greater level makes possible the creation of nested bookmarks.

Figure 4-46. *Hyper Link tab options*

The lower part of the Hyper Link tab is dedicated to the link definition toward an external source or a position in the document. Through the Hyperlink target option, it is possible to specify whether the exploration of a particular link has to be made in the current window (this is the predefined setting and the target is Self) or in a new window (the target is Blank). This kind of behavior control makes sense only in certain output formats such as HTML and PDF.

The following text outlines some of the remaining options in the Hyper Link tab.

Hyperlink Type Option

JasperReports provides five types of built-in hypertext links: Reference, LocalAnchor, LocalPage, RemoteAnchor, and RemotePage.

Reference

The Reference link indicates an external source that is identified by a normal URL. This is ideal to point to a servlet, for example, to manage record drill-down functionalities. The only expression required is the hyperlink reference expression.

LocalAnchor

To point to a local anchor means to create a link between two locations into the same document. It can be used, for example, to link the titles of a summary to the chapters they refer to.

To define a LocalAnchor, it is necessary to specify a hyperlink anchor expression, which will have to produce a valid anchor name.

LocalPage

If instead of pointing to an anchor, you want to point to a specific current report page, you need to create a LocalPage link. In this case, it is necessary to specify the page number you are pointing to by means of a hyperlink page expression (the expression has to return an Integer object).

RemoteAnchor

If you want to point to a particular anchor that resides in an external document, you use the RemoteAnchor link. In this case, the URL of the external file pointed to will have to be specified in the Hyperlink Reference Expression field, and the name of the anchor will have to be specified in the Hyperlink Anchor Expression field.

RemotePage

This link allows you to point to a particular page of an external document. Similarly, in this case the URL of the external file pointed to will have to be specified in the Hyperlink Reference Expression field, and the page number will have to be specified by means of the hyperlink page expression.

■**Caution** Not all export formats support hypertext links.

Hyperlink Parameters

Sometimes you will need to define some parameters that must be "concatenated" to the link. The Link parameters table provides a convenient way to define them. The parameter value can be set using an expression.

Custom Hyperlink Types

Sometimes the hyperlink string requires a complex custom elaboration in order to be generated. JasperReports provides a way to plug into the engine a custom hyperlink producer factory that can generate the hyperlink string having as input a JRPrintHyperlink object. The custom factory will be associated with a custom hyperlink type (basically a name like "myHyperlinkType"). You can put your custom hyperlink type name in the Hyperlink type combo box, which is editable for this purpose.

CHAPTER 5

Fonts and Styles

You can save time defining the look of your elements by using styles. A *style* is a collection of pre-defined properties that refer to aspects of elements (like background color, borders, and font). You can define a default style for your report that all undefined properties of your elements refer to by default.

Fonts describe the characteristics (shape and dimension) of text. In JasperReports, you can specify the font properties for each text element. With previous versions, you could define a set of global fonts named *report fonts* and associate them with a text element, and the global fonts would then be used for the text contained in the element. However, note that report fonts are now deprecated, so you want to define a style instead of a report font. In effect, a style contains all the information about a font and works much like a report font.

Working with Fonts

Usually a font is defined by the following basic characteristics:

- Font name (font family)

- Font dimension

- Attributes (bold, italics, underlined, barred, etc.)

If a report is to be exported as a PDF file, JasperReports needs the following additional information:

PDF font name: The name of font (it could be a predefined PDF font or the name of a TTF file present in the classpath)

PDF embedded: A flag that specifies whether an external TrueType font (TTF) file should be included in the PDF file

PDF encoding: A string that specifies the name of the character encoding

If the report is not exported to PDF format, the font used is the one specified by font name and enriched with the specified attributes. In the case of a PDF document, PDF font name identifies the font used and its attributes (bold, italics, etc.). Other attributes are ignored since they are inherited from the specified PDF font.

Using TTF Fonts

You can use an external True Type font. To do so, the external fonts (files with `.ttf` extensions) must appear in the classpath. This is necessary both during design time (during the use of iReport) and during production (when the report is produced by an external Java program, Swing program, or servlet).

Caution Avoid adding hundreds of TrueType fonts to the classpath because this slows down the start of iReport. For Windows in particular, avoid adding the `%WINDIR%\fonts` directory to the classpath.

In the Font name combo box in the Font tab of the element properties window, only the system fonts, managed by the Java Virtual Machine (JVM), are shown (see Figure 5-1). These are usually inherited by the operating system. Therefore, to select an external TTF font to use in non-PDF reports, install it on your system before use.

Figure 5-1. *Font definition*

After installing, all available external fonts are listed in the PDF font name combo box (see Figure 5-2).

Figure 5-2. *List of TTF fonts*

This combo box displays first a list of PDF built-in fonts, and then all TTF files found in the classpath on startup. At this point, there is no way to rescan the classpath to update the list without restarting iReport.

If the font is not available at design time, edit the TTF file name directly in the combo box. Please note that if the file is not found when the report is run, this will generate an error.

If the selected font is an external TTF font, to ensure that the font is viewed correctly in the exported PDF, select the PDF Embedded check box.

Font Loading and Font Paths

Scanning the whole classpath to look for TTF files and loading all classes used to read TTF files (provided by iText) is really expensive in terms of startup time. For these reasons, iReport provides several ways to limit the time wasted by these processes. If you don't use external fonts at all, you can disable the TTF font loading at startup in the General tab of the Options window (Options ➤ Settings). If during your work you need to use external fonts, the menu command Options ➤ Reload fonts will do what you avoided during startup.

To limit the number of directories to scan when looking for fonts, you can define a special *fonts path*. This is composed of a set of directories belonging to the classpath, so you can be sure that JasperReports will find the requested fonts to fill a report (see Figure 5-3).

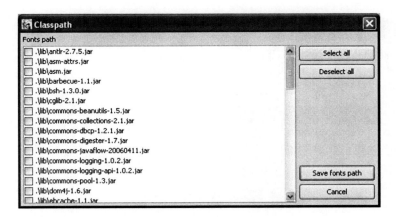

Figure 5-3. *Fonts path window*

To define the fonts path, select Options ➤ Fonts path and check all the directories and JARs that must be scanned when looking for fonts.

A void fonts path will not be considered, and the whole classpath will be used instead.

Character Encoding

Correct character encoding is crucial in JasperReports, particularly when you have to print in PDF format. Therefore, it is very important to choose the right PDF encoding for characters.

The encoding specifies how characters are to be interpreted. In Italian, for example, to print correctly accented characters (such as è, ò, à, and ù), you must use *CP1252* encoding (Western European ANSI, also known as WinAnsi). However, some JVM versions (those prior to version 1.4) do not support this encoding; these versions require *Cp1252* encoding (the only difference is the "p" written in lowercase).

iReport has a rich set of predefined encoding types in the PDF Encoding combo box in the Font tab of the element properties window.

If you have problems with reports containing nonstandard characters in PDF format, make sure that all the fields have the same encoding type and check the charset used by the database from which the report data is read.

Use of Unicode Characters

You can use Unicode syntax to write non-Latin-based characters (such as Greek, Cyrillic, and Asian characters). For these characters, specify Unicode code in the expression that identifies the field text. For example, to print the euro symbol, use the Unicode \u20ac character escape.

■**Caution** The expression \u20ac is not simple text; it is a Java expression that identifies a string containing the € character. If you write this text into a static text element, "\u20ac" will appear; the value of a static field is not interpreted as a Java expression (this only happens with the text fields).

Working with Styles

To define a new style, select Styles from the Format menu. This opens a window for managing report styles (see Figure 5-4).

Style name	Default	
Default	Yes	New
Header1		Modify
Footer		Set as default
		Delete

Figure 5-4. *Styles window*

This list is the same as in the styles library pane in the main window, shown in Figure 5-5 (the combo box on top of the pane must be set to Report styles).

In the Styles window, press the New button to add a new style.

You can define many properties for a style. Leave the default value when you don't want to set a specific value for a property. To reset a value, click the Reset button, shown here:

Figure 5-5. *Styles library pane showing the report styles*

The only mandatory field in the Style definition window, shown in Figure 5-6, is the Style name. All other fields are optional.

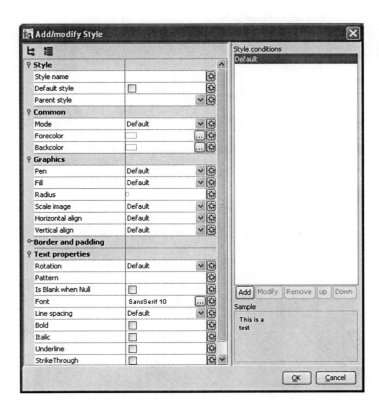

Figure 5-6. *Style definition window*

It is possible to specify a style to be the default style of a report (you can have only one default style in a report). If a default style is present, all the element properties that have an unspecified value will implicitly inherit a value from the default style.

The Parent style property defines the style from which the current one inherits default properties.

The other properties fall into the following four categories: common properties, graphics properties, border and padding properties, and text properties. For details about each of these properties, refer to Chapter 4.

In the Common tab of the element properties window for each text element is a combo box labeled Style. To apply a style to an element, choose a value from the list.

Caution The copy/paste style items in the pop-up menu in the main design window (see Figure 5-7) simply copy or paste the graphic properties of one element to another. They do not refer to the *Style property* of the element, shown in Figure 5-8.

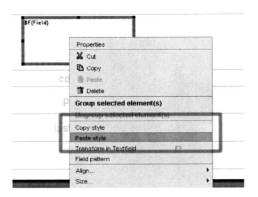

Figure 5-7. *Copy/paste style items in the pop-up menu don't refer to the style property.*

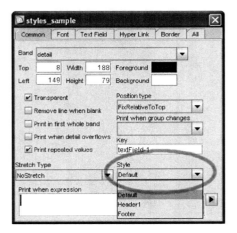

Figure 5-8. *Element properties window—Style property*

Creating Style Conditions

Starting with JasperReports 1.2, you can make your styles dynamic using *conditions*. For example, you can set the forecolor of a text field to black if the field value is positive and to red when it is negative. To do that, add a condition to the Style conditions list, which adds a new set of values to the style (see Figure 5-9). You can override all default style values; these new values will be used when the condition is true.

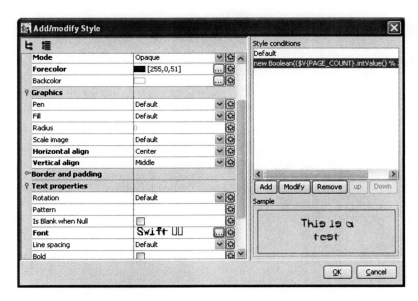

Figure 5-9. *Conditional style*

Sometimes you can't see the changes in your final report even if the condition is true, especially when adding a style to old JRXML files (earlier than JasperReports version 1.2). This happens because iReport used to save all the attribute values of elements in the JRXML file. When an attribute of an element is explicitly defined, the style value is overridden, and the conditional style is not applied. (Starting from iReport 1.2, this kind of behavior has changed.)

Reusing Styles Through the Styles Library

Instead of repeatedly defining similar styles for each report, you can define a style in the styles library and reuse it in other reports. To do this, drag a style from the library over an element. If the style is not yet present in the report, it is added, and the Style attribute of the element is set to the name of the selected style.

iReport comes with a set of completely modifiable predefined styles.

To use the library, select Styles library from the combo box above the library pane in the main window.

An image in the background of the list informs you that the styles panel is displaying the report styles (Figure 5-10) or the list of saved styles in the library (Figure 5-11).

Figure 5-10. *Report styles image*

Figure 5-11. *Styles library image*

If you want to specify a style present in the library be the default style for new reports, you need to choose in the Options window (Options ➤ Settings) a value for the Default Style property (in the property group Report Defaults in the General tab). From then on, every time a new report is created, the specified style will be copied into the new report and set as the default style.

To add, modify, and delete styles, use the buttons on the right of the combo box above the pane (see Figure 5-12).

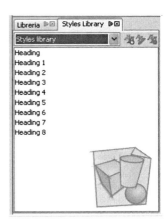

Figure 5-12. *Styles can be organized in the styles library.*

■**Caution** Once a library style has been applied to a report, any later changes to that library style will not be updated in the report style.

Library styles are saved in the styleLibrary.xml file located in the same directory as config.xml (by default, <user home>/.ireport/).

A Word About Report Fonts

The use of report fonts is deprecated—use styles instead.

In case you do run into report fonts when working in iReport, understand that iReport does not manage the report font optimally. iReport limits itself to setting the property values of the selected report font to the selected element and to copying all the attributes of the global font to the text element. In fact, global fonts were created to economize the XML source by avoiding having to specify all the font characteristics for every single field. Since this work is completely automated in iReport, optimizing has little importance. However, because of this, the attempt to centralize report font management is bypassed, because JasperReports uses the attributes specified at the element level and they are always specified by iReport. More simply, if a global report font is used in a text element, its characteristics are saved with the text element and essentially override the global report font.

You cannot currently define a set of fonts to be used in more than one report.

CHAPTER 6

■ ■ ■

Fields, Parameters, and Variables

In a report, there are three groups of objects that can store values: *fields*, *parameters*, and *variables*. These objects are used in expressions, they can change their values during print progression, and they are typed, that is, all these objects have a type that corresponds to a Java class such as String or Double.

Fields, parameters, and variables have to be declared in the report in order to be used. By selecting View from the main menu, you will find, among other choices, the Fields, Variables, and Parameters submenus. Each of these three submenus allows you to view the window for managing all these objects (see Figure 6-1).

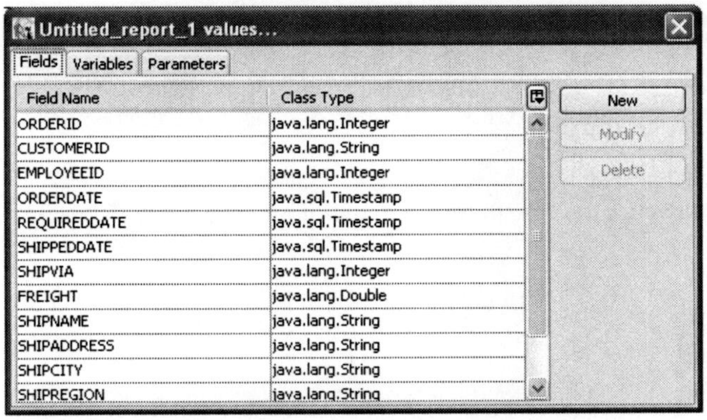

Figure 6-1. *Window for managing fields, variables, and parameters*

Through this values window, it is possible to declare, modify, and remove fields, variables, and parameters. The same operations available in this window are available in the Document structure panel as well (see Figure 6-2).

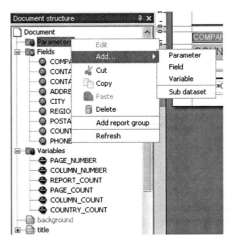

Figure 6-2. *Management of fields, variables, and parameters from the Document structure panel*

Let's take a closer look at these objects, starting with fields.

Working with Fields

A report is commonly created starting from a datasource: the datasources in JasperReports are always organized in a set of records that are composed of a series of fields exactly like the results of a SQL query.

In the window that appears when you select View ➤ Fields, in the Fields tab, you can view declared fields. In order to declare a field, click the New button, and the window shown in Figure 6-3 will appear.

Figure 6-3. *Adding a new field*

The fields are identified by a name, by a type, and by an optional description. Starting from JasperReports 1.0.0, fields can be of any type. This simplifies working with JavaBean datasources where casting from java.lang.Object to the actual report field class is no longer required in expressions; now you can refer to a field by using the following syntax, where field_name can be an arbitrary string:

$F{*field_name*}

So, if you want to deal with a field named MyPerson as an it.businesslogic.Person object, you would write

((it.businesslogic.Person)$F{MyPerson})

Starting from JasperReports 1.3.2, you can use custom name/value pair properties for report fields (and report parameters) to store extra information about a field. By clicking the Edit field properties button in the Add/modify field dialog box shown earlier in Figure 6-3, you can open the window in Figure 6-4 to edit a field's properties.

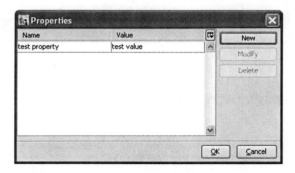

Figure 6-4. *Editing field properties*

Custom properties can be read and used by external applications.

The number of fields in a report could be really high (possibly reaching the hundreds). For this reason, in iReport, different tools exist for the declaration of fields retrieved by particular datasource typologies.

Registration of Fields of a SQL Query

The most widely used tool is the one that allows you to declare or *record* the fields of a SQL query in order to use them in a report. To do this, it is necessary first of all to open the Report query dialog box by clicking the button shown here:

The dialog box for the query definition will appear, as shown in Figure 6-5. It will be used to fill the report (if the report is really created starting from a SQL query).

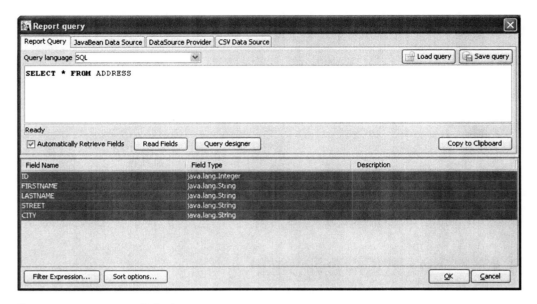

Figure 6-5. *Report query dialog box*

After being sure that the connection to the DBMS is active, insert a query, for example:

```
select * from customers
```

iReport will run the SQL query, and it will analyze its result in order to propose available fields to you. By selecting the fields, you register them in the values window (see Figure 6-6).

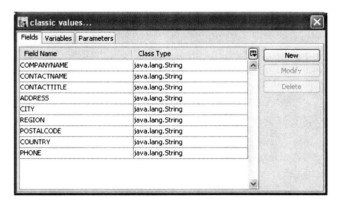

Figure 6-6. *Fields retrieved from a query*

■**Caution** To register the fields, it is necessary to select them from the list; if the query contains some mistakes, deselect the Automatically Retrieve Fields check box in the Report query dialog box and read the fields manually with the Read Fields button.

The current status of Automatically Retrieve Fields is remembered by iReport even after a restart.

In this case, all the fields will be of type String: in general, the type set for the fields is based on the original SQL type, which can be matched with a string, an integer, and so forth.

Accessing the SQL Query Designer

You can create queries in the Report queries dialog box via a visual query designer. You open this tool by clicking the button labeled Query designer (a JDBC connection must be active, and the selected language must be SQL).

This SQL query designer, which comes from the SQLeonardo project, provides a drag-and-drop way to create queries (see Figure 6-7).

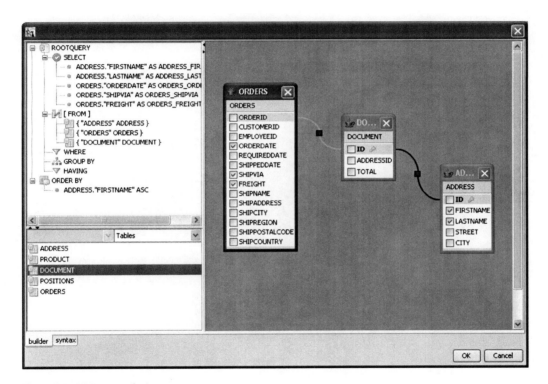

Figure 6-7. *SQL query designer*

To create a simple query, drag some tables into the main pane and select some fields.

Registration of the Fields of a JavaBean

One of the most advanced features of JasperReports is the capability to manage datasources that are not based on a simple SQL query. This is the case for JavaBean collections, where Java objects substitute for records. In this case, the "fields" are object attributes (or attributes of attributes).

By selecting the JavaBean Datasource tab in the Report query dialog box, you can register fields that are read by a specified Java object. For example, Figure 6-8 shows the fields for the following object:

```
it.businesslogic.ireport.examples.beans.PersonBean
```

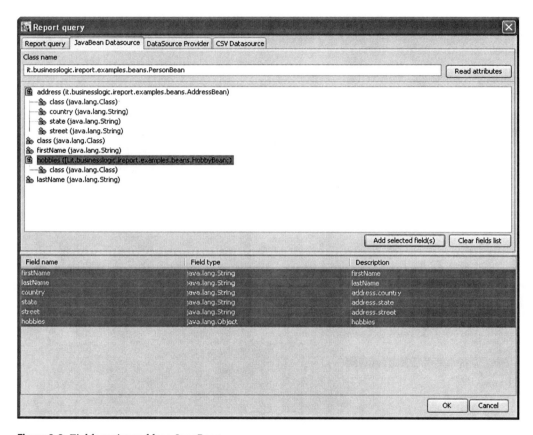

Figure 6-8. *Fields registered by a JavaBean*

By clicking the Read attributes button, you can explore the object. When browsing the object, you can see scalar attributes or other objects. By double-clicking an object, you can access its attributes.

In order to add a field to the list, select a tree node and click the Add selected field(s) button. The path to the attribute will be stored in the field description.

Displaying a Field with a Text Field

To print a field in a Text Field element, you will need to set the expression and the text field type correctly in the Text Field tab of the element properties window (see Figure 6-9). If necessary, you can also define a pattern for formatting the field.

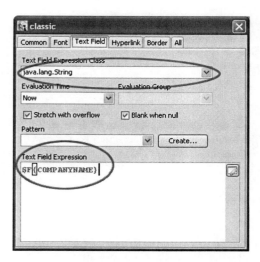

Figure 6-9. *Element properties for printing the field*

It is possible to automate the setting of the expression and of the type by dragging a field from the fields list into the desired report band.

Working with Parameters

Parameters are values usually passed to the report from the program that creates the print of the report. They can be used for guiding particular behaviors during runtime (such as the application of a condition in a SQL query) and for supplying additional data to the print context such as an Image object containing a chart or a string with the report title.

As with fields, parameters are also typed and must be declared at design time (see Figure 6-10). The parameter types can be arbitrary.

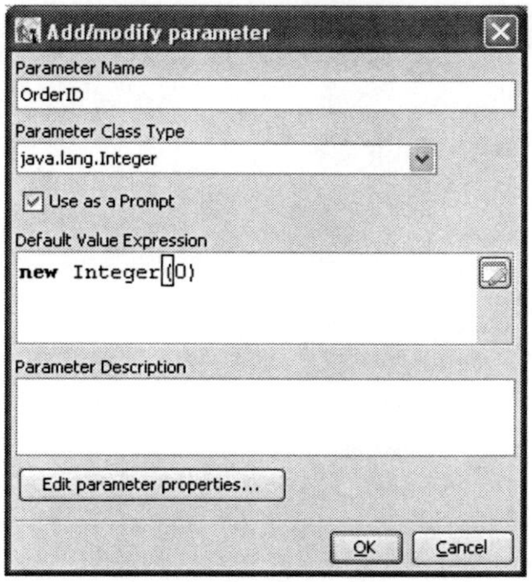

Figure 6-10. *Adding a new parameter*

At the moment, the property Use as a Prompt in the Add/modify parameter dialog box is not used by iReport, and it is not relevant for printing. It is a mechanism introduced by JasperReports to allow applications to collect parameters entered directly by the user.

In an expression, you refer to a parameter by using the following syntax, in which *parameter_name* is an arbitrary string:

```
$P{parameter_name}
```

A parameter can assume a default value if the application does not pass an explicit value for that parameter to the report. Parameters (and variables as well) are Java objects, so it is incorrect to use an expression for a default value of type Double such as

```
0.123
```

You must create an instance of the Double object this way:

```
new Double(0.123)
```

As for fields, you can define a set of name/value pairs so you can store extra information about a parameter in your report. Such properties are normally used by external applications.

Click the Edit parameter properties button to bring up the dialog box shown earlier in Figure 6-4, where you can edit property information for parameters.

Using Parameters in a Query

Parameters may be used to filter a SQL query. Suppose you want to print information about a particular customer identified by customer ID (not known at design time). Your query will be as follows:

```
select * from customers
where CUSTOMERID = $P{MyCustomerId}
```

MyCustomerId is a parameter declared as an integer. JasperReports will transform this query to

```
select * from customers where CUSTOMERID = ?
```

It will run this SQL using a prepared statement by passing the MyCustomerId value as a query parameter. If you would like to pass the parameter value directly, you can use this special syntax:

```
$P!{parameter_name}
```

This allows you to replace the parameter name in the query with its value. For example, if you have a parameter named MyWhere with the value of where CUSTOMERID = 5, the query

```
select * from customers   $P!{CUSTOMERID}
```

will be transformed into

```
select * from customers   where CUSTOMERID = 5
```

by using this syntax.

Passing Parameters from a Program

Parameters are passed from a program "caller" to the print generator through a class that extends the java.util.Map interface.

Consider the code in Listing 2-2 in Chapter 2, in particular the following lines:

```
...
HashMap hm = new HashMap();
        ...
JasperPrint print = JasperFillManager.fillReport(
                                fileName,
                                hm,
                        new JREmptyDataSource());
...
```

fillReport is a key method that allows you to print a report by passing the file name as a parameter—in this case, a dummy datasource (JREmptyDataSource) and a parameter map that is empty and is represented by a java.util.HashMap object.

To use a parameter that contains the title of your report, you can proceed this way:

1. Declare the parameter as described previously. The parameter will be of the type java.lang.String and named REPORT_NAME (see Figure 6-11).

Figure 6-11. *Definition of the REPORT_NAME parameter*

2. Add into the title band a Text Field element with the following expression: $P{ REPORT_NAME}.

3. Modify the program code:

```
...
HashMap hm = new HashMap();
hm.put("REPORT_NAME","This is the title of the report");
        ...
JasperPrint print = JasperFillManager.fillReport(
                                fileName,
                                hm,
                        new JREmptyDataSource());
```

You have inserted into the parameter map a value for the REPORT_NAME parameter.
Figures 6-12 and 6-13 show the passed parameter at design time and when printed, respectively.

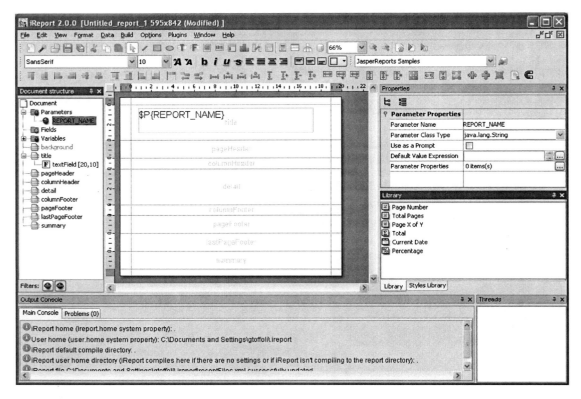

Figure 6-12. *Using a parameter to print the report title*

You do not need to pass the values of all parameters declared in a report unless you want to set
a value for a parameter by the program explicitly. JasperReports will use the default value expression
(which you can specify in the Add/modify parameter dialog box) to calculate the predefined value
of the parameter; the empty expression is synonymous to null.

In reality, this example is not very interesting because the data type passed is a simple string.
However, it is possible to pass some much more complex objects such as an image (java.awt.Image)
or a datasource instance usable to feed a particular subreport. It is important to fill a parameter
with an object having the same type as the declared type for the parameter. Otherwise, a
ClassCastException will be thrown.

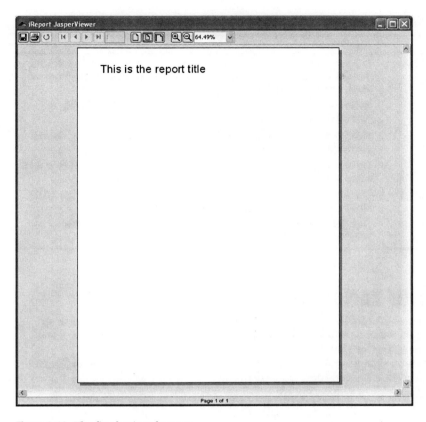

Figure 6-13. *The final printed report*

Built-in Parameters

JasperReports provides some built-in parameters (they are internal to the reporting engine) that are readable but not modifiable by the user. These parameters are presented in Table 6-1.

Table 6-1. *Built-in Parameters*

Parameter	Description
REPORT_PARAMETERS_MAP	This is the java.util.Map passed to the fillReport method, and it contains the parameter values defined by the user.
REPORTCONNECTION	This is the JDBC connection passed to the report when the report is created through a SQL query.
REPORT_DATASOURCE	This is the datasource used by the report when it is not using a JDBC connection.
REPORT_SCRIPTLET	This represents the scriptlet instance used during creation. If no scriptlet is specified, this parameter uses an instance of net.sf.jasperreports.engine.JRDefaultScriptlet. Starting from JasperReports 1.0.0, an implicit cast to the provided scriptlet class is performed. This simplifies many expressions that use the provided scriptlet class.

Continued

Table 6-1. *Continued*

Parameter	Description
IS_IGNORE_PAGINATION	You can switch the pagination system on or off by setting a value for this parameter (it must be a Boolean object). By default, pagination is used, except for exporting to HTML or Excel formats.
REPORT_LOCALE	This is used to set the locale used to fill the report. If no locale is provided, the system default will be used.
REPORT_TIME_ZONE	This is used to set the time zone used to fill the report. If no locale is provided, the system default will be used.
REPORT_MAX_COUNT	This is used to limit the number of records filling a report. If no value is provided, no limit will be set.
REPORT_RESOURCE_BUNDLE	This is the resource bundle loaded for this report. See Chapter 10 for how to provide a resource bundle for a report.
REPORT_VIRTUALIZER	This defines the class for the report filler that implements the JRVirtualizer interface for filling the report.

Working with Variables

Variables are objects used to store the results of calculations such as subtotals, sums, and so on.

Variables are typed, the same as fields and parameters are. You must declare the Java type of which they are instances (the variable class type).

Figure 6-14 shows the dialog box for the creation of a new variable. Following is a list describing the meaning of each field in this dialog box.

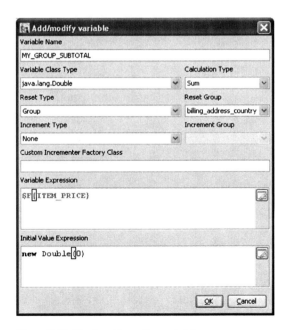

Figure 6-14. *Declaration of a variable*

Variable Name: This is the name of the variable. Similar to fields and parameters, you refer to a variable using the following syntax in an expression, where *variable_name* is an arbitrary string:

$V{*variable_name*}

Variable Class Type: Similar to parameters, variables do not have restrictions regarding the object type that they can assume. In the combo box, you can see some of the most common types such as java.lang.String and java.lang.Double.

Calculation Type: This is the type of a predefined calculation used to store the result by the variable. When the predefined value is Nothing, it means "don't perform any calculation automatically." JasperReports performs the specified calculation by changing the variable's value for every new record that is read from the datasource. To perform a calculation of a variable means to evaluate its expression (defined in the Variable Expression area). If the calculation type is Nothing, JasperReports will assign the variable the value that resulted from the evaluation of the variable expressions. If a calculation type is other than Nothing, the expression result will represent a new input value for the chosen calculation, and the variable value will be the result of this calculation. The calculation types are listed in Table 6-2.

Table 6-2. *Calculation Types for Variables*

Calculation Types	Description
Nothing	No type calculation is performed. It is used when the calculation type is intrinsic to the expression that is specified and valuated for each new record.
Count	This counts how many times the expression result is different from null. It is not the same as Sum, which makes real sums based on the expression's numerical value.
Distinct Count	This counts the number of different expression results; the order of expression evaluation does not matter.
Sum	This adds to each iteration the expression value to the variable's current value.
Average	This calculates the arithmetic average of all the expressions received in input.
Lowest	This returns the lowest expression value received in input.
Highest	This returns the highest expression value received in input.
StandardDeviation	This returns the standard deviation of all the expressions received in input.
Variance	This returns the variance of all the expressions received in input.
System	This does not make any calculation, and the expression is not evaluated. In this case, the report engine keeps only the last value set for this variable in memory. This setting can be used to store the calculation result performed, for example, one returned from a scriptlet.

Reset Type: This specifies when a variable value has to be reset to the initial value or simply to null. The variable reset concept is fundamental when you want to make some group calculations such as subtotals or averages. The reset types are listed in Table 6-3.

Table 6-3. *Variable Reset Types*

Reset Types	Description
None	The initial value expression is always ignored.
Report	The variable is initialized only once at the beginning of report creation by using the initial value expression.
Page	The variable is initialized again in each new page.
Column	The variable is initialized again in each new column (or in each page if the report is composed of only one column).
Group	The variable is initialized again in each new group (the group specified in the Reset group setting).

Reset Group: This specifies the group that determines the variable reset if the Group reset type is selected.

Increment Type: This specifies when a variable value has to be evaluated; the variable reset concept is fundamental when you want to make some group calculations such as subtotals or averages. The increment types are the same as the calculation types listed in Table 6-2.

Increment Group: This specifies the group that determines the variable increment if the Group increment type is selected.

Custom Incrementer Factory Class: This is the name of a Java class that increases the JRIncrementerFactory interface, which is useful for defining operations such as the sum for nonnumerical types.

Variable Expression: This is the Java expression that identifies the input value of the variable to each iteration.

Initial Value Expression: This is an expression for evaluating the variable's initial value.

Built-in Variables

As with the parameters, JasperReports provides some built-in variables (which are directly managed by the reporting engine). These variables are readable but not modifiable by the user. Table 6-4 lists the built-in variables.

Table 6-4. *Built-in Variables*

Built-in Variable	Description
PAGE_NUMBER	Contains the current number of pages. At "report" time, this variable will contain the total number of pages.
COLUMN_NUMBER	Contains the current number of columns.
REPORT_COUNT	Contains the current number of records that have been processed.
PAGE_COUNT	Contains the current number of records that have been processed in the current page.
COLUMN_COUNT	Contains the current number of records that have been processed during the current column creation.
*group_name*_COUNT	Contains the current number of records that have been processed for the group specified as a variable prefix.

CHAPTER 7

■ ■ ■

Bands and Groups

In this chapter, I will explain how to manage bands and groups by using iReport. In Chapter 3, you learned how reports are structured, and you have seen how the report is divided into bands, horizontal portions of a page that are printed and modified in height according to band properties and content. Here, you will see how to adjust the properties of bands. You will also learn how to use groups and how to create some breaks in a report.

Modifying Bands

JasperReports divides a report into eight main bands and the background (nine bands in total). To these two other bands can be added: the group footer and the group header.

By clicking the Bands button shown here:

it is possible to bring up a list of bands present in your report (see Figure 7-1).

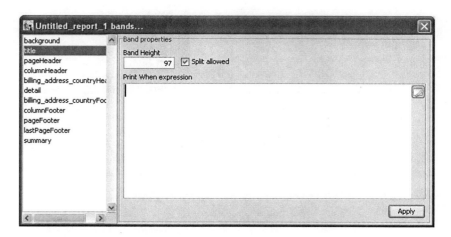

Figure 7-1. *Bands list and properties window*

Through this window, you can modify the main properties of a band: specify its height, expressed in pixels (through the Band Height option); indicate whether the band breaks if it overflows the page (by enabling the Split allowed check box option); and include an expression (in the Print When expression area) that must return a Boolean object, which determines whether the band gets printed. In this case, the empty expression represents implicitly the following:

```
new Boolean(true)
```

indicating that the band is always printed. In this expression, you can use fields, variables, and parameters, as long as the expression produces a Boolean object as a result.

The same band properties can be modified using the band properties sheet by selecting the band node in the Document structure panel: the properties sheet is normally located on the right of the main window (see Figure 7-2). This approach permits you to modify the same property of more than a single band at time.

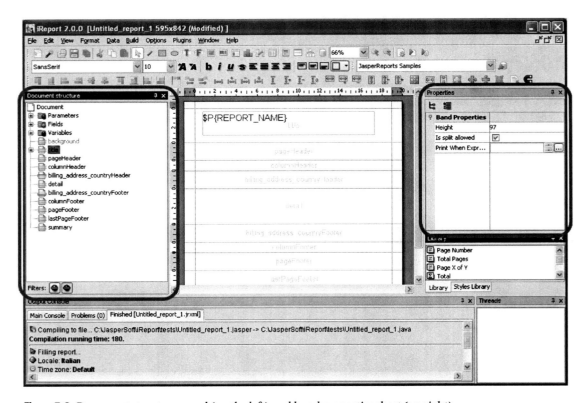

Figure 7-2. *Document structure panel (on the left) and band properties sheet (on right)*

Even if it is specified explicitly, the band height can increase if one or more of the elements it contains grows vertically (it can happen for Text Field elements whose contents exceed the specified dimensions or for Subreport elements). JasperReports guarantees that the band height is never less than that specified.

Note In order to resize a band, you can use the band properties sheet or the bands list and properties window, setting a value directly for the band in the Band Height field, or use the mouse by moving the cursor over the lower margin of the band and dragging it toward the bottom or the top of the page (see Figure 7-3).

A double-click on the lower margin allows you to resize the band by adapting the height to the content.

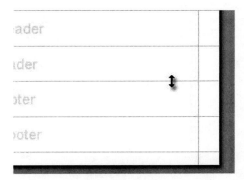

Figure 7-3. *Movement of the lower margin of a band*

Tip If one or more consecutive bands have zero height, it is possible to increase a band's dimensions by moving toward the bottom the lower margin in the band that precedes it while pressing down the Shift key.

By moving an element from one band to another, the band with which the element is associated is changed automatically.

Working with Groups

Groups allow you to organize the records of a report to better structure the report content. A group is defined through an expression. JasperReports evaluates this expression: a new group begins when the expression value changes.

I will explain the use of the groups by walking you through an example step by step. Suppose you have a list of people: you want to create a report where the names of these people are grouped based on the initial letter (like in a phone book). Run iReport and open a new empty report. Next, you will take the data from a database by using a SQL query (a JDBC connection to the Northwind database must already be configured and tested). The first thing you have to consider is the order of record selection: JasperReports doesn't dictate order of records coming from a datasource; for this reason, when you think about a report containing some groups, you have to order the records in the right way yourself. For this example, use the following SQL query:

```
select * from customers order by CONTACTNAME
```

The selected records will be ordered according to the name of the selected customers. Select the CONTACTNAME and COUNTRY fields through the Report query dialog box (see Figure 7-4).

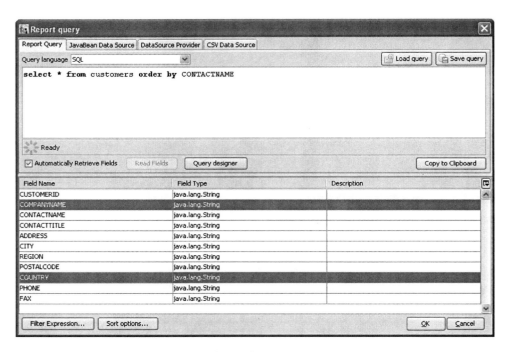

Figure 7-4. *The query extracts the ordered records.*

Before continuing on with creating your group, make sure that everything works correctly by inserting in the details band the CONTACTNAME and COUNTRY fields (move them from the Document structure panel to the detail band, as shown in Figure 7-5), and then compile and create the report. To make things a bit more complex, divide the detail into two columns (Chapter 3 discusses how to specify the number of columns in a report). The result should be similar to that of Figure 7-6.

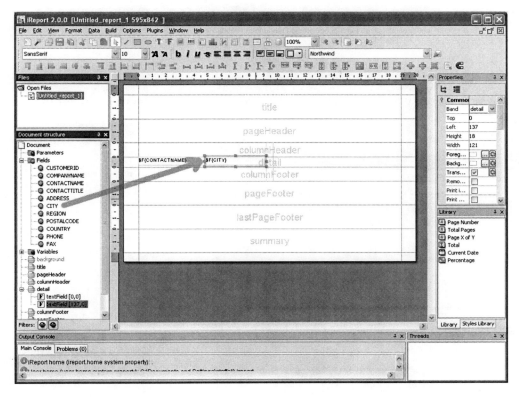

Figure 7-5. *The report without groups*

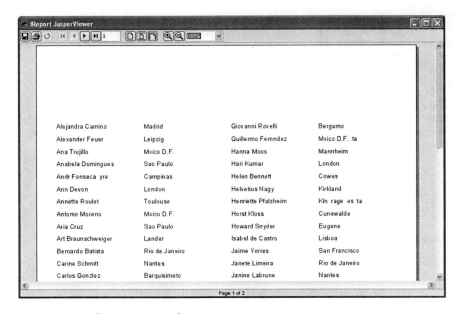

Figure 7-6. *A preliminary printed report*

Now on to grouping the data. By clicking the Groups button, shown here:

you bring up the report groups window through which you manage report groups, as shown in Figure 7-7.

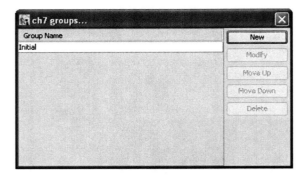

Figure 7-7. *Report groups window*

Click the New button and in the dialog box that appears, insert a new group named, for example, Initial (see Figure 7-8).

Figure 7-8. *Specifying group properties*

A group is identified by several properties:

Group Name: This specifies the group name, which will be used to name the two bands to associate with the group: the header and the footer.

Start on a New Column: If this option is selected, it forces a column break at the end of the group (that is, at the beginning of a new group); if there is only one column in the report, a column break becomes a page break.

Start on a New Page: If this option is selected, it forces a page break at the end of the group (that is, at the beginning of a new group).

Reset Page Number: This option resets the number of pages at the beginning of a new group.

Print header on each page: If this option is selected, it prints the group header on all the pages on which the group's content is printed (if the content requires more than one page for the printed report).

Min height to Start New Page: If the value is other than 0, JasperReports will start to print this group on a new page, if the available space is less than the minimum specified. This option is usually used to avoid dividing by a page break a report section composed of two or more elements that you want to remain together (such as a title followed by the text of a paragraph).

Group Expression: This is the expression that JasperReports will evaluate against each record. When the expression changes in value, a new group is created. If this expression is empty, it is equal to null, and since a null expression will never change in value, the result is a single group header and a single group footer, respectively, after the first column header and before the last column footer.

Group Header Band Height: This is the band height representing the group header: as for all bands, it is possible to modify this value also from the bands list and properties window (refer back to Figure 7-1).

Group Footer Band Height: This is the band height representing the group footer: as for all bands, it is possible to modify this value also from the bands list and properties window (refer back to Figure 7-1).

For this example, you name the group Initial (referring to the initial letter of the names); now you will tell it to start on a new column (selecting the Start on a New Column option). Your group expression has to return the first letter of each name, but an expression like the following:

```
$F{CONTACTNAME}.substring(0,1)
```

would be not sufficient to do what you want, because there is no guarantee that the CONTACTNAME field is not null and that the length is greater than or equal to one. In fact, if CONTACTNAME is null, the expression evaluation generates a `NullPointerException`, and if CONTACTNAME is a zero-length string, the expression evaluation generates an `ArrayOutOfBoundException`. In order to prevent these exceptions, you have to test these two bad cases with a conditional expression like this:

```
( ($F{CONTACTNAME} != null && $F{CONTACTNAME}.length() > 0) ?
      $F{CONTACTNAME}.substring(0,1) : "")
```

You use the Java constraint

```
( condition ) ? value1 : value2
```

which returns *value1* if the *condition* is true and *value2* if the *condition* is false. In particular, if CONTACTNAME is null or its length is zero, it is returned an empty string; otherwise, it is returned the first character of the name.

Once you have added the new group, two new bands appear in the design window: these are labeled InitialHeader and InitialFooter. Insert in the InitialHeader band a text field with the expression used for the group (see Figure 7-9).

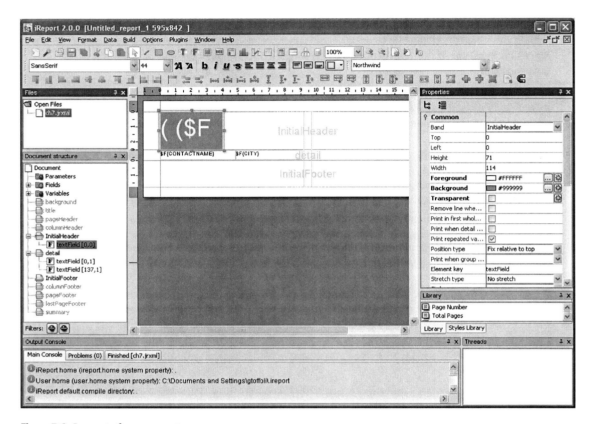

Figure 7-9. *Layout of your report*

Figure 7-10 shows the final result.

The number of possible groups contained in a report is arbitrary, and a group can be contained in a parent group, and itself contain other children groups. The result is a *groups list*.

It is possible to change the priority of a group with respect to another through the Move Up and Move Down buttons present in the report groups window (shown previously in Figure 7-7).

To change the priority of a group means also to change the position of the bands composing it. The higher the priority, the further the group bands are from the detail band.

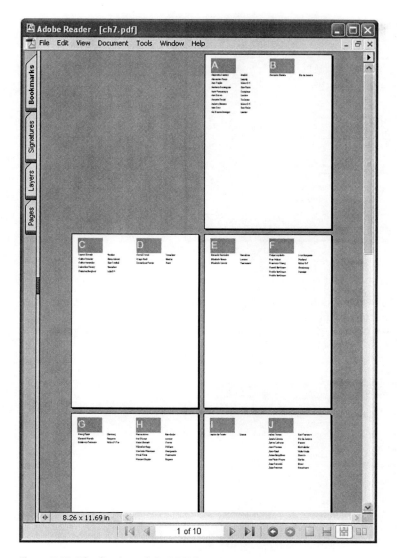

Figure 7-10. *The final result in PDF format*

Group Wizard

To simplify and speed up the creation of a group, iReport provides a convenient wizard that can be run by selecting Edit ➤ New Report Group Wizard.

The Report Group Wizard becomes unbelievably useful when a group is based on a report object, like a field or a variable. In this case, after you set the group name, you select the desired object from the Group by the following report object combo box (see Figure 7-11).

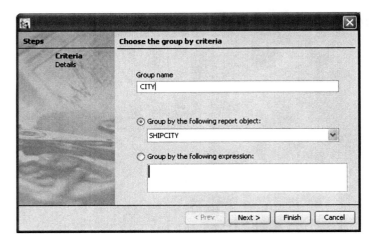

Figure 7-11. *Report Group Wizard—step 1*

Alternatively, it's possible to set a more complex expression by selecting the Group by the following expression radio button option and filling the field below it.

In the next step, shown in Figure 7-12, you can decide whether or not to display the group header and the group footer.

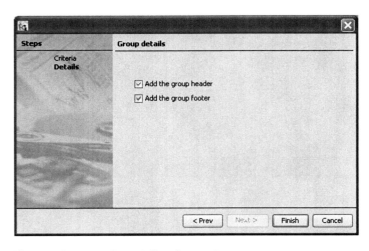

Figure 7-12. *Report Group Wizard—step 2*

Groups and Record Order

As mentioned earlier, JasperReports by default does not order data records from a datasource. For this reason, when you create a group, you are responsible for providing the right order of records to JasperReports. This task is trivial when dealing with SQL queries, where an order by clause can do the job, but it's also simple when using other kinds of datasources such as an XML datasource. In this case, you must be sure that the order of provided data is compatible with the report groups to avoid several equal results of the same group expression value (which will produce more groups than desired).

If you cannot provide the data in the right order, you can use the Sort options of JasperReports to force an in-memory sorting of your records (the "Sorting and Filtering Records" section in Chapter 9 explains how to do just that).

CHAPTER 8

■■■

Subreports

Subreports represent one of the most advanced functionalities of JasperReports, and they make possible the realization of very complex reports. The aim is to be able to insert a report into another report created with modalities similar to the first one.

You have seen that to create a printed report you need three things: a JASPER file, a parameters map (it can be empty), and a datasource (or a JDBC connection). In this chapter, I will explain how to pass these three objects to a subreport through its parent report and by creating dynamic connections that are able to filter the records of the subreport based on the parent's data. Then I will explain how to return information regarding the subreport creation to the parent report.

Creating a Subreport

As I have already said, a subreport is a real report composed of its own XML source and compiled in a JASPER file. To create a subreport means to create a normal report. You have to pay attention only to the print margins, which are usually set to zero for subreports. The horizontal dimension of the report should be as large as the element into which it will be placed in the parent report. It is not necessary that the Subreport element be exactly as large as the subreport; however, in order to avoid unexpected results, it is always better to be precise.

In the parent report it is possible to insert a subreport using the Subreport tool, shown here:

What is created is an element similar to the Rectangle element.

The Subreport element dimensions are not really meaningful because the subreport will occupy all the space it needs without being cut or cropped. You can think of a Subreport element as defining the position of the top-left corner to which the subreport will be aligned.

Linking a Subreport to the Parent Report

To link the subreport to the parent report means to define three things: how to recover the JASPER object that implements the subreport, how to feed it with data, and how to set the value for the subreport parameters. All this information is defined through the Subreport and Subreport (Other) tabs of the element properties window (see Figures 8-1 and 8-2).

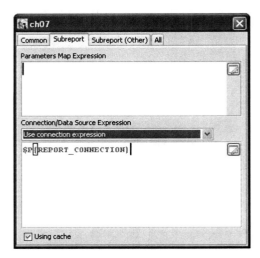

Figure 8-1. *Subreport tab options*

Figure 8-2. *Subreport (Other) tab options*

First, let's take a look at how subreport parameters are set.

Passing Parameters

Just as a report is invoked from a program using the `fillReport` method, a parameters map is passed during a subreport's creation; in reality, this map is managed directly by the reporting engine, but you can insert parameter name/object pairs into this map at runtime. Although the Parameters Map Expression option is probably the method least used to set values of subreport parameters, it is the first property of the Subreport element encountered in the Subreport tab; it allows you to define an expression, the result of which must be a `java.util.Map` object. Using this method, it is possible, for example, to pass to the master report (from your program) a parameter containing a map, and then to pass this map to the subreport by including in an expression the name of the parameter (for example, $P{myMap}) that contains the map. It is also possible to pass to the child report the same parameters map that was provided to the parent by using the built-in parameter `REPORT_PARAMETERS_MAP`: in this case, the right expression would be $P{REPORT_PARAMETERS_MAP}.

If you leave the Parameters Map Expression field blank, an empty map will be passed to the subreport (this is not true if you define some subreport parameter values as you'll see soon in the section "A Step-by-Step Example"). The limitation of this mechanism is the immutability of the parameters passed in the map. In order to get around this limitation, JasperReports allows you to define some parameter name/object pairs where the value of each object can be created through an expression. You can see the Subreport parameters table earlier in Figure 8-2. Also, in this case, the interface is quite self-explanatory: by clicking the Add button, you can bring up a dialog box in which it is possible to add a new parameter that will feed the parameters map of the subreport (see Figure 8-3).

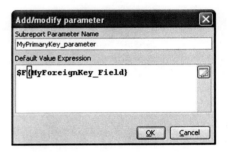

Figure 8-3. *Adding a new parameter*

The parameter name has to be the same as the one declared in the subreport. The names are *case sensitive*, which means capitalization counts. If you make an error typing the name or the inserted parameter has not been defined, no error is thrown (but something would probably end up not working, and you would be left to wonder why).

In the Default Value Expression area, you supply a classic JasperReports expression, in which you can use fields, parameters, and variables. The return type has to be congruous with the parameter type declared in the subreport; otherwise, an exception of `ClassCastException` will occur at runtime.

One of the most common uses of subreport parameters is to pass the key of a record printed in the parent report in order to execute a query in the subreport through which you can extract the records referred to (report headers and lines).

Specifying the Datasource

To set the subreport datasource means to tell JasperReports how to retrieve data to fill the subreport. There are two big datasource groups: JDBC connections and datasources.

Using a JDBC connection to fill the parent report makes the use of the subreport simple enough. In this case, a *connection expression* defines a `java.sql.Connection` object that is already linked to the database (you will see how to specify this type of expression later in this chapter in the section "A Step-by-Step Example"). It is possible to pass this already opened connection through the parameters map explicitly, but the simplest thing is to use the predefined `REPORT_CONNECTION` parameter containing the connection passed to the `fillReport` method from the calling application. By using a connection expression, you ensure the report will be created starting from the SQL query contained in the subreport.

The use of a datasource is more complex (even if it is sometimes necessary when a connection like JDBC is not being used), but it is extremely powerful. It involves writing a datasource expression that returns the `JRDataSource` instance with which to fill the subreport. Depending on what you want to achieve, it is possible to pass the datasource that will feed the subreport through a parameter. If the parent report is executed using a datasource, this datasource is stored in the `REPORT_DATASOURCE` built-in parameter; unlike the `REPORT_CONNECTION` parameter, the `REPORT_DATASOURCE` should never be used to feed a subreport. A datasource is in general a *consumable* object that is usable for feeding a report only once, so a datasource will satisfy the needs of a single report (or subreport). Therefore, the parameter technique is not suitable when every record of the master report has got its own subreport (unless there is only one record in the master report). When I explain datasources in Chapter 9, you will see how this problem is easily solved by using custom datasources, and how to create subreports using different types of connections and datasources.

Specifying the Subreport

To specify what JASPER file to use to create the subreport, you must set a *subreport expression* (you will see how to specify this type of expression later in this chapter in the section "A Step-by-Step Example"). The type of object returned from this expression has to be selected from the combo box that precedes the expression field (refer back to Figure 8-2). Table 8-1 lists the possible object types.

Table 8-1. *Possible Return Types of the Subreport Expression*

Possible Return Types	Description
net.sf.jasperreports.engine.JasperReport	The JASPER file preloaded in a JasperReport object
java.io.InputStream	An open stream of the JASPER file
java.net.URL	A URL that identifies the location of the JASPER file
java.io.File	A file object that identifies the JASPER file
java.lang.String	The name of the JASPER file

If the expression is a string, it uses the `JRLoader` class to load the file starting from the specified location. Specifically, the string is at first interpreted as a URL. In case of a `MalformedURLException` being returned, the string is interpreted as a physical path to a file; if the file does not exist, the string is interpreted as a Java resource. This means that if you refer to a file, the string has to contain the absolute path for that file, or you have to put your JASPER file in the classpath and refer to it using a Java resource path.

A Step-by-Step Example

Let's put into practice what you have learned in the previous sections. Say you want to print an orders list with rows containing order details. You will use a JDBC connection to the database Northwind: the three tables to use are Orders, Customers, and Order Details.

Open an empty report and click the button shown here:

Insert the query for the parent report:

```
select * from orders
```

From the available fields list keep only ORDERID, ORDERDATE, and CUTOMERID so that you simplify the example (to remove unwanted fields from the list, select them and click the Cancel button). Click the OK button: the three fields will be registered automatically in the report (see Figures 8-4 and 8-5).

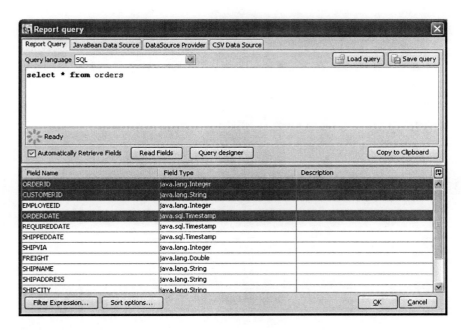

Figure 8-4. *Selecting the report master fields*

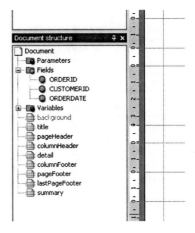

Figure 8-5. *The selected fields are registered among the report fields.*

Drag the three fields into the detail band, as shown in Figure 8-6, save the report named as you like (for example, `master.jrxml`), and print this simple report before proceeding with the subreport. Your results should resemble what you see in Figure 8-7.

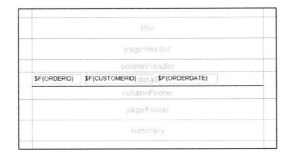

Figure 8-6. *Adding the selected fields to the detail band*

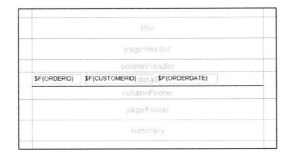

Figure 8-7. *Test of the report master*

Next, you will construct the first subreport to display the information about the customer of each order (CUSTOMER).

In the same way you constructed the report master, prepare this second report by adding to the parameters list the CUSTOMERID parameter, type java.lang.String. The query of this subreport will use this parameter as follows: SELECT * FROM CUSTOMERS WHERE CUSTOMERID = $P{CUSTOMERID} (see Figure 8-8).

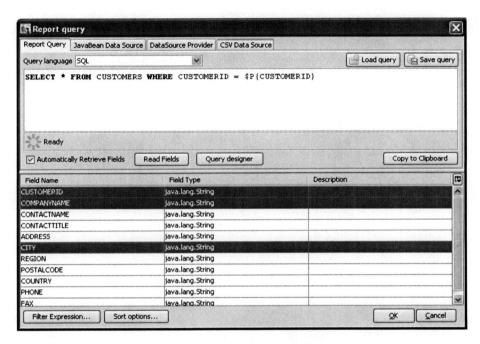

Figure 8-8. *The query of the first subreport (customers.jrxml)*

In order to correctly read the query fields, it is necessary to associate a default value for the parameter (for example, the empty string "").

In the subreport, all the page margins are usually removed because it will be inserted into the master report as a simple element. Figure 8-9 shows how the subreport layout should look.

| $F{CUSTOMERID} | $F{COMPANYNAME} | | $F{CITY} |

Figure 8-9. *Design of the subreport*

Save the subreport (for example, with the name customers.jrxml) and insert a Subreport element into the master report. The vertical dimension of this element is not important, because when you print the report, JasperReports will use all the vertical space necessary (see Figure 8-10).

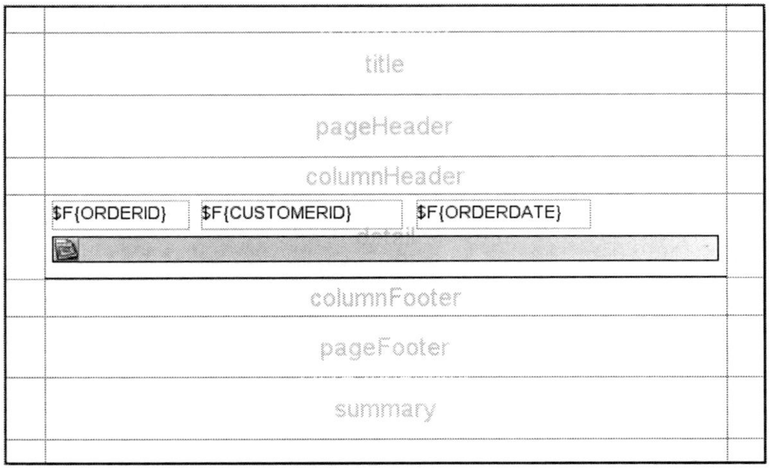

title	
pageHeader	
columnHeader	
$F{ORDERID} $F{CUSTOMERID} $F{ORDERDATE}	
columnFooter	
pageFooter	
summary	

Figure 8-10. *TheSubreport element in the master report (height is not meaningful)*

When you insert the Subreport element, the Subreport Wizard automatically opens. You don't want to use this wizard at this point (I will show you how to work with the Subreport Wizard later in the section "Using the Subreport Wizard"), so select the option "Just create the subreport element" and click Finish. To begin setting the subreport properties, open the element properties window and click the Subreport tab.

Select Use connection expression in the combo box under Connection/Datasource Expression and specify $P{REPORT_CONNECTION} as the expression that stores the JDBC connection used to fill the parent (see Figure 8-11).

Figure 8-11. *Connection to use for feeding the subreport*

In the Subreport (Other) tab, specify where to find the customer.jasper file (that is, the file that contains the subreport) and how to create or modify the parameters that bind the subreport to the master report (see Figure 8-12).

Figure 8-12. *Location of the JASPER file and parameters to bind the subreport to the master report*

As the expression for your subreport, simply specify the name of the JASPER file you created to use as the subreport. By using iReport, you ensure that the subreport will be found when you specify its name without an absolute path, because the directory where the subreport is stored will automatically be added to the classpath, and so the subreport will be found not as a file but as a Java resource through the ClassLoader. In other cases, it could be necessary to specify the directory path where the subreport is located as parameter and to specify an expression like this:

$P{PATH_TO_SUBREPORTS} + java.io.File.separator + "customers.jasper"

In order to extract each customer's data and to view it in the subreport, you have to fill the CUSTOMERID parameter of customers.jasper. To do so, add a new line in the parameters table of the subreport by specifying the parameter name of the subreport and give it an expression that creates the value to give to the parameter. In this case, the parameter will be CUSTOMERID and the expression will be $F{CUSTOMERID}, which is the value of the corresponding field in the master report.

Compile master.jrxml and customers.jrxml and run the parent report. Your results should resemble Figure 8-13.

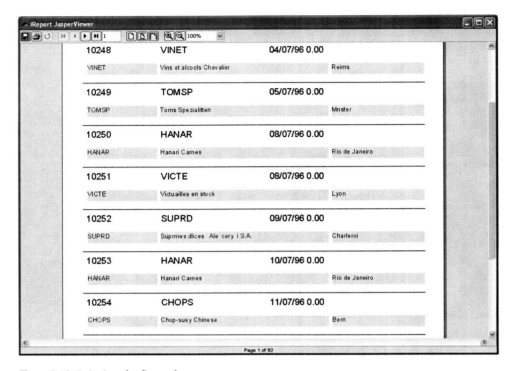

Figure 8-13. *Printing the first subreport*

Proceed with the second subreport to view order details. Once again, start from an empty report, remove the margins, and define the parameter to link to the master report: in this case, use the ORDERID parameter declared as java.lang.Integer, and insert the query for the selection of the order detail rows: select * from orderDetails where ORDERID = $P{ORDERID} (see Figure 8-14).

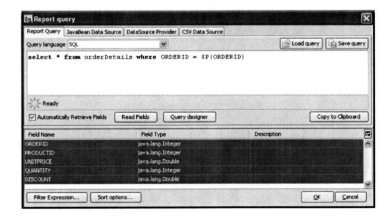

Figure 8-14. *Query for the second subreport*

Set the height of the unused bands to zero (all except for the detail band) and insert in the detail band the fields you want to print (see Figure 8-15).

Figure 8-15. *Design of the second subreport*

Save the file in the same directory as the master with the name details.jrxml and compile it in order to generate details.jasper.

Add the subreport to the master report, as shown in Figure 8-16, and specify the file name of the new subreport and the binding for the ORDERID field.

The file name to specify will be details.jasper (having previously saved the subreport with the name details.jrxml).

Add the parameter of the ORDERID subreport with the value $F{ORDERID} (see Figure 8-17).

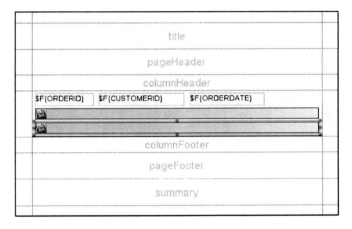

Figure 8-16. *The second subreport added to the master report*

Figure 8-17. *Second subreport's properties*

Now compile the master report once more and print it. The final result should be something like what you see in Figure 8-18.

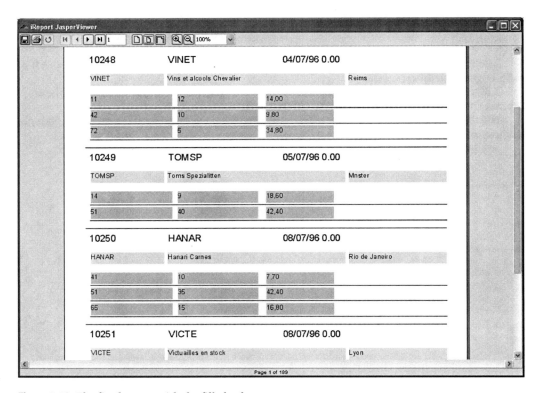

Figure 8-18. *The final report with the filled subreports*

Returning Values from a Subreport

It is often necessary to retrieve information, such as totals or the number of records, from within a subreport.

JasperReports versions 1.0.0 and later provide a new feature that allows users to retrieve values from within a subreport. This mechanism works much the same as passing input parameters to subreports. The idea is to save values calculated during the filling of the subreport into variables in the master report.

Bindings between calculated values and local variables can be set in the Subreport return values tab in the lower part of the Subreport (Other) tab of the element properties window (see Figure 8-19).

Figure 8-19. *Subreport return values*

To create a new binding between a local variable and a calculated value from a subreport, click the Add button. A window opens, as shown in Figure 8-20.

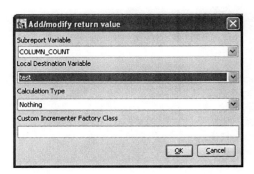

Figure 8-20. *Binding a local variable to a calculated value*

At this point, select a calculated value from the subreport (in this case, the value is a variable from the subreport), as well as the local variable that will contain the returned value. Since iReport doesn't recognize variables defined within a subreport, the first combo box is writable.

Next, select a calculation type. If you want a subreport value to be returned as is, select the value Nothing. Otherwise, several calculations can be applied. For example, if the desired value is the average of the number of records within a subreport that is invoked repeatedly, set the calculation type to Average.

■**Caution** When you create a new variable in your master report to be used like a container for a returned value, set the variable calculation type to System in the Add/modify variable dialog box. The effective calculation type performed on the variable values is the one defined in the dialog box shown in Figure 8-20.

The value coming from the subreport is available only when the whole band containing the subreport is printed. If you need to print this value using a text field placed in the same band as your subreport, set the evaluation time of the text field to Band.

You can find additional details and information on returning parameters in *The Definitive Guide to JasperReports* by Teodor Daniciu, Lucian Chirita, Sanda Zaharia, and Ionut Nedelcu (Apress, 2007).

Using the Subreport Wizard

To simplify inserting a subreport, starting from iReport 1.2.1, a wizard for creating subreports automatically starts when a Subreport element is added to a report.

You can use the Subreport Wizard, shown in Figure 8-21, to create a brand new report that will be referenced as a subreport or to refer to an existing report. In the latter case, if the report you choose contains one or more parameters, the wizard provides an easy way to define a value for each of them.

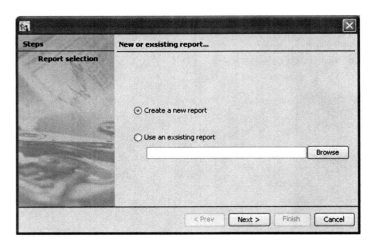

Figure 8-21. *Subreport Wizard*

Create a New Report via the Subreport Wizard

If you are adding a subreport to an open report that has previously been saved, the Subreport Wizard can create a new report for you that will be used as a subreport.

The steps to create the new report are very similar to those you follow in the Report Wizard:

1. Select a connection or datasource; if the datasource requires a query (like a JDBC or Hibernate connection), you can write it in the text area or load it from a file.

2. Select fields.

3. Select the layout.

4. Save the new subreport and subreport expression definition.

There is currently no way to define groups for the subreport using the Subreport Wizard. You can add groups after the automatic creation of the report using the report groups window (View ➤ Report groups).

The subreport expression is used to refer to the subreport JASPER file. The wizard lets you do this in one of two ways:

1. Store the path part of the subreport URI in a parameter, as shown in Figure 8-22, to make it modifiable at runtime by setting a different value for the parameter (the subreport path is the default value).

2. Save the complete path in the expression.

If the subreport is created in the same directory as the master report, the path value is set to a zero-length string. Please note that at runtime this works only if the subreport is present in the classpath.

The subreport is not compiled when created. To test your report, you must compile it.

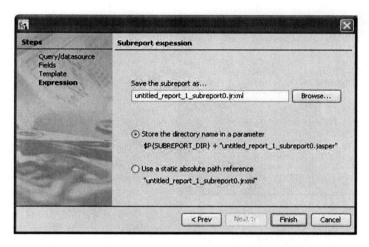

Figure 8-22. *Specifying a subreport expression in the Subreport Wizard*

When you create a new subreport, you can't specify parameters. You will be able to add parameters and use them in the subreport query after the report is created. At this point, to filter your subreport query, follow these steps:

1. Add a parameter to the report implementing your subreport.

2. Use that parameter in your query with the typical syntax $P{*MyParam*} (or $!P{*MyParam*} if the parameter must be concatenated with the query as is).

3. In the master report, open the element properties window of the Subreport element and add an entry in the Subreport parameters list setting an expression for the subreport parameter (see the section "Passing Parameters" earlier in this chapter for more details).

If your subreport is not based on a SQL or HQL query, you must still set the subreport datasource expression to successfully run your report.

As mentioned earlier, you can use the Subreport Wizard to create a brand new report that will be referenced as a subreport or to refer to an existing report. In the latter case, if the chosen report contains one or more parameters, the wizard provides an easy way to define a value for each of them.

Specifying an Existing Report in the Subreport Wizard

You can point to an existing report as a subreport through the Subreport Wizard. To do this, the first step is to select a JRXML or a JASPER file in the first screen of the wizard. (The JASPER file must have been created with JasperReports version 1.2.0 or greater.)

The second step of the wizard manages expressions for the connection or the datasource used to fill the subreport (see Figure 8-23).

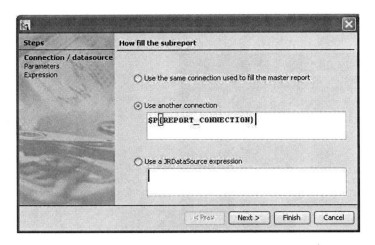

Figure 8-23. *Specifying a connection/datasource expression*

You can select the *Use the same connection used to fill the master report* radio button option when using a JDBC-based subreport. The JDBC connection is passed to the subreport to execute it.

To specify a different JDBC connection, select the Use another connection radio button option.

Finally, to use a JRDataSource object to fill the subreport, select Use a JRDataSource expression and write an expression capable of returning a JRDataSource object.

If the selected report contains parameters, they are listed in the next step (see Figure 8-24). For each parameter, you can set a value by choosing an object from the combo boxes. The combo box contains a set of suggested values. Of course, you can write your own expression, but no expression editor is provided in this context.

Finally, you must designate how to generate the subreport expression. Just as for a new subreport, there are two options: store the path in a parameter to set it dynamically, or set a hard-coded path (see Figure 8-25).

All choices can be modified after you leave the Subreport Wizard.

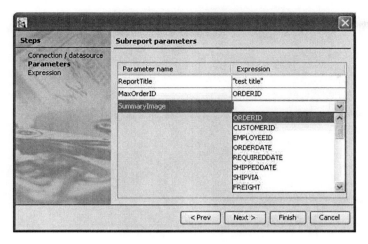

Figure 8-24. *Specifying subreport parameters*

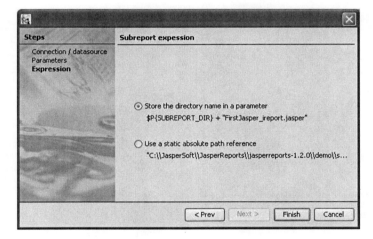

Figure 8-25. *Specifying a subreport expression*

CHAPTER 9

■ ■ ■

Datasources and Query Executers

There are several ways in JasperReports to provide data to fill a printed report; for example, you can put a SQL query directly inside a report and provide a connection to a database against which to execute the query and read the resulting record set.

iReport provides direct support for a rich set of query languages, including SQL, HQL, EJBQL, and MDX, and supports other languages like XPath (XML Path Language).

Moreover, in iReport, you can use custom languages by registering pluggable engines called *query executers* to interpret and execute the report query.

If you don't want to use a query language, or you simply don't want to put the query inside the report, you can use a JasperReports datasource: basically a JR datasource is an object that iterates on a record set organized like a simple table. All the datasources implement the JRDataSource interface. JasperReports provides many ready-to-use implementations of datasources to wrap generic data structures, like arrays or collections of JavaBeans, result sets, table models, CSV and XML files, and so on. In this chapter, I will present some of these datasources, and you will see how easy it is to create a custom datasource in order to fit any possible need.

Finally, you will see how to define a custom query language and a custom query executer to use it.

iReport provides support for all these things: you can define JDBC (Java Database Connectivity) connections to execute SQL queries, set up Hibernate connections using Spring, and test your own JRDataSource or custom query language.

How a JasperReports Datasource Works

JasperReports is a record-set-oriented engine: this means that to print a report, you have to provide a set of records. When the report is run, JasperReports will iterate on this record set, creating and filling the bands according to the report definition. Bands, groups, variables—their elaboration is strictly tied to the record set used to fill the report. This is why JasperReports defines only one query per report. Multiple queries/datasources can be used when inserting subreports or defining sub-datasets, each one with their own query (or datasource), fields, parameters, variables, and so on. Subdatasets are only used to feed a crosstab or a chart.

Each record contains a set of fields. These fields must be declared in the report in order to be used, as explained in Chapter 6.

But what is the difference between using a query inside a report and providing data using a JRDataSource? Basically, there is no difference. In fact, what happens behind the scenes when a query is used instead of a JRDataSource is that JasperReports executes the query using a built-in or user-defined query executer that will produce a JRDataSource. There are circumstances where providing a JDBC connection to the engine and using a query defined at report level can simplify the use of subreports.

A `JRDataSource` is a consumable object, which means that you cannot use the same instance of `JRDataSource` to fill more than one report or subreport. A typical error is try to use the same `JRDataSource` object (e.g., provided to the report as parameter) to feed a subreport placed in the detail band: if the detail band is printed more than once (normally it is printed for every record present in the main datasource), the subreport will be filled for each main record, and every time the subreport will iterate on the same `JRDataSource` provided. However, this will only give results the first time the datasource is used.

At the end of this chapter, you will know how to avoid this kind of error, and you'll have all the tools to decide the best way to fill your report: using a query in a language supported by JasperReports, a built-in datasource, a custom datasource, or finally a custom query language with the relative query executer.

Understanding Datasources and Connections in iReport

iReport allows you to manage and configure different types of datasources to fill reports. These datasources are stored in the iReport configuration and activated when needed.

When I talk about datasources, you need to understand there is a distinction between real datasources (or objects that implement the `JRDataSource` interface) and connections, used in combination with a query defined inside the report. In addition, the term *datasource* used in JasperReports is not the same as the concept in `javax.sql.Datasource`, which is a means of getting a physical connection to the database (usually with JNDI lookup). The datasource object I refer to in the JasperReports realm already has concrete data inside itself.

Here is a list of datasource and connection types provided by iReport:

- JDBC connection
- JavaBeans set datasource
- XML datasource
- CSV datasource
- Hibernate connection
- Spring-loaded Hibernate connection
- JR datasource provider
- Custom datasource
- Mondrian OLAP connection
- XML/A connection
- EJBQL connection
- Empty datasource

Finally, there is a special mode to execute a report, called *query executer mode*, that you can use to force creation of the report without passing any connection to or datasource for the report engine.

All the connections are "opened" and passed directly to JasperReports during report generation. For many connections, JasperReports provides one or more built-in parameters that can be used inside the report for several purposes (e.g., to fill a subreport that needs the same connection as the parent).

The XML datasource allows you to take data from an XML document. A CSV (comma-separated values) datasource allows you to open a CSV file for use in a report. The JavaBean set datasource, custom datasource, and JR datasource provider allow you to print data using purposely written Java classes. The Hibernate connection provides the environment to execute HQL (Hibernate Query Language) queries (this connection can be configured using Spring, too). EJBQL (Enterprise JavaBean Query Language) queries can be used with an EJBQL connection, and MDX queries can be used with a native direct connection to a Mondrian server or with the standard XML/A interface to interrogate a generic OLAP database. An empty datasource is something like a generator of records having zero fields. This kind of datasource is used for test purposes or to achieve very particular needs.

Connections and datasources are managed through the menu command Data ➤ Connections/Data Sources, which opens the configured connections list (see Figure 9-1).

Name	Data Source Type	Default	
Mysql OPTIGEZ	Database JDBC connection	☐	New
JasperReports Samples	Database JDBC connection	☐	Modify
XML test	XML file data source	☐	
XML Addressbook	XML file data source	☐	Delete
XML Orders	XML file data source	☐	
ECG_sample_datasource	Custom JRDataSource	☐	Set as Default
My new connection 2	Database JDBC connection	☐	
Northwind	Database JDBC connection	☑	Import...
EJBQL Test	EJBQL connection	☐	
Salseforce Data Source	SalesForce data source	☐	Export...

Figure 9-1. *List of configured datasources*

As mentioned previously, a connection and a datasource are different objects. However, from this point on, unless a distinction needs to be made, I will use these two words interchangeably.

Even if you keep an arbitrary number of datasources ready to use, iReport always works with only one source or connection at a time. You can set the active datasource in several ways. The most easy and intuitive is to select the right datasource from the combo box located on the toolbar (see Figure 9-2).

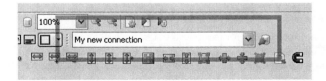

Figure 9-2. *To use a datasource, choose it in this combo box.*

You can alternatively set the active datasource by selecting from the main window Data ➤ Set Active Connection and choosing the desired datasource from the list that appears, as shown in Figure 9-3.

Figure 9-3. *List of the available datasources*

Finally, you can set the active datasource by selecting a datasource in the Connections/Datasources dialog box and clicking the Set as Default button (see Figure 9-4).

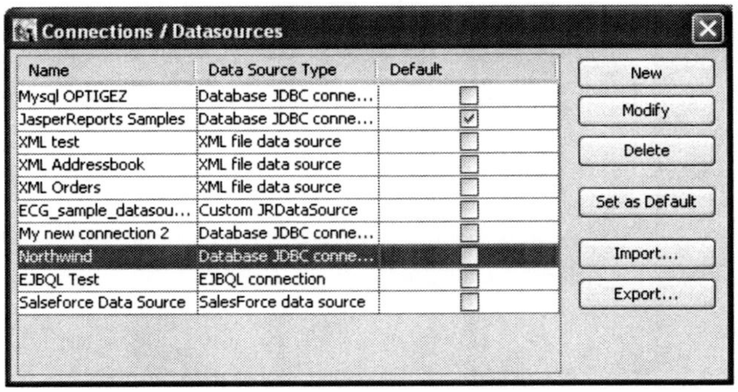

Figure 9-4. *iReport provides the Set as Default button to allow you to set the active datasource.*

If no datasource is selected, it is not possible to fill a report with data. An active connection is no longer required to use the Report Wizard, but of course it can help a lot if you are designing, for example, an SQL query-based report.

Creating and Using JDBC Connections

A JDBC connection allows you to use a relational DBMS (or in general whatever is accessible through a JDBC driver) as a datasource. To set a new JDBC connection, click the New button in the Connections/Datasources dialog box (shown earlier in Figure 9-1) to open the interface for creation of a new connection (or datasource). From the list, select Database JDBC connection to bring up the window shown in Figure 9-5.

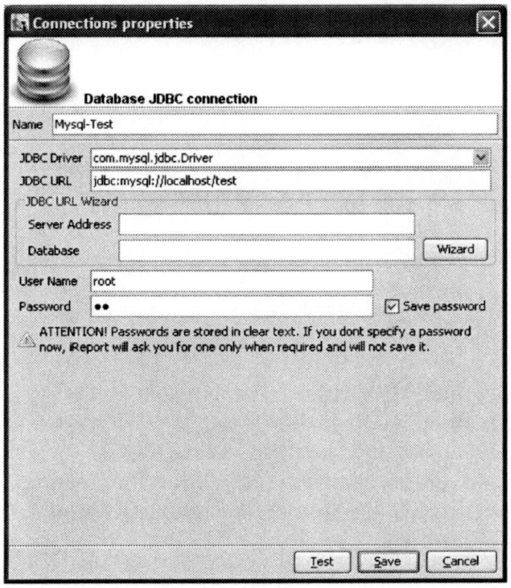

Figure 9-5. *Creation of a JDBC connection*

The first thing to do is to name the connection (possibly using a significant name, such as Mysql—Test). iReport will always use the specified name to refer to this connection.

In the JDBC Driver field, you specify the name of the JDBC driver to use for the connection to the database. The combo box proposes the names of all the most common JDBC drivers.

Thanks to the JDBC URL Wizard, it is possible to automatically construct the JDBC URL to use for the connection to the database by inserting the server name and the database name in the correct text fields. Click the Wizard button to create the URL.

Enter a username and password to access the database. By means of a check box option, you can save the password for the connection.

Caution iReport saves the password in clear text in the configuration file located in `<USER_HOME>/.ireport/config.xml`.

If the password is empty, it is better if you specify that it be saved.

After you have inserted all the data, it is possible to verify the connection by clicking the Test button. If everything is OK, the dialog box shown in Figure 9-6 will appear.

Figure 9-6. *Connection to the DB successfully tested*

At the end of the test, remember to set the created connection as the active connection to use it (iReport 2.0.0 does this automatically).

In general, the test can fail for a lot of reasons, the most frequent of which are the following:

- A ClassNotFoundError exception was thrown.

- The URL is not correct.

- Parameters are not correct for the connection (database is not found, the username or password is wrong, etc.).

Let's take a closer look at these issues.

ClassNotFoundError

The ClassNotFoundError exception occurs when the required JDBC driver is not present in the classpath. For example, suppose you wish to create a connection to an Oracle database. iReport has no driver for this database by default, but you could be deceived by the presence of the oracle.jdbc.driver.OracleDriver driver in the JDBC drivers list shown in the window for creating new connections. If you were to select this driver, when you test the connection, the program will throw the ClassNotFoundError exception, as shown in Figure 9-7.

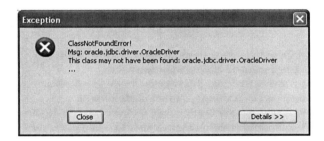

Figure 9-7. *Driver not found error*

What you have to do is to add the JDBC driver for Oracle, which is a file named classes12.zip (or classes11.zip for older versions) to the classpath (which is where the JVM searches for classes). As iReport uses its own class loader, it will be enough to copy the classes12.zip file into the iReport lib directory and perform the test again without restarting the program.

The lib directory is the right place to insert JAR archives (with a .jar or .zip extension). If the driver is not a JAR version, but it is shipped as an uncompressed directory (for example a com directory containing the hierarchy of all driver classes), the most correct place to dynamically add those classes to the classpath is in the classes directory (present in the home of iReport), so you would copy the driver directory there.

URL Not Correct

If an incorrect URL is specified (for example, due to a typing error), you'll get an arbitrary exception when you click the Test button. The exact cause of the error can be deduced by the stack trace available in the exception dialog box.

In this case, if possible, it is better to use the JDBC URL Wizard to build the JDBC URL and try again.

Parameters Not Correct for the Connection

The less-problematic error scenario is one where you try to establish a connection to a database with the wrong parameters (username or password is not valid, database specified is nonexistent, etc.). In this case, the same database will return a message that will be more or less explicit about the failure of the connection.

Working with Your JDBC Connection

When the report is created by using a JDBC connection, you specify a SQL query to extract the records to print from the database. This connection can also be used by a subreport or, for example, by a personalized lookup function for the decoding of particular data. For this reason, JasperReports puts at your disposal a special parameter named REPORT_CONNECTION of the java.sql.Connection type that can be used in whatever expression you like, with the parameters syntax as follows: $P{REPORT_CONNECTION}

This parameter contains exactly the java.sql.Connection class passed to JasperReports from the calling program.

The use of JDBC or SQL connections represents the simplest and easiest way to fill a report. (The details for how to create a SQL query are explained in Chapter 6.)

Fields Registration

In order to use SQL query fields in a report, you need to *register* them (it is not necessary to register all the selected fields—those effectively used in the report are enough). For each field, you must specify its name and type. Table 9-1 shows the mapping of the SQL types to the corresponding Java types.

Table 9-1. *Conversion of SQL and Java Types*

SQL Type	Java Object
CHAR	String
VARCHAR	String
LONGVARCHAR	String
NUMERIC	java.math.BigDecimal
DECIMAL	java.math.BigDecimal
BIT	Boolean
TINYINT	Integer
SMALLINT	Integer
INTEGER	Integer
BIGINT	Long
REAL	Float
FLOAT	Double
DOUBLE	Double

Continued

Table 9-1. *Continued*

SQL Type	Java Object
BINARY	byte[]
VARBINARY	byte[]
LONGVARBINARY	byte[]
DATE	java.sql.Date
TIME	java.sql.Time
TIMESTAMP	java.sql.Timestamp

Table 9-1 does not include the BLOB and CLOB types and other special types such as ARRAY, STRUCT, and REF because these types cannot be managed automatically by JasperReports. (However, it is possible to use them by declaring them generically as Object and by managing them by writing supporting static methods. The BINARY, VARBINARY, and LONGBINARY types should be dealt with in a similar way. With many databases, BLOB and CLOB can be declared as java.io.InputStream.

Whether a SQL type is converted to a Java object depends on the JDBC driver used.

For the automatic registration of SQL query fields, iReport uses a mapping a little bit more simplified than that proposed in Table 9-1.

Sorting and Filtering Records

The records coming from a datasource (or from the execution of a query through a connection) can be ordered and filtered. Sort and filter options can be set from the Report query dialog box by clicking the buttons labeled Sort options and Filter Expressions.

The filter expression must return a Boolean object: TRUE if a particular record can be kept, FALSE otherwise.

The sorting is based on one or more fields. Each field can be sorted using an ascending or a descending order.

Using JavaBeans Set Datasources

A JavaBeans set datasource allows you to use some JavaBeans as data to fill a report. In this context, a JavaBean is a Java class that employs a series of *getter* methods, with the following syntax:

```
public returnType getXXX()
```

where *returnType* (the return value) is a generic Java class or a primitive type (such as int, double, etc.).

In order to create a connection of this type, after clicking New in the Connections/Datasources dialog box, select JavaBeans set data source in the list of datasource types to bring up the dialog box shown in Figure 9-8.

Once again, the first thing to do is to specify the name of the new datasource.

The JavaBeans set datasource uses an external class (named Factory) to produce some objects (the JavaBeans) that constitute the data to pass to the report. Enter your Java class (the complete name of which you specify in the Factory class field) that has a static method to instantiate different JavaBeans and to return them as a collection (java.util.Collection) or an array (Object[]). The method name and the return type have to be specified in the other fields of the window.

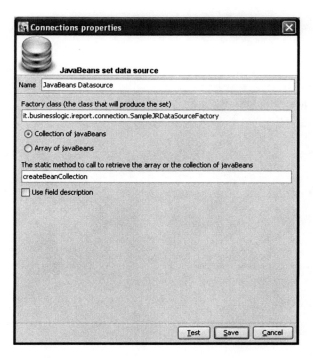

Figure 9-8. *Creation of a JavaBean set datasource*

Let's see how to write this Factory class. Suppose that your data is represented by Person objects; following is the code of this class, which shows two fields: name (the person's name) and age.

```
public class Person
{
    private String name = "";
    private int age = 0;

    public Person(String name, int age)
    {
        this.name = name;
        this.age = age;
    }

    public int getAge()
    {
      return age;
    }

    public String getName()
    {
      return name;
    }
}
```

Your class, which you will name TestFactory, will be something similar to this:

```
public class TestFactory
{
    public static java.util.Collection generateCollection()
    {
        java.util.Vector collection = new java.util.Vector();

        collection.add(new Person("Ted",  20) );
        collection.add(new Person("Jack", 34) );
        collection.add(new Person("Bob",  56) );
        collection.add(new Person("Alice",12) );
        collection.add(new Person("Robin",22) );
        collection.add(new Person("Peter",28) );

        return collection;
    }
}
```

Your datasource will represent five JavaBeans of Person type.
The parameters for the datasource configuration will be as follows:

- *Factory name*: **TestFactoryDataSource**
- *Factory class*: **TestFactory**
- *Method to call*: **generateCollection**
- *Return type*: **Collection of JavaBean**

Fields of a JavaBean Set Datasource

One peculiarity of a JavaBeans set datasource is the fields are exposed through getter methods. This means that if the JavaBean has a getXyz method, xyz is a record field.

In this example, the Person object shows two fields: name and age; register them in the fields list as String and Integer, respectively.

Create a new empty report, open the values window, and add the two fields (see Figure 9-9).

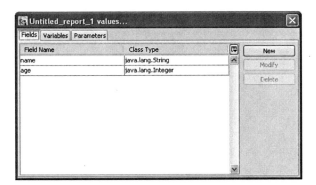

Figure 9-9. *Registering the JavaBean Person fields*

Move the fields into the detail band and run the report. Figure 9-10 shows how your report should appear during design time, while Figure 9-11 shows the result of the printed report filled with JavaBeans set.

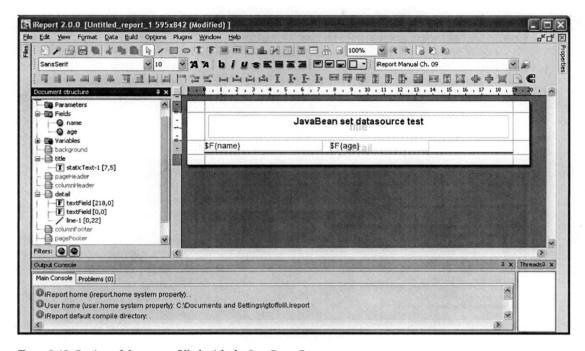

Figure 9-10. *Design of the report filled with the JavaBean Person*

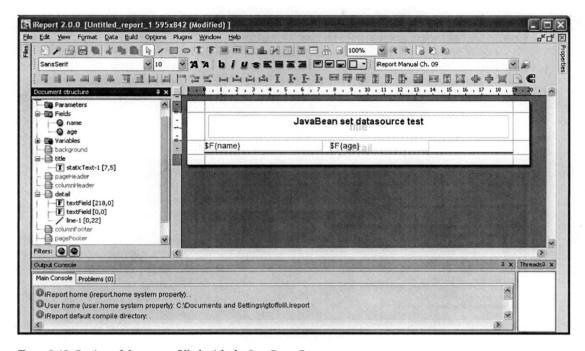

Figure 9-11. *The final result of the report using a JavaBean set datasource*

To refer to an attribute of an attribute, you can use a special notation dividing attributes with dots. For example, to access the `street` attribute of the `Address` bean contained in the `Person` bean, you can use the syntax `address.street`. The real call would be `bean.getAddress().getStreet()`.

If the flag Use field description is set when you are specifying the properties of your JavaBeans set datasource, the mapping between JavaBean attribute and field value is done using the field description and not the field name. In this case, the datasource will consider only the description to look up the field value, and the field can have any name.

iReport provides a visual tool to map JavaBean attributes to report fields. To use it, open the Report query dialog box, go to the JavaBean Data Source tab, insert the full class name of the bean you want to explore, and click the Read attributes button. The tree that appears will be populated with the attributes of the specified bean class (see Figure 9-12). If some attributes are Java objects as well, they can be explored by double-clicking them to look for other attributes. To map a field, simply select an attribute name and press the Add Selected Field(s) button.

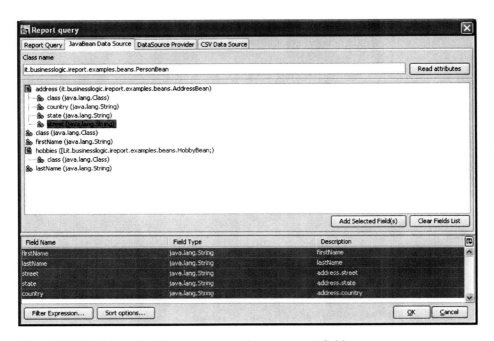

Figure 9-12. *Exploring a JavaBean to map attributes to report fields*

Using XML Datasources

XML documents can be used as datasources from iReport version 0.4.0 on, thanks to the support provided by JasperReports. Versions prior to 0.4.0 were using a particular version of this datasource developed by the iReport team. Because of the greater flexibility of the JasperReports version, the old implementation is no longer supported.

An XML document is typically a tree structure that need not necessarily be a table. For this reason, you must configure the datasource to indicate what nodes of the XML documents have to be selected and presented as records. To do this, you use an XPath expression to define a node set. The specifics of XPath are available at `http://www.w3.org/TR/xpath`.

Some examples will be useful to help you know how to define the node selection.

Consider the XML file in Listing 9-1. It is a hypothetical address book in which different people appear, grouped in categories. At the end of the categories list, a second list, of favorite objects, appears.

In this case, it is possible to define different node set types. The choice is determined by how you want to organize the data in your report.

Listing 9-1. *Example XML File*

```
<addressbook>
   <category name="home">
      <person id="1">
          <lastname>Davolio</lastname>
          <firstname>Nancy</firstname>
      </person>
      <person id="2">
          <lastname>Fuller</lastname>
          <firstname>Andrew</firstname>
      </person>
      <person id="3">
          <lastname>Leverling</lastname>
      </person>
  </category>
  <category name="work">
      <person id="4">
          <lastname>Peacock</lastname>
          <firstname>Margaret</firstname>
      </person>
</category>
  <favorites>
      <person id="1"/>
      <person id="3"/>
</favorites>
</addressbook>
```

To select only the people contained in the categories (that is, all the people in the address book), use the following expression:

```
/addressbook/category/person
```

Four nodes will be returned. These are shown in Listing 9-2.

Listing 9-2. *Node Set with Expression /addressbook/category/person*

```
<person id="1">
          <lastname>Davolio</lastname>
          <firstname>Nancy</firstname>
</person>
<person id="2">
          <lastname>Fuller</lastname>
          <firstname>Andrew</firstname>
      </person>
<person id="3">
          <lastname>Leverling</lastname>
      </person>
<person id="4">
          <lastname>Peacock</lastname>
          <firstname>Margaret</firstname>
</person>
```

If you want to select the people appearing in the favorites node, the expression to use is

```
/addressbook/favorites/person
```

The returned nodes will be two, as shown in Listing 9-3.

Listing 9-3. *Node Set with Expression /addressbook/favorites/person*

```
<person id="1"/>
<person id="3"/>
```

Here you should include an expression that is a bit more complex than the last example in order to see XPath's power: the idea is to select the person nodes belonging to the work category. The expression to use is the following:

```
/addressbook/category[@name = "work"]/person
```

The expression will return only one node, that with an ID equal to 4, as shown in Listing 9-4.

Listing 9-4. *Node Set with Expression /addressbook/category[@name = "work"]/person*

```
<person id="4">
        <lastname>Peacock</lastname>
        <firstname>Margaret</firstname>
</person>
```

After you have created an expression for the selection of a node set, you proceed to the creation of an XML datasource.

Open the window for creating a new datasource and select XML File data source from the list of connection types to bring up the dialog box shown in Figure 9-13.

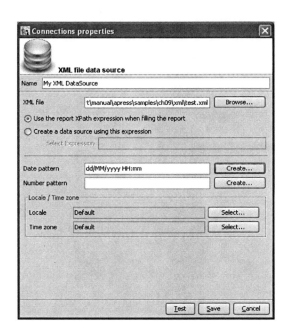

Figure 9-13. *Creation of an XML file datasource*

The only mandatory information to specify is the XML file name. You can provide a set of nodes to the engine selected using a predefined static XPath expression. Alternatively, the XPath expression can be set directly inside the report. In that case, the report engine will take care of performing the node selection according to the expression specified. The advantage of this solution is the ability to use parameters inside the XPath expression, which acts like a real query on the supplied XML data.

From JasperReports 1.3.1 on, you can specify Java patterns to convert dates and numbers from plain strings to more appropriate Java objects (like Date and Double). For the same purpose, you can define a specific locale and time zone to use when parsing the XML stream.

Registration of the Fields for an XML Datasource

In the case of an XML datasource, besides the type and the name, the definition of a field in the report needs a particular expression inserted as a field description. As the datasource aims always at one node of the selected node set, the expressions are "relative" to the present node.

To select the value of an attribute of the present node, use the following syntax:

```
@<name attribute>
```

For example, to define a field where to store the ID of a person (attribute id of the node person), it is sufficient to create a new field, name it, and set the description to

```
@id
```

Similarly, it is possible to get to the child nodes of the present node. For example, if you want to refer to the lastname node, child of person, use the following syntax:

```
lastname
```

To move to the parent value of the present node (for example, to determine the category to which a person belongs), use a slightly different syntax:

```
ancestor::category/@name
```

The ancestor keyword indicates that you are referring to a parent node of the present node; in particular, you are referring to the first parent of category type, of which you want to know the value of the name attribute.

Now, let's see everything in action. Prepare a simple report with the registered fields shown in Table 9-2.

Table 9-2. *Registered Fields for Example Report*

Field Name	Description	Type
id	@id	Integer
lastname	lastname	String
firstname	firstname	String
category	ancestor::category/@name	String

iReport 2.0 provides a drag-and-drop interface to map XML nodes to report fields: to use it, open the Report query dialog box and select XPath as the query language. If the active connection is a valid XML datasource, the associated XML document will be shown in a tree view. To register the fields, set the record nodes by right-clicking a person node and selecting Set record node (generate XPath), as shown in Figure 9-14; the record nodes will become bold. Then drag the required nodes or attributes in the field list to map them to report fields. iReport will guess the correct XPath expression to use and will create the fields for you. You can modify the generated field name and set a more suitable field type.

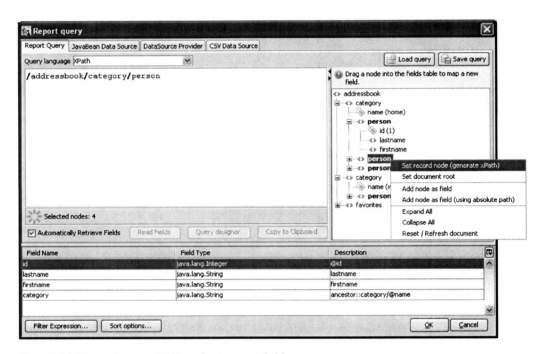

Figure 9-14. *The tool to map XML nodes to report fields*

Insert the different fields into the detail band (as shown in Figure 9-15). The XML file used to fill the report is that shown previously in Listing 9-2. The XPath expression for the node set selection specified in the definition of the connection is

```
/addressbook/category/person
```

The final result appears in Figure 9-16.

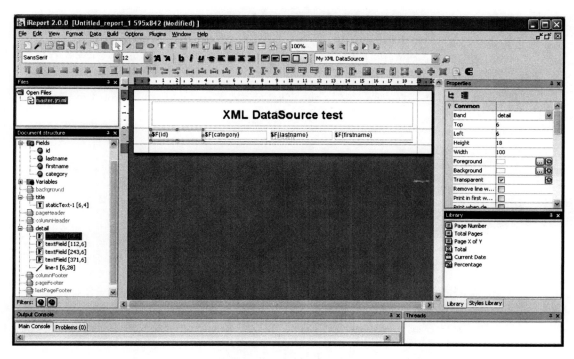

Figure 9-15. *Design of the report for testing an XML file datasource*

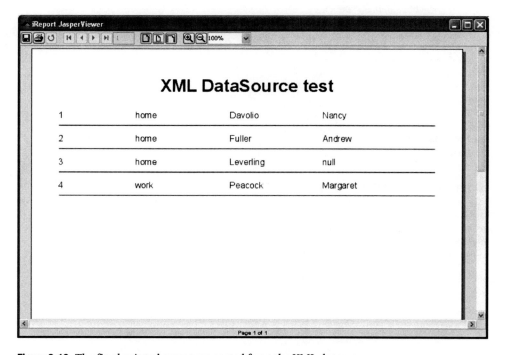

Figure 9-16. *The final printed report generated from the XML datasource*

XML Datasource and Subreport Elements

A node set allows you to identify a series of nodes that represent, from a JRDataSource point of view, some records. However, when the XML document is very complex, it may be necessary to see other node sets that are in the main nodes. Take into consideration the XML in Listing 9-5. This is a slightly modified version of the document presented in Listing 9-1: for each person node, a hobbies node is added, which contains a series of hobby nodes, and one or more e-mail addresses.

Listing 9-5. *Complex XML Example*

```xml
<addressbook>
    <category name="home">
        <person id="1">
            <lastname>Davolio</lastname>
            <firstname>Nancy</firstname>
            <email>davolio1@sf.net</email>
            <email>davolio2@sf.net</email>
            <hobbies>
                <hobby>Music</hobby>
                <hobby>Sport</hobby>
            </hobbies>
        </person>
        <person id="2">
            <lastname>Fuller</lastname>
            <firstname>Andrew</firstname>
            <email>af@test.net</email>
            <email>afullera@fuller.org</email>
            <hobbies>
                <hobby>Cinema</hobby>
                <hobby>Sport</hobby>
            </hobbies>
        </person>
        <person id="3">
            <lastname>Leverling</lastname>
            <email>leverling@xyz.it</email>
        </person>
    </category>
    <favorites>
        <person id="1"/>
        <person id="3"/>
    </favorites>
</addressbook>
```

What you want to produce is a document more elaborate than those you have seen until now; for each person, you want to view an e-mail address and hobbies.

To obtain such a document, it is necessary to use subreports—in particular, you will need a subreport for an e-mail addresses list, one for hobbies, and one for favorite people. To generate these subreports, you need to understand how to produce new datasources to feed them. In this case, you use the JRXmlDataSource, which exposes two extremely useful methods:

```
public JRXmlDataSource dataSource(String selectExpression)
```

and

```
public JRXmlDataSource subDataSource(String selectExpression)
```

The difference between the two is that the former values the expression of node selection by referring to the document root node; the latter values this expression starting from the selected node.

Both methods are used in the datasource expression of a Subreport element to produce dynamically the datasource to pass to that element. The most important thing is that this mechanism allows you to make the datasource production and the expression of node selection dynamic.

In this case, the expression to create the datasource that will feed the subreport of the e-mail addresses will be

```
((net.sf.jasperreports.engine.data.JRXmlDataSource)
        $P{REPORT_DATA_SOURCE}).subDataSource("/person/email")
```

which says, "Starting from the present node (person), give me back all the email nodes that are direct descendants."

The expression for the hobbies subreport will be similar, except for the node selection:

```
((net.sf.jasperreports.engine.data.JRXmlDataSource)
    $P{REPORT_DATA_SOURCE}).subDataSource("/person/hobbies/hobby")
```

You declare the master report's fields as in Table 9-2 earlier. In the subreport, you have to refer to the present node value, so the field expression will be simply a dot (.), as shown in Figure 9-17.

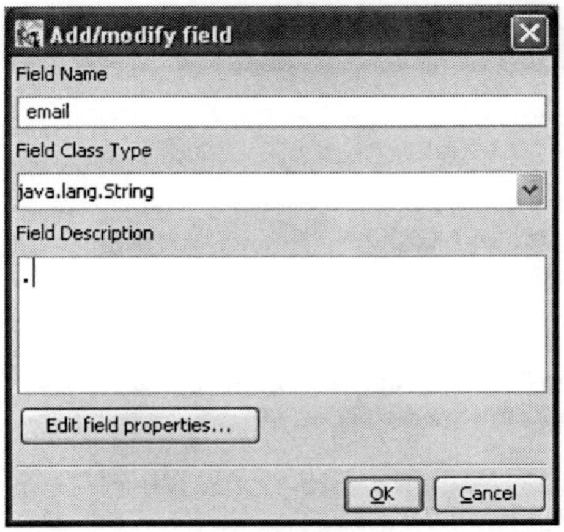

Figure 9-17. *The present record value for the email field*

Proceed with building your three reports: addressbook.jasper, email.jasper, and hobby.jasper.

In the master report, addressbook.jrxml, insert a group named CATEGORY, of which you associate the expression for the category field ($F{category}), as shown in Figure 9-18. In the CATEGORY header band, insert a field through which you will view the category name. By doing this, the names of the different people will be grouped for the category (as in the XML file).

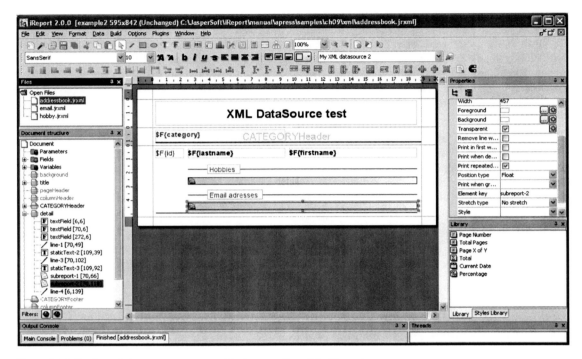

Figure 9-18. *Design of the master report with the e-mail and hobby subreports*

In the detail band, position the id, lastname, and firstname fields. Underneath these fields, add the two Subreport elements, the first for the hobbies, the second for the e-mail addresses.

The e-mail and hobby subreports are identical except for the expression of the only field present in these subreports and the declaration of the field to print (see Figure 9-19). The two reports should be as large as the Subreport elements in the master report, so reduce the margins to zero.

Compile and execute the report. If everything is OK, you will see the printed report shown in Figure 9-20, which displays the groups of people in home and work categories and the subreports associated with every person on the list.

As this example demonstrates, the real power of the XML datasource is the versatility of XPath, which allows navigation of the node selection in a refined manner.

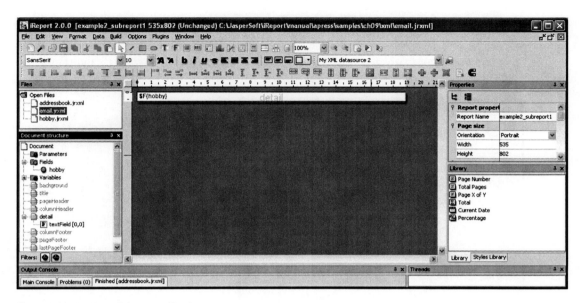

Figure 9-19. *Design of the e-mail subreport*

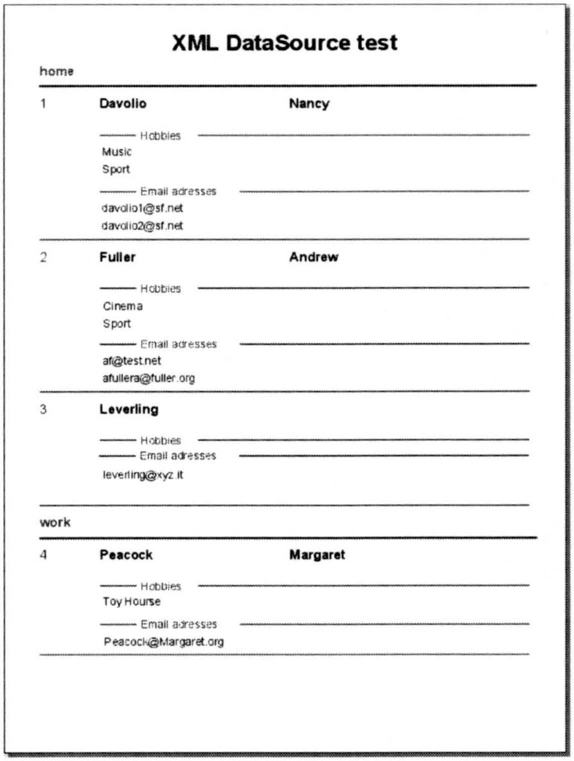

Figure 9-20. *Final printed report with subreports generated from an XML datasource*

Using Remote XML File Datasources

You can create a datasource that points to a remote XML file that is accessible by an RL. Figure 9-21 shows the dialog box in which you specify properties for such a datasource when creating it.

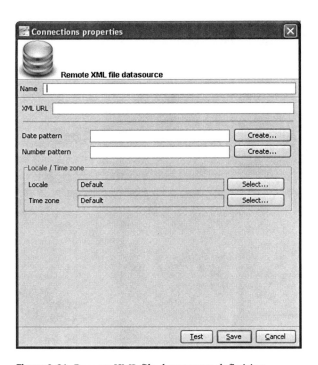

Figure 9-21. *Remote XML file datasource definition*

You can specify Java patterns to convert dates and numbers from plain strings to more appropriate Java objects (like Date and Double). For the same purpose, you can specify a locale and time zone to use when parsing the XML stream.

For remote XML datasources, iReport supports the following built-in parameters:

- XML_URL: The URL to access

- XML_USERNAME: The username to use when accessing this URL

- XML_PASSWORD: The password for the username specified by XML_USERNAME

Since you may want to generate the XML file on the fly, your report can also pass parameters to the remote XML datasource using these parameters:

- XML_GET_PARAM_*parameter name*

- XML_POST_PARAM_*parameter name*

Using CSV Datasources

Initially, the datasource for CSV documents was a very simple datasource proof of concept to show how to implement a custom datasource. The CSV datasource interface was improved when JasperReports 1.2 added a native implementation to fill a report using a CSV file.

To create a connection based on a CSV file, click the New button in the Connections/Datasources dialog box and select File CSV datasource from the datasource types list to bring up the dialog box shown in Figure 9-22.

Figure 9-22. *Configuration of a CSV datasource*

Set a name for the connection and choose a CSV file. Then declare the fields in this datasource. If the first line in your file contains the names for each column, click the Get column names from the first row of the file button and select the Skip the first line check box option. This forces JasperReports to skip the first line (the one containing your column labels). In any case, the column names read from the file are used instead of the declared ones, so avoid modifying the names "registered" with the Get column names button.

If the first line of your CSV file doesn't contain the column names, set a name for each column. If you can't think of meaningful names, use names like COLUMN_0, COLUMN_1, and so on.

■Caution If you define more columns than the ones available, you'll get an exception at report filling time.

If your CSV file uses nonstandard characters to separate fields and rows, you can adjust the default setting for separators using the second tab labeled Separators, shown in Figure 9-23.

Figure 9-23. *Second Separators tab*

Registration of the Fields for a CSV Datasource

When you create a CSV datasource, you must define a set of column names, which will be used as fields for your report. To add them to the fields list, set your CSV datasource as the active connection and open the Report query dialog box. Go to the tab labeled CSV Datasource and click the Get fields from datasource button, as shown in Figure 9-24.

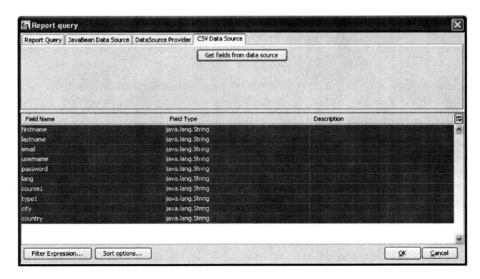

Figure 9-24. *Adding column names to the fields list*

By default, iReport sets the class type of all fields to java.lang.String. If you are sure that the text of a particular column can be easily converted to a number, a date, or a Boolean value, set the correct field type yourself once your fields are added to your report.

The pattern used to recognize a timestamp (or date) object can be configured at the datasource level by selecting the Use custom date format check box option.

Using JREmptyDataSource

JasperReports provides a special datasource named JREmptyDataSource. It is the datasource used to create a report when the following button is clicked:

This source returns true to the next method for the record number (by default only one), and always returns null to every call of the getFieldValue method. It is like having some records without fields, that is, an empty datasource.

The two constructors of this class are

```
public JREmptyDataSource(int count)
public JREmptyDataSource()
```

The first constructor indicates how many records to return, and the second sets the number of records to one.

To use more than one empty record in iReport, hold the Shift key when you click the button shown previously in this section. A dialog box to choose the number of records to generate appears, as shown in Figure 9-25.

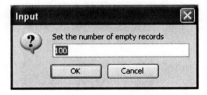

Figure 9-25. *Setting the number of empty records*

iReport provides a way to define an instance of this kind of datasource from the Connections/ Datasources dialog box, too, so you can use it like a normal datasource.

Using HQL and Hibernate Connections

Starting with version 1.2, JasperReports provides a way to use HQL directly in your report. To do so, first set up a Hibernate connection. Expand your classpath to include all classes, JARs, and configuration files used by your Hibernate mapping. In other words, iReport must be able to access all the

`*.hbm.xml` files you plan to use, the JavaBeans declared in those files, the `hibernate.cfg.xml` file, and other optional JARs used (e.g., those that access the database under Hibernate).

To add these objects to the classpath, select Options ➤ Classpath from the main window.

Once you've expanded the classpath, open the Connections/Datasources dialog box, click the New button, and choose Hibernate connection as your datasource type. This brings up the dialog box shown in Figure 9-26.

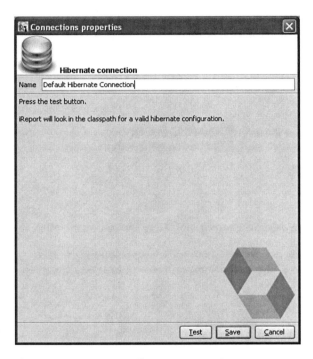

Figure 9-26. *Creating a Hibernate connection*

Click the Test button to be sure that `hibernate.cfg.xml` is in the classpath.

Currently, iReport works only with a single Hibernate configuration (that is, the first `hibernate.cfg.xml` file found in the classpath).

If you use the Spring framework, you can use a Spring configuration file to define your connection. In this case, you'll need to set the configuration file name and the session factory bean ID (see Figure 9-27).

Now that a Hibernate connection is available, use an HQL query to select the data to print. You can use HQL in the same way you use SQL: open the Report query dialog box (Edit ➤ Report Query) and choose HQL as the query language from the combo box on top (see Figure 9-28).

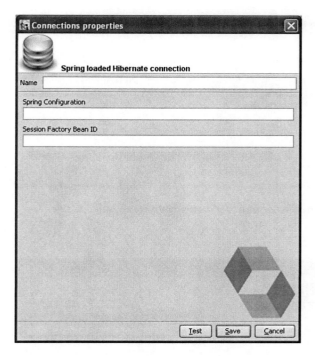

Figure 9-27. *Hibernate connection loaded using Spring*

Figure 9-28. *Specifying HQL for a query*

When you enter an HQL query, iReport tries to retrieve the available fields. According to the JasperReports documentation, the field mappings are resolved as follows:

- If the query returns one object per row, a field mapping can be one of the following:
    - If the object's type is a Hibernate entity or component type, the field mappings are resolved as the property names of the entity/component. If a select alias is present, it can be used to map a field to the whole entity/component object.
    - Otherwise, the object type is considered scalar, and only one field can be mapped to its value.

- If the query returns a tuple (object array) per row, a field mapping can be one of the following:

  - *A select alias*: The field will be mapped to the value corresponding to the alias.

  - *A property name prefixed by a select alias and a "."*: The field will be mapped to the value of the property for the object corresponding to the alias. The type corresponding to the select alias has to be an entity or component.

Caution Due to a defect addressed in iReport 1.2.0, if the query doesn't return any rows, no fields are listed and a `null` exception is caught.

Starting from iReport 1.2.4, a new interface is provided to navigate result objects (see Figure 9-29).

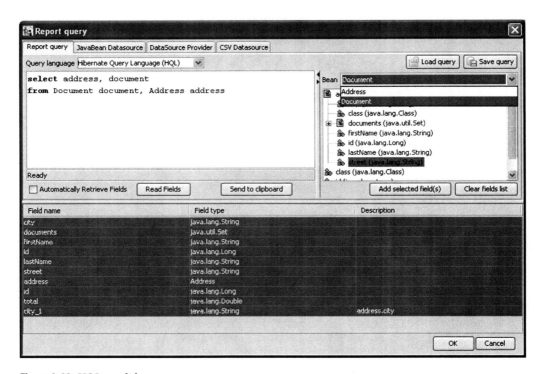

Figure 9-29. *HQL result browser*

In this way, it's easy to map an attribute of an object present in a resulting record to a report field. Beans available in each record are listed in the combo box on top of the object tree.

To add a field from the tree, select the corresponding node and click the Add selected field(s) button.

Understanding the JRDataSource Interface

Before proceeding with the implementation of a personalized JRDataSource, it is necessary to understand how the JRDataSource interface works. Every JRDataSource must implement these two methods:

```
public boolean next()
public Object  getFieldValue(JRField jrField)
```

The first method is useful to move a virtual cursor to the next record: in fact, data shown by a JRDataSource is ideally organized into tables. The next method returns true if the cursor is positioned correctly in the subsequent record, false if there are no other records.

Every time that JasperReports executes a next method, all the fields declared in the report are filled, and all the expressions (starting from those associated with the variables) are calculated again; subsequently, it will be decided whether to print the header of a new group, to go to a new page, and so on. When next returns false, the report is ended by printing all final bands (group footer, column footer, last page footer, and the summary). The next method can be called as many times as there are records present (or represented) from the datasource instance.

The method getFieldValue is called by JasperReports after a call to next results in a true value. In particular, getFieldValue is executed for every single field declared in the report (see Chapter 6 for the details on how to declare a report field). In the call, a JRField object is passed as a parameter; in it is the name of the field of which you want to obtain the value. The type of Java object that you expect is given back by the call, as well as the field description (used sometimes to specify information useful for the datasource to extract the field value).

The type of return value of the getFieldValue method has to be adequate to that declared in the JRField parameter, except for when a null is returned. If the type of the field was declared as java.lang.Object, the method can return an arbitrary type. In this case, if required, a cast can be used in the expressions. In Chapter 6, as an example, you saw the it.businesslogic.Person field used in the following syntax:

```
((it.businesslogic.Person)$F{MyPerson})
```

How to Implement a New JRDataSource

Sometimes the JRDataSource supplied with JasperReports cannot completely satisfy your needs. In these cases, it is possible to write a new JRDataSource. This operation is not complex: in fact, all you have to do is create a class that implements the JRDataSource interface (see Listing 9-6) that exposes two simple methods: next and getFieldValue.

Listing 9-6. *The JRDataSource Interface*

```
Package net.sf.jasperreports.engine;

public interface JRDataSource
{
     public boolean next() throws JRException;
     public Object  getFieldValue(JRField jrField) throws JRException;
}
```

The next method is useful to move records represented by the datasource. It has to return true if a new record to elaborate exists and false otherwise.

If the next method has been called positively, the getFieldValue method has to return the value of the requested field (or null if the requested value is not found or does not exist). In particular, the requested field name is contained in the JRField object passed as a parameter. Also, JRField is an interface through which it is possible to get the information associated to a field: the name, the description, and the Java type that represents it (as mentioned previously in the "Understanding the JRDataSource Interface" section).

Now try writing your personalized datasource. The idea is a little original: you have to write a datasource that explores the directory of a file system and returns the found objects (files or directories). The fields you will make to manage your datasource will be the file name, which you will name FILENAME; a flag that indicates whether the object is a file or a directory, which you will name IS_DIRECTORY; and the file size, if available, which you will name SIZE.

There will be two constructors for your datasource: the former will receive as a parameter the directory to scan, the latter will not have parameters (and will use the current directory to scan).

Just instantiated, the datasource will look for the files and the directories present in the way you indicate and fill an array with the files it finds.

The next method will increase the index variable that you will use to keep track of the position reached in the array files, and it will return true until you reach the end of the array.

Listing 9-7 shows the JRDataSource interface to implement.

Listing 9-7. *The JRFileSystemDataSource Class Implementing the JRDataSource Interface*

```
import net.sf.jasperreports.engine.*;
import java.io.*;

public class JRFileSystemDataSource implements JRDataSource
{
        File[] files = null;
        int    index = -1;

        public JRFileSystemDataSource(String path)
        {
            File dir = new File(path);
            if (dir.exists() && dir.isDirectory())
            {
                    files = dir.listFiles();
            }
        }

        public JRFileSystemDataSource()
        {
            this(".");
        }

        public boolean next() throws JRException
        {
            index++;
            if (files != null && index < files.length)
            {
                    return true;
            }
            return false;
        }


        public Object  getFieldValue(JRField jrField) throws JRException
```

```
        {
                File f = files[index];
                if (f == null) return null;
                if (jrField.getName().equals("FILENAME"))
                {
                        return f.getName();
                }
                else if (jrField.getName().equals("IS_DIRECTORY"))
                {
                        return new Boolean(f.isDirectory());
                }
                else if (jrField.getName().equals("SIZE"))
                {
                        return new Long(f.length());
                }
                // Field not found...
                return null;
        }
}
```

The getFieldValue method will return the requested file information. Your implementation does not use the information regarding the return type expected by the caller of the method, but it assumes that the name has to be returned as a string, the flag IS_DIRECTORY as a Boolean object, and the file size as a Long object. In the next section, you will learn how to use your personalized datasource in iReport and test it.

Using a Personalized JRDataSource with iReport

iReport provides support for almost all the datasources supplied by JasperReports such as JRXmlDataSource, JRBeanArrayDataSource, and JRBeanCollectionDataSource.

To use your personalized datasources, a special connection is provided; it is useful for employing whichever JRDataSource you want to use through some kind of factory class that provides an instance of that JRDataSource implementation. This factory class is just a simple Java class useful for testing your datasource and using it to fill a report in iReport.

The idea is the same as what you have seen for the JavaBeans set datasource: it is necessary to write a Java class that creates the datasource through a static method and returns it.

For example, if you want to test the JRFileSystemDataSource in the previous section, you need to create a simple class like that shown in Listing 9-8.

Listing 9-8. *Class for Testing a Personalized Datasource*

```
import net.sf.jasperreports.engine.*;

public class TestFileSystemDataSource
{
        public static JRDataSource test()
        {
                return new JRFileSystemDataSource("/");

        }
}
```

This class, and in particular the static method that will be called, will execute all the necessary code for instancing correctly the datasource. In this case, you create a new JRFileSystemDataSource object by specifying a way to scan the directory root ("/").

Now that you have defined the way to obtain a JRDataSource that you have prepared and made ready to be used, create the connection through which it will be used.

Create a new connection as you normally would, select Custom JRDataSource from the datasource type list, and specify a datasource name such as Test FileSystemDataSource (or whatever name you wish), as shown in Figure 9-30.

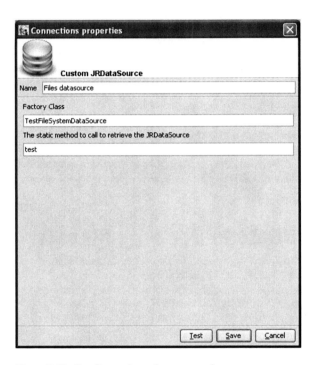

Figure 9-30. *Configuration of a custom datasource*

Next, specify the class and the method to use to obtain an instance of your JRFileSystemDataSource: TestFileSystemDataSource and test.

Prepare a new report with fields managed by the datasource. No method to find the fields managed by a datasource exists because you are using a custom JRDataSource. In this case, you know that the JRFileSystemDataSource manages three fields and their names and types: FILENAME (String), IS_DIRECTORY (Boolean), and SIZE (Long). After you have created these fields, insert them in the report's detail band as shown in Figure 9-31.

Divide the report into two columns, and in the column header band insert File name and Size tags. Then add two Image elements, one representing a document and the other an open folder. In the Print when expression setting of the Image element that is placed in the foreground, insert the expression $F{IS_DIRECTORY}.

Figure 9-32 shows what the printed report should look like.

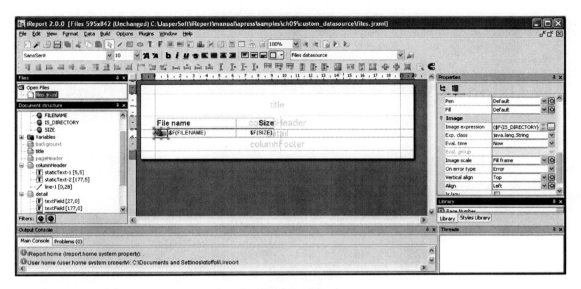

Figure 9-31. *Design window for the report using JRFileSystemDataSource*

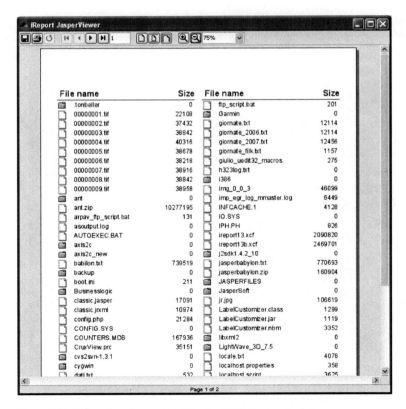

Figure 9-32. *The printed report fed by the JRFileSystemDataSource*

In this example, the class that instantiated the JRFileSystemDataSource was very simple. However, you can use more complex classes, such as one that obtains the datasource by calling an Enterprise JavaBean, or by calling a web service.

Using MDX and OLAP (Mondrian) Connections

iReport supports MDX queries executed against a Mondrian OLAP server (http://mondrian.sourceforge.net/). The measure values extracted using MDX are mapped to report fields using a special syntax.

In order to use MDX, you have to configure a connection to a Mondrian server, which requires the following items:

- A configured JDBC connection pointing to the data
- The URL of an XML file containing the definition of the schema: cubes, hierarchies, and so forth

To create a Mondrian OLAP connection, follow these steps:

1. From the Connections/Datasources dialog box, click New. In the list of datasource types, select Mondrian OLAP connection as the connection type. This brings up the dialog box shown in Figure 9-33.

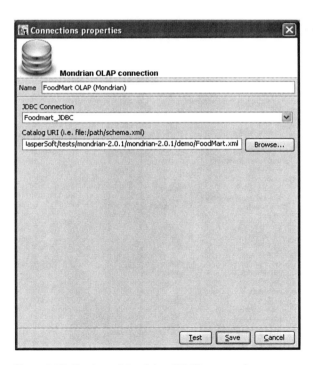

Figure 9-33. *Setting a Mondrian OLAP connection*

2. Select from the combo box the connection pointing to the cube data, and set the schema location.

3. Click Test to verify that the connection works properly.

It's not possible to specify an OLAP connection with the Report Wizard, so you will continue this example of MDX usage with a blank report. In the JasperReports distribution, in the demo/sample/mondrian/metadata directory, you will find a sample schema (FoodMart.xml). You can use this schema together with the foodmart sample database provided by Mondrian.

4. Set the new OLAP connection as the active connection (by selecting it from the datasources combo box in the toolbar).

5. Create a new blank report (File ➤ New Document), and click OK to accept the default values.

6. Open the Report query dialog box (Data ➤ Report Query) and set MDX as the query language in the Query language combo box at the top of the Report Query tab.

7. Insert in the text area the following MDX query:

```
SELECT {[Measures].[Unit Sales],
        [Measures].[Store Sales]} ON COLUMNS,
        {[Product].members} ON ROWS
FROM [Sales]
WHERE [Time].[1997].[Q2]
```

and click the button Read Fields.

At this point the right side of the query area will be filled with the measures, dimensions, and hierarchies selected in the query (see Figure 9-34).

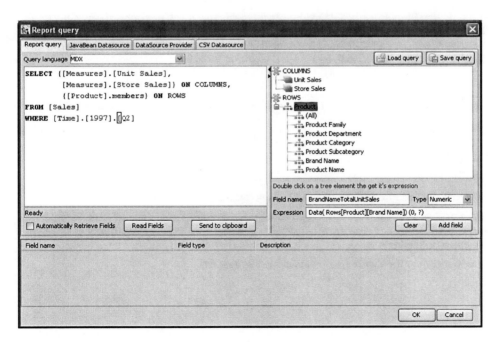

Figure 9-34. *MDX measures, dimensions, and hierarchies*

Now that you have the query metadata shown as a tree, you can start to define the field mapping.

Figure 9-35 shows the query result displayed using JPivot to give you an idea of the MDX result.

Product	Measures	
	● Unit Sales	● Store Sales
–All Products	62,610	132,666.27
–Drink	5,895	11,914.58
–Alcoholic Beverages	1,699	3,506.37
–Beer and Wine	1,699	3,506.37
–Beer	417	810.25
–Good	71	129.02
Good Imported Beer	46	74.52
Good Light Beer	25	54.50
–Pearl	99	142.34
Pearl Imported B~	44	40.04

Figure 9-35. *MDX result displayed using JPivot*

To begin defining the field mapping, proceed by creating the two fields to map the Unit Sales and Store Sales measures:

1. Double-click the Unit Sales item in the tree under the COLUMNS branch.

2. Set Field name to Unit Sales and Expression to `Data([Measures].[Unit Sales],?)`.

Please note that iReport is not able to identify the field type; it will be your responsibility to set the correct type (text, numeric, date, or Boolean).

The expression proposed by iReport is a typical expression to identify a specific cell in the MDX result collection. The syntax is as follows:

`Data(Measure, Tuple)`

The question mark in the example expression is a way to simply point to the current cell.

3. Next, set the type to Numeric and click Add field to add the field to the fields list. Remember to select all desired fields in the bottom table before clicking OK to close the Report query dialog box.

4. Repeat the preceding steps to add the Store Sales measure to the fields list, too.

5. Close the Report query dialog box, and check for the new two fields in the Library tab.

6. Drag the two new fields into the detail band, put a couple labels in the column header band, a title in the title band, and set the Unit Sales and Store Sales text field patterns to #,##0.00, as shown in Figure 9-36.

7. Run the report. The results should resemble Figure 9-37.

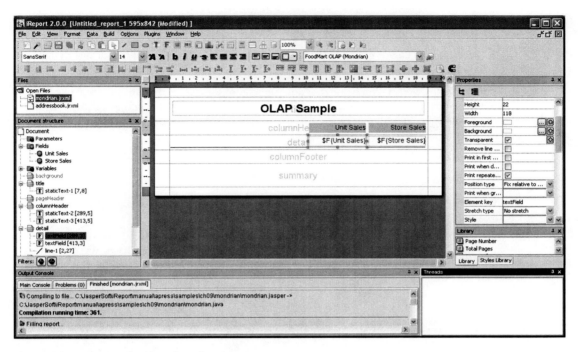

Figure 9-36. *Designing the MDX-based report*

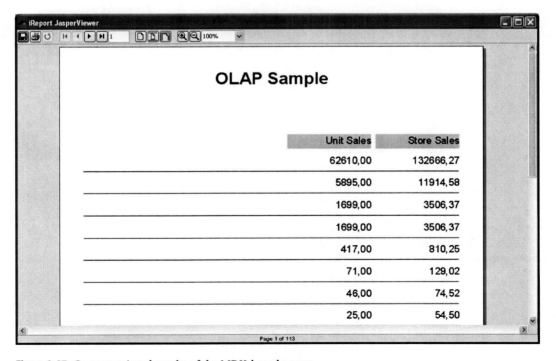

Figure 9-37. *Current printed results of the MDX-based report*

Now you can map to some other report fields all the values coming from the Product dimension. Start by adding a field to store the product name.

8. Return to the Report query dialog box. Click the Clear button to reset the form to define a field.

When you deal with a dimension that does not contains measures, you have to define a field yourself. You start by setting the field name: Product_Name. If you want to simply get the member name as a field value, double-click the desired member (the item Product Name in the tree). The following expression

```
Rows[Product][Product Name]
```

exactly represents the name of the product member labeled Product Name.

9. As just described, add to the report fields all the hierarchy levels: Family, Department, Category, Subcategory, Brand, and Product Name.

10. Next, use the Report Group Wizard (Edit ➤ New Report Group Wizard) to create some groups to aggregate data (see Figure 9-38). Starting from Family, add a group for each level in the hierarchy (excluding Product Name, as it's the maximum detail that you can reach).

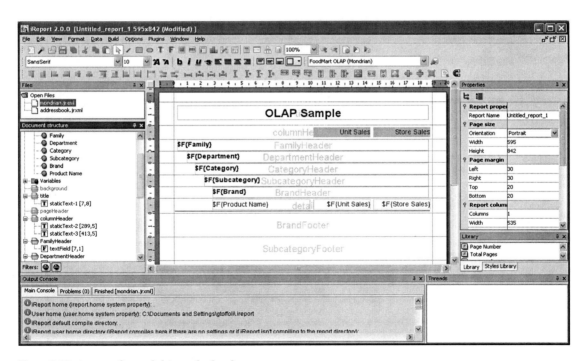

Figure 9-38. *A group for each hierarchy level*

Finally, you want use MDX to calculate some subtotals. In effect, all this data is contained in the OLAP cube, and it does not make sense to calculate it again using JasperReports variables. The syntax to map a subtotal is as follows:

```
Data(set)(tuple)
```

11. To calculate the total of Unit Sales for all products, use the expression

```
Data( Rows[Product][(All)] )([Measures].[Unit Sales],?)
```

12. Add the subtotal of the Unit Sales for the category level and the grand total of the same measure:

- UnitSalesCategoryTotal:

```
Data( Rows[Product][Product Category] )([Measures].[Unit Sales],?)
```

- UnitSalesGrandTotal:

```
Data( Rows[Product][(All)] )([Measures].[Unit Sales],?)
```

Both the fields are of type `java.lang.Number`.

Figure 9-39 shows how your report should look in the design pane, and Figure 9-40 shows a section of the printed report.

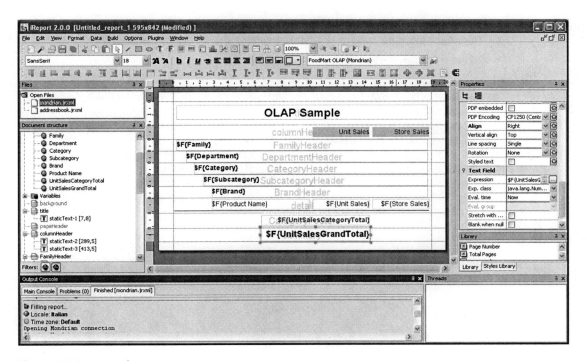

Figure 9-39. *Some totals*

Figure 9-40. *The totals fields extracted by the data*

Working with an XML/A Connection

JasperReports 1.3 introduced support for XML for Analysis (XML/A) datasources. In iReport, a new connection of type XML/A has been added to support this kind of datasource. The requirements to configure an XML/A connection are as follows:

- The URL that exposes the XML/A service
- The datasource name (meaning a datasource provided by the XML/A server)
- The catalog against which an MDX query is executed

Optionally, the cube to use can be specified.

To query the server in order to get the available datasources, catalogs, and relative cubes, click the button labeled Get metadata, shown in Figure 9-41, when you are specifying properties for a new XML/A datasource.

An XML/A connection can be used in JasperReports only by specifying a special query executer for the MDX language. Alternatively, this kind of connection can be used with a special MDX query executer created by Cincom, an American software and services provider.

iReport 1.3.1 introduced the username and password fields, though they are not currently supported by the Cincom query executer; these credentials are used when HTTP authentication is required for the specified URL.

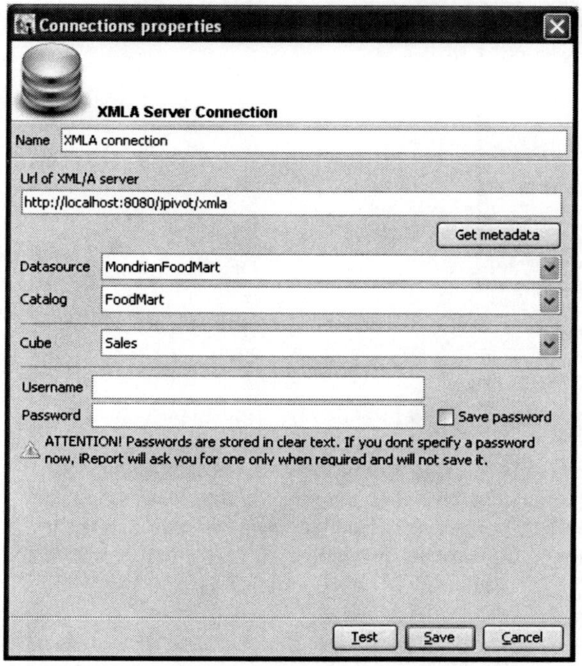

Figure 9-41. *XML/A connection definition*

Using an XML/A Connection with JasperReports

In JasperReports, each language is tied to a query executer, which you will learn more about in the section "Custom Languages and Query Executers" later in the chapter. For now, what you need to know is that the default query executer defined for the "mdx" language is

```
net.sf.jasperreports.olap.JRMondrianQueryExecuterFactory
```

This class assumes that a Mondrian connection (instead of an XML/A connection) is passed to the report engine in order to execute the MDX query saved into the report. Therefore, this query executer cannot work using a generic XML/A connection. To get around this, the solution is to change the default query executer for the language MDX, or better, define a new language, for instance "mdx2", and associate with it the right executer called

```
net.sf.jasperreports.olap.xmla.JRXmlaQueryExecuterFactory
```

This can be done in iReport by opening the Query executers window (Options ➤ Query executers) and clicking New to bring up the dialog box in Figure 9-42, in which you create the new language definition.

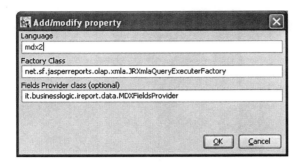

Figure 9-42. *Specifying a new language definition*

The new language mdx2 will employ the query executer provided by JasperReports to allow you to use XML/A datasources.

To help you with the field mapping, when editing a query of type mdx2, you can display the same interface that appears in the Report query dialog box when dealing with the MDX language. In effect, you are always using the MDX language, but in this particular context you are using the language name to point JasperReports to the right query executer to use. You achieve that by setting the following class as the fields provider:

```
it.businesslogic.ireport.data.MDXFieldsProvider
```

which is the default fields provider used by iReport for the MDX language.

Here comes a little problem: the mapping tool for MDX (described in detail previously in the section "Using MDX and OLAP (Mondrian) Connections") does not work with XML/A datasources, but only using Mondrian directly. This is a limitation that will be addressed in the future. The current workaround to create the mapping easily is to use a Mondrian connection at design time.

When the report is executed, the JRXmlaQueryExecuterFactory puts at your disposal three built-in parameters: XMLA_URL, XMLA_DATASOURCE, and XMLA_CATALOG, all of type String.

Using an XML/A Connection with the Cincom MDX Query Executer

iReport contains a custom query executer contributed by Cincom. It can run MDX queries against an XML/A connection, and the assigned language name is xmla-mdx. Again, the name actually refers to the MDX language, but the report engine will look for the query executer "registered" for this language name, for instance:

```
net.sf.jasperreports.engine.query.JRXmlaQueryExecuterFactory
```

The implementation of this query executer is contained in cincom-jr-xmla.jar, which makes available at runtime three built-in parameters: XMLA_URL, XMLA_DS, and XMLA_CAT, all of type String.

When an MDX query is specified in the Report query dialog box, the available fields can be read with the Read Fields button, as shown in Figure 9-43.

You will notice that the mapping syntax is quite different from the one used by the native MDX query executers of JasperReports. This makes the two implementations incompatible.

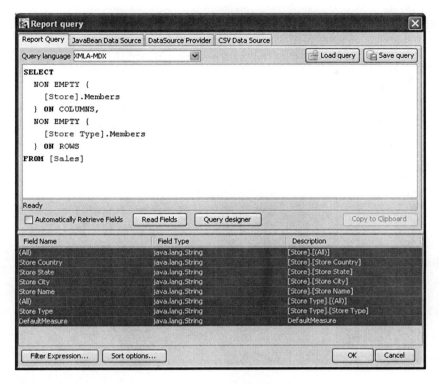

Figure 9-43. *Field mapping using an XML/A connection*

Using the MDX Query Editor Rex

To facilitate the creation of MDX queries, iReport is integrated with Rex (waRehouse EXplorer), an open source visual designer for MDX queries (see Figure 9-44). Rex requires an XML/A connection to work, so it cannot be used through a direct Mondrian connection (as required by the field mapping tool integrated in iReport).

Basically, Rex is a visual MDX query builder. It lets you explore the dimensions provided by the OLAP cube, and drag the desired measures and members into the builder tree in the center of the window, as shown in Figure 9-44. You can test your query, see the result, and when ready, you can bring the query into iReport to use it with the current report.

As with all the tools to design the report query, to start Rex, open the Report query dialog box, select XMLA-MDX from the Query language combo box, and press the button Query designer.

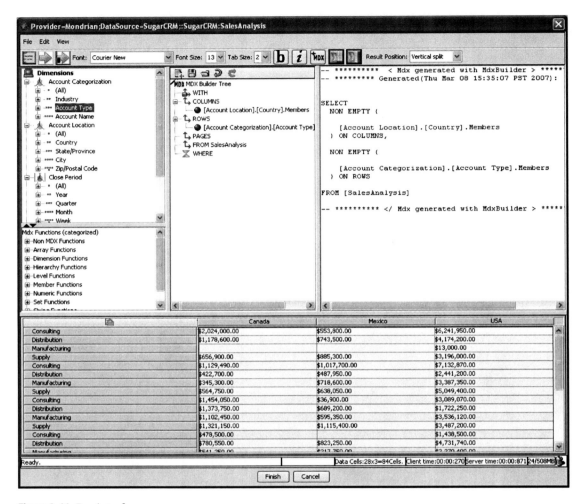

Figure 9-44. *Rex interface*

Using an EJBQL Connection

EJBQL, or Enterprise JavaBeans Query Language, is a language for performing queries on sets of entity beans managed by a persistence container. You can find more info about EJBQL at http://java.sun.com/j2ee/tutorial/1_3-fcs/doc/EJBQL.html. EJBQL is very similar to HQL, and iReport provides for both a similar interface to explore result sets and map report fields.

The first step to create an EJBQL query-based report is to configure a connection with the persistence manager (see Figure 9-45). JasperReports comes with a sample based on Toplink, a persistence manager from Oracle.

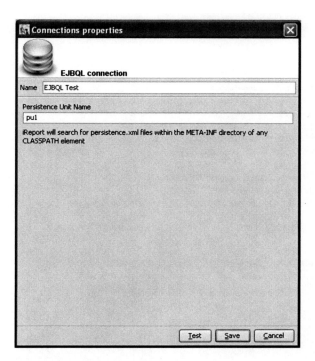

Figure 9-45. *Configuring an EJBQL datasource*

In order to run the sample, you have to add to the iReport classpath (by selecting Options ➤ Classpath) the two JARs located inside the directory demo/samples/ejbql/lib (in JasperReports version 1.2.3 and greater) and the directory demo/samples/ejbql/build/classes as well (first ensuring you have compiled all required classes in this sample folder using Ant and the provided build.xml file).

In the classes directory just included in the classpath is a META-INF subdirectory containing persistence.xml, an XML file that defines one or more persistence units with relative properties and settings.

iReport will look for this file (if more than one persistence.xml file is available in the classpath, only the first will be considered). The only key information that you must provide is the name of the persistence unit to use (in this case, the name is pu1 according to the persistence.xml file provided by JasperReports (the content of which is shown in Listing 9-9). The database used is the HSQLDB shipped with JasperReports.

Listing 9-9. *The Content of the persistence.xml File*

```
<persistence xmlns="http://java.sun.com/xml/ns/persistence" version="1.0">
    <persistence-unit name="pu1">
        <!-- Provider class name is required in Java SE -->
        <provider>
          oracle.toplink.essentials.ejb.cmp3.EntityManagerFactoryProvider
        </provider>
        <!-- All persistence classes must be listed -->
```

```
        <class>Person</class>
        <class>Movie</class>
        <class>Cast</class>
        <class>Varia</class>
        <properties>
            <!-- Provider-specific connection properties -->
            <property name="toplink.jdbc.driver" value="org.hsqldb.jdbcDriver"/>
            <property name="toplink.jdbc.url" value="jdbc:hsqldb:/JasperSoft/➥
                JasperReports/jasperreports-1.2.3/demo/samples/ejbql/db"/>
            <property name="toplink.jdbc.user" value="sa"/>
            <property name="toplink.jdbc.password" value=""/>
            <!-- Provider-specific settings -->
            <property name="toplink.logging.level" value="DEBUG"/>
            <property name="toplink.platform.class.name" value=
                "oracle.toplink.essentials.platform.database.HSQLPlatform"/>
        </properties>
    </persistence-unit>
</persistence>
```

An EJBQL query can return for each row, from the JasperReports point of view, a single Java object, or a mixed set of objects and scalar values.

In the first case, iReport provides a way to navigate a single object in order to map nested attributes to report fields (see Figure 9-46).

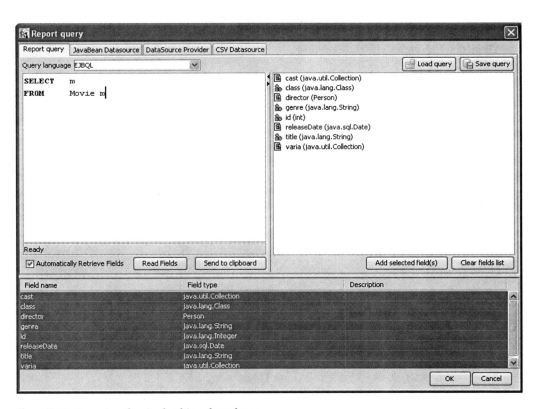

Figure 9-46. *Browsing the single object–based row*

If more than one object/value is present in a result row, fields can be mapped to the result columns only using as the field name COLUMN_*x*, where *x* is the column number (starting from 1), as shown in Figure 9-47.

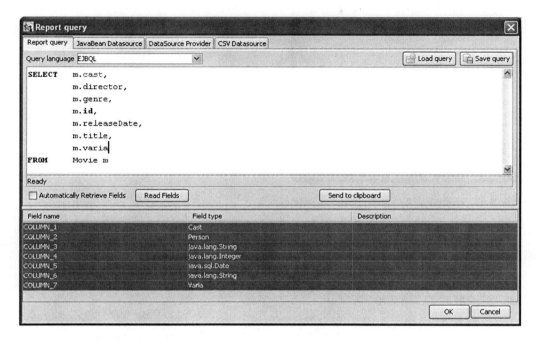

Figure 9-47. *Multicolumn results*

Running an EJBQL Query from a Subreport

When using an EJBQL datasource, subreports can be filled in two ways: using a field coming from the main result set and of type `java.util.Collection`, or passing to the subreport what is needed to execute a new EJBQL query.

In the first case, you assume the collection contains a set of JavaBeans, and you wrap this collection using a `JRBeanCollectionDataSource`. The datasource expression to fill a subreport showing all the persons in the cast of a movie, for example, might look like this:

```
new JRBeanCollectionDataSource($F{cast})
```

Otherwise, if you still want query data using EJBQL, you have to pass to the subreport the instance of the entity manager responsible for gathering data. This can be done by adding a parameter to the subreport named `JPA_ENTITY_MANAGER` with `$P{JPA_ENTITY_MANAGER}` as the value (see Figure 9-48). This built-in parameter contains exactly the instance of the entity manager you need.

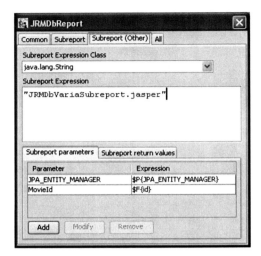

Figure 9-48. *Connection of a subreport that uses EJBQL*

You will not include a connection/datasource expression for the Subreport element, so you set the combo box in the Subreport tab to Don't use connection or datasource.

Please note that you can still pass the JPA_ENTITY_MANAGER parameter even if you want to fill a subreport using a Bean collection; this way, you can preserve the ability to fill nested subreports that are based on an EJBQL query.

Running an EJBQL-Based Report from a Java Application

In order to execute a report that uses an EJBQL query inside your application, you have to provide the report engine an instance of the entity manager responsible for gathering data (exactly as it happens when filling a subreport).

```
EntityManagerFactory emf =
            Persistence.createEntityManagerFactory("pu1", new HashMap());
EntityManager em = emf.createEntityManager();

try
{
    Map parameters = new HashMap();
    parameters.put(
                    JRJpaQueryExecuterFactory.PARAMETER_JPA_ENTITY_MANAGER,
                    em);

    JasperFillManager.fillReportToFile(fileName, parameters);

    em.close();

}
finally
{
    if (em.isOpen())  em.close();
    if (emf.isOpen()) emf.close();
}
```

To pass the entity manager instance, you have to insert it into the map used to set the report parameters, using as object key the constant JRJpaQueryExecuterFactory.PARAMETER_JPA_ENTITY_MANAGER.

Importing and Exporting Datasources

To simplify the process of sharing datasource configurations, iReport provides a mechanism to export and import datasource definitions.

To export one or more datasources, select from the Connections/Datasources dialog box the items to export and click the Export button (see Figure 9-49). iReport will ask you to name the file and indicate the destination where to store the exported information. The created file is a simple XML file and can be edited with a common text editor, if needed. A file exported with iReport can be imported by clicking Import. Since an exported file can contain more than one datasource or connection definition, the import process will add all the datasources found in the specified file to the current list.

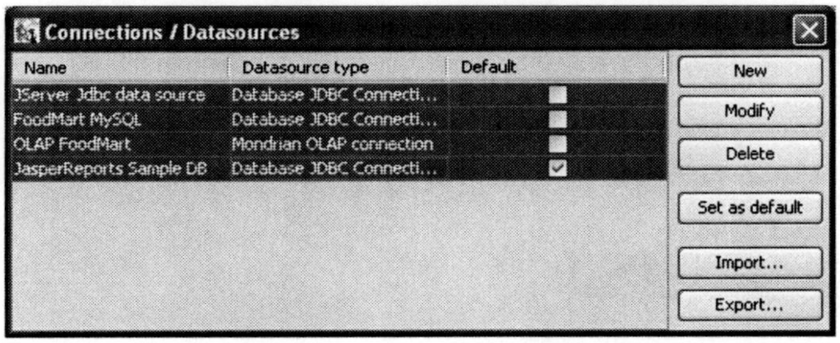

Figure 9-49. *Export and import datasources via the Connections/Datasources dialog box.*

If a duplicated datasource name is found during the import, iReport will postfix a number to the imported datasource name, as shown in Figure 9-50.

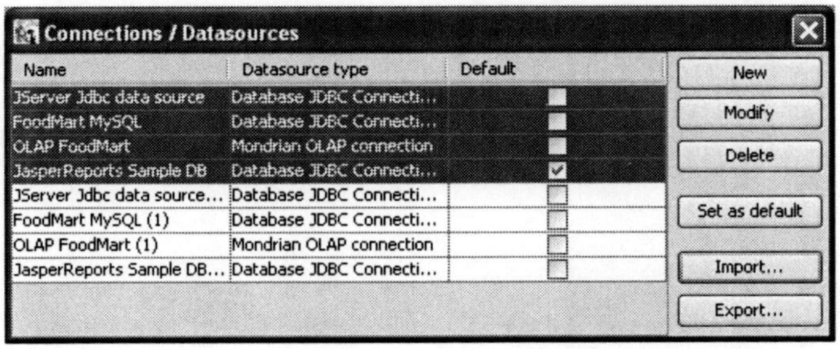

Figure 9-50. *Imported datasources (not selected)*

JasperReports Datasource Providers

JasperReports provides an interface to standardize the use of a custom JRDataSource in GUI tools. To create and use this kind of object, write a class that implements the interface net.sf. jasperreports.engine.JRDataSourceProvider.

```
public interface JRDataSourceProvider
{

    public boolean supportsGetFieldsOperation();

    public JRField[] getFields(JasperReport report)
        throws JRException, UnsupportedOperationException;

    public JRDataSource create(JasperReport report)
        throws JRException;

    public void dispose(JRDataSource dataSource)
        throws JRException;
}
```

This kind of object can be used in the Report query dialog box to get the datasource fields (if the datasource provider supports this feature).

To use a datasource provider, simply create a new connection of type JRDataSourceProvider and set the class that implements your provider (see Figure 9-51).

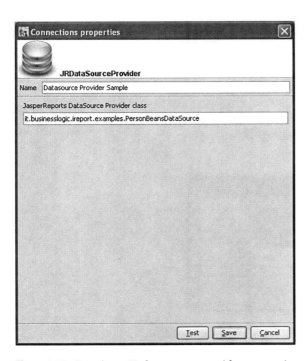

Figure 9-51. *Creating a JR datasource provider connection*

The following is sample code of a JR datasource provider that can be used to wrap
JRFileSystemDataSource:

```
import net.sf.jasperreports.engine.JRDataSource;
import net.sf.jasperreports.engine.JRDataSourceProvider;
import net.sf.jasperreports.engine.JRException;
import net.sf.jasperreports.engine.JRField;
import net.sf.jasperreports.engine.JasperReport;
import net.sf.jasperreports.engine.design.JRDesignField;
/*
 * JRFileSystemDataSourceProvider.java
 *
 */

public class JRFileSystemDataSourceProvider implements JRDataSourceProvider {

    /** Creates a new instance of JRFileSystemDataSourceProvider */
    public JRFileSystemDataSourceProvider() {
    }

    public boolean supportsGetFieldsOperation() {
        return true;
    }

    public JRField[] getFields(JasperReport jasperReport)
        throws JRException,  UnsupportedOperationException {

        JRField[] fields = new JRField[3];

        JRDesignField field1 = new JRDesignField();
        field1.setName("FILENAME");
        field1.setValueClass(String.class);
        field1.setValueClassName(String.class.getName());
        fields[0] = field1;


        JRDesignField field2 = new JRDesignField();
        field2.setName("IS_DIRECTORY");
        field2.setValueClass(Boolean.class);
        field2.setValueClassName(Boolean.class.getName());
        fields[1] = field2;

        JRDesignField field3 = new JRDesignField();
            public void dispose(JRDataSource jRDataSource) throws JRException {
    }
}
```

When the getFields method is called by iReport to get the fields list, a special instance of the
JasperReport object is provided to the method. This instance is not the real compiled version of the
report that is being edited, but rather an ad hoc instance containing the specified query (and relative language), all the report custom properties, and all the parameters with their default value
expressions.

Creating Custom Languages and Query Executers

One of the most exciting improvements since JasperReports 1.2.6 is the ability to use custom languages inside iReport to perform a query. Currently, JasperReports provides native support for the following query languages: SQL, HQL, XPath, EJBQL, and MDX.

A custom language is a query language that is not natively supported by JasperReports and that will be used by the report query through which data to print will be selected. A custom language is tied to a query executer, an object that will be used by JasperReports to process the custom query and get data as a JRDataSource object.

In order to use a new language, you have to register it: this can be done from the Query executers window (Options ➤ Query executers). A new language can be added by simply setting the language name and the Factory class used to get an instance of the query executer (see Figure 9-52).

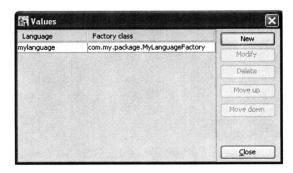

Figure 9-52. *Adding a new language via a query executer*

Be sure that all the classes and JARs required by the query executer are in the classpath.

At this point, you will be able to use the new query language in the report, set it, and enter an appropriate query in the Report query dialog box (see Figure 9-53).

Figure 9-53. *Using the newly added report query language*

■**Caution** Currently, iReport does not provide any mechanism to automatically get the fields from a custom query.

Creating a Query Executer for a Custom Language

It's time to learn the ropes. You want to create a query executer capable of getting as query input some lines organized as a CSV file: for each row, you will have a set of fields separated by a comma. The query that you want to process will be something like the following:

```
"Dow",    12194.13, 27.80
"Nasdaq", 2413.21, 18.56
"S&P 500", 1396.71,  3.92
```

As you can see, you are not defining a real query language, you are simply putting text data where a query should be . . . but this example does not lose any of its generality: you have some text (the query), and your query executer will try to process this query and provide a result in the form of a JRDataSource object.

Please note that the query can always accept parameters using the canonical syntax $P{*parameter name*}. The responsibility for managing query parameters belongs to the query executer.

A query executer is composed of two objects: the query executer factory and the actual query executer. When a query is processed, JasperReports instantiates the query executer factory, matching the language of the report query, and calls the method createQueryExecuter, passing as arguments a JRDataset (a structure to manage fields, parameters, variables, queries, and query languages declared in the report) and a map containing the values provided for each parameter. This method will return an instance of a JRQueryExecuter that provides the method createDatasource: the engine will call it to get the datasource to fill the report. Figure 9-54 provides a schema that shows this process.

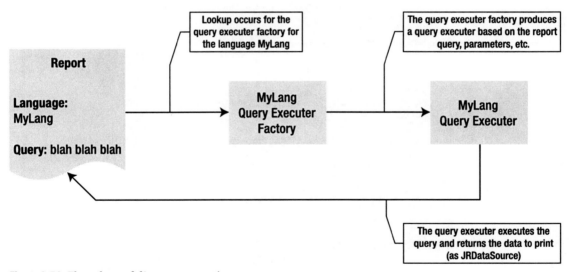

Figure 9-54. *Flow chart of the query execution*

Let's start with the query executer factory. JasperReports provides an interface to create this kind of object:

```java
package net.sf.jasperreports.engine.query;

import java.util.Map;

import net.sf.jasperreports.engine.JRDataset;
import net.sf.jasperreports.engine.JRException;
import net.sf.jasperreports.engine.JRValueParameter;


/**
 * Factory classes used to create query executers.
 * For each query language, a query executer factory must be created
 * and registered as a JR property.
 * Query executer factory instances must be thread-safe as they are cached
 * and used as singletons.
 */
public interface JRQueryExecuterFactory
{
    /**
     * Returns the built-in parameters associated with this query type.
     * These parameters will be created as system-defined parameters for each
     * report/dataset having a query of this type.
     * The returned array should contain consecutive pairs of parameter
     * names and parameter classes
     * (e.g. <code>{"Param1", String.class, "Param2", "List.class"}</code>).
     * @return array of built-in parameter names and types associated
     * with this query type
     */
    public Object[] getBuiltinParameters();


    /**
     * Creates a query executer.
     * This method is called at fill time for reports/datasets having a
     * query supported by
     * this factory.
     * @param dataset the dataset containing the query, fields, etc.
     * @param parameters map of value parameters (instances of
     * {@link JRValueParameter JRValueParameter})
     *       indexed by name
     *
     * @return a query executer
     * @throws JRException
     */
    public JRQueryExecuter createQueryExecuter(
                        JRDataset dataset, Map parameters) throws JRException;

    /**
     * Decides whether the query executers created by this factory support
     * a query parameter type.
     * This check is performed for all $P{..} parameters in the query.
     *
     * @param className the value class name of the parameter
     * @return whether the parameter value type is supported
     */
    public boolean supportsQueryParameterType(String className);
}
```

The methods to implement are three: getBuiltinParameters, createQueryExecuter, and supportsQueryParameterType.

The first method returns an array containing names and types of built-in parameters that the query executer makes available. This feature is useful when the query is executed against some kind of session object or a connection to an external entity, like a database, or a server. For example, the query executer factory for SQL provides the built-in parameter REPORT_CONNECTION, storing the java.sql.Connection instance used to execute the query; this object can be used by subreports to execute their SQL queries. Similarly, the query executer factory for HQL provides as a parameter the Hibernate session required to perform the query.

The second method (createQueryExecuter) is responsible for creating the query executer instance, making it possibly the most important one of the three.

Finally, you can filter the accepted parameter types by implementing the supportsQueryParameterType method, which returns true if the class name given as an argument is accepted, and false otherwise.

In this implementation, you will not return any built-in parameter, and you will accept all types of parameters (actually, your query executer factory will ignore any parameters, avoiding processing the $P{} directives of the query).

Here is the code:

```
import java.util.Map;
import net.sf.jasperreports.engine.JRDataset;
import net.sf.jasperreports.engine.JRException;
import net.sf.jasperreports.engine.JRQuery;
import net.sf.jasperreports.engine.query.JRQueryExecuter;
import net.sf.jasperreports.engine.query.JRQueryExecuterFactory;

/**
 *
 */
public class CSVQueryExecuterFactory implements JRQueryExecuterFactory {

    public Object[] getBuiltinParameters() {
        return new Object[]{};
    }

    public JRQueryExecuter createQueryExecuter(JRDataset jRDataset, Map map)
                                                        throws JRException {
        JRQuery query = jRDataset.getQuery();
        String queryString = query.getText();

        return new CSVQueryExecuter(queryString);
    }

    public boolean supportsQueryParameterType(String string) {
        return true;
    }

}
```

The query executer has a simple interface too. Again, there are three methods: one that will produce the JRDataSource to fill the report (createDatasource), another to clean up everything at the end of the execution (close), and finally a method to interrupt the query execution (cancelQuery).

```
/**
 * Query executer interface.
 * An implementation of this interface is created when the input data
 * of a report/dataset is specified by a query.
 * The implementation will run the query and create a JRDataSource
 * from the result.
 * The query executers would usually be initialized by a JRQueryExecuterFactory
 * with the query and the parameter values.
 */
public interface JRQueryExecuter
{
    /**
     * Executes the query and creates a JRDataSource out of the result.
     *
     * @return a JRDataSource wrapping the query execution result.
     * @throws JRException
     */
    public JRDataSource createDatasource() throws JRException;

    /**
     * Closes resources kept open during the datasource iteration.
     * This method is called after the report is filled or the dataset is
     * iterated.
     * If a resource is not needed after the datasource has been created,
     * it should be released at the end of createDatasource.
     */
    public void close();

    /**
     * Cancels the query if it's currently running.
     * This method will be called from a different thread if the client
     * decides to cancel the filling process.
     *
     * @return <code>true</code> iff the query was running and it has been
     * cancelled
     * @throws JRException
     */
    public boolean cancelQuery() throws JRException;
}
```

This very simple query executer will do nothing when the close and the cancelQuery methods are invoked. The main method, createDatasource, will create an instance of JRCsvDataSource providing the report query as the CSV stream to process; the aim, in fact, is to return a JRDataSource object. Your CSVQueryExecuter will look as follows:

```
package it.businesslogic.ireport.examples.queryexecuter;

import it.businesslogic.ireport.connection.JRCSVDataSource;
import java.io.StringReader;
import net.sf.jasperreports.engine.JRDataSource;
import net.sf.jasperreports.engine.JRException;
import net.sf.jasperreports.engine.data.JRCsvDataSource;
import net.sf.jasperreports.engine.query.JRQueryExecuter;
```

```
public class CSVQueryExecuter implements JRQueryExecuter {

    private String fileContent;

    /** Creates a new instance of CSVQueryExecuter */
    public CSVQueryExecuter(String fileContent) {
        this.fileContent = fileContent;
    }

    public JRDataSource createDatasource() throws JRException {

        JRCsvDataSource csvds = new JRCsvDataSource(
                    new StringReader( fileContent ));
        return csvds;
    }

    public void close() {
    }

    public boolean cancelQuery() throws JRException {
        return true;
    }
}
```

Simple, right? Now that you have the query executer and the query executer factory, you can try your new language in iReport. Configure iReport as shown earlier to use the new factory with the language "csv" (or any other name you prefer). Create a new report and the required fields (the JRCsvDataSource uses field names like COLUMN_0, COLUMN_1, etc., all with type String). Specify your CSV data by setting the query language to csv, and run the report.

The query executer mechanism opens the door to making an infinite number of possible implementations and new languages available for JasperReports. Using this feature, it's easy to create, for example, support for Oracle store procedures, and most smart developers will be able to support a full range of programming languages such as JavaScript, Ruby, and Groovy as query languages.

Working with a Fields Provider

When you write a query in the Report query dialog box, be it a simple SQL statement or a very long and complex expression in a custom language, it is very useful to have a tool capable of analyzing the query and, if necessary, executing it, in order to detect and extract the available fields, or a tool to help you with field mapping, or a visual designer in which you can easily design the query itself.

iReport provides natively some such tools for SQL, HQL, EJBQL, and MDX: for example, when editing an SQL query, the list of available fields can be read using the Read Fields button, and when editing an HQL query, you can explore the result to select the fields you desire.

To extend these capabilities or replace the ones available for a specific language, you can write a *fields provider*: through this interface, a visual designer, a tool to help with field mapping, and a tool to read available fields from a query can be provided for each language type.

A fields provider is plugged into iReport similarly to the way a query executer is—by using the Query executers window (Options ➤ Query executers). Table 9-3 lists the default values of the query executer factory and the report provider class for each language defined.

Table 9-3. *Default Language Query Executer Factory and Fields Provider Classes*

Language	Query Executer Factory	Fields Provider Class
sql (or SQL)	net.sf.jasperreports.engine.query. JRJdbcQueryExecuterFactory	it.businesslogic.ireport.data. SQLFieldsProvider
hql (or HQL)	net.sf.jasperreports.engine.query. JRHibernateQueryExecuterFactory	it.businesslogic.ireport.data. HQLFieldsProvider
ejbql (or EJBQL)	net.sf.jasperreports.engine.query. JRJpaQueryExecuterFactory	it.businesslogic.ireport.data. EJBQLFieldsProvider
mdx (or MDX)	net.sf.jasperreports.olap. JRMondrianQueryExecuterFactory	it.businesslogic.ireport.data. MDXFieldsProvider
xmla-mdx	net.sf.jasperreports.engine.query. JRXmlaQueryExecuterFactory	it.businesslogic.ireport.data. CincomMDXFieldsProvider
xPath (or XPath)	net.sf.jasperreports.engine.query. JRXPathQueryExecuterFactory	N/A

The fields provider interface is defined in it.businesslogic.ireport.FieldsProvider. Here is the code of the interface:

```
package it.businesslogic.ireport;

import it.businesslogic.ireport.gui.ReportQueryDialog;
import java.awt.Component;
import java.util.Map;
import net.sf.jasperreports.engine.JRDataset;
import net.sf.jasperreports.engine.JRException;
import net.sf.jasperreports.engine.JRField;


/**
 * Returns true if the provider supports the
 * getFields(IReportConnection,JRDataset,Map) operation. By returning true in
 * this method the datasource provider indicates that it is able to introspect
 * the datasource and discover the available fields.
 *
 * @return true if the getFields() operation is supported.
 */
public boolean supportsGetFieldsOperation();

/**
 * Returns the fields that are available from a query of a specific language
 * The provider can use the passed-in report to extract some additional
 * configuration information such as report properties.
 * The IReportConnection object can be used to execute the query.
 *
 * @param con the IReportConnection active in iReport.
 * @param the JRDataset that will be filled using the datasource created by
 * this provider. The passed-in report can be null. That means that no compiled
 * report is available yet.
 * @param parameters map containing the interpreted default value of each
 * parameter
 * @return a nonnull fields array. If there are no fields, then an empty array
 * must be returned.
```

```
 *
 * @throws UnsupportedOperationException is the method is not supported
 * @throws JRException if an error occurs.
 */
public JRField[] getFields(
                IReportConnection con,
                JRDataset reportDataset,
                Map parameters )
                    throws JRException, UnsupportedOperationException;


/**
 * Returns true if the getFields can be run in a background thread each time
 * the user changes the query.
 * This approach cannot be valid for fields providers that require much time to
 * return the list of fields.
 */
public boolean supportsAutomaticQueryExecution();


/**
 * Returns true if the fields provider can run its own query designer
 */
public boolean hasQueryDesigner();


/**
 * Returns true if the fields provider can run its own editor
 */
public boolean hasEditorComponent();


/**
 * This method is used to run a query designer for the specific language.
 * @param con the IReportConnection active in iReport.
 * @param query the query to modify
 * @param reportQueryDialog the parent reportQueryDialog. It can be used to get
 * all (sub)dataset information with reportQueryDialog.getSubDataset();
 *
 */
public String designQuery(
                IReportConnection con,
                String query,
                ReportQueryDialog reportQueryDialog)
                    throws JRException, UnsupportedOperationException;



/**
 * The component that will stay on the right of the query panel. To listen for query
 * changes, the component must implement the interface FieldsProviderEditor.
 * The component will be visible only when a query change is successfully executed.
 * The component can store the reference to the report query dialog in which it
 * will appear.
 */
public FieldsProviderEditor getEditorComponent(
                        ReportQueryDialog reportQueryDialog );


}
```

Technically, there are seven methods to implement (supportsGetFieldsOperation, getFields, supportsAutomaticQueryExecution, hasQueryDesigner, hasEditorComponent, designQuery, getEditorComponent) four of which define what the specific fields provider is able to do, and three related to three main tasks: designing the query, reading the fields, and providing a fields editor.

supportsGetFieldsOperation indicates whether the fields provider implementation is able to get the fields from the query (i.e., executing it, as happens for the SQL). If this method returns true, iReport assumes that the method getFields returns a nonnull array of fields (net.sf.jasperreports.engine.JRField).

hasQueryDesigner and hasEditorComponent return true if the fields provider implementation supports visual query designing and has a tool to edit field mapping, respectively.

These methods are called when a language is selected in the Report query dialog box. iReport looks for the matching fields provider and, if available, enables/disables the Read Fields and Query designer buttons according to the return values (see Figure 9-55).

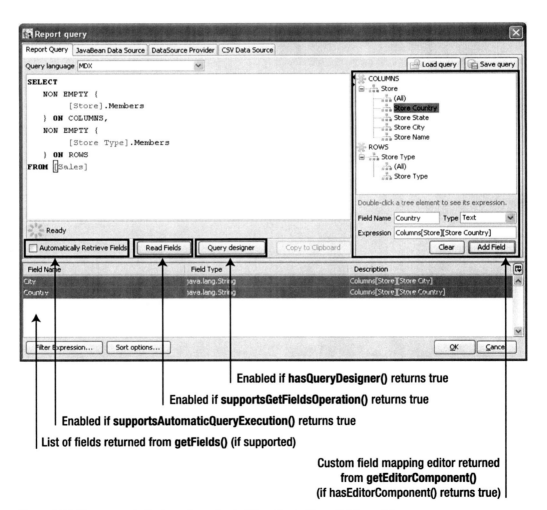

Figure 9-55. *Components that can be activated/deactivated by a field provider*

If an editor component is available, it is displayed on the right of the query text area.

Every time you change the query text, if both supportsAutomaticQueryExecution and supportsGetFieldsOperation return true, and the Automatically Retrieve Fields check box option is selected, the method getFields is called. The resulting JRField array is used to populate the fields list.

If the editor component is present, it can receive a query-changed event through the FieldsProviderEditor interface (implemented by the components returned by the getEditorComponent method).

If the method hasQueryDesigner returns true, the Query designer button will be enabled. When clicked, iReport will call the method designQuery, passing as parameters the currently selected instance of IReportConnection, the query string to edit (which can be blank), and a reference to the Report query dialog box (which can be null). The method must return a string containing the new query, or null if the operation was canceled by the user.

Sample implementations of fields providers are available in the iReport source code, in the package it.businesslogic.ireport.data.

Creating Custom iReport Connections

When working in iReport, it is not always easy to take advantage of the great flexibility intrinsic in JasperReports in terms of datasources. Especially with the advent of pluggable query executers that enabled the use of custom languages, the custom JRDataSource is simply not enough. For this reason, iReport 1.3.3 introduced a more generic way to define a custom connection, making pluggable any implementation of IReportConnection. This class represents a very generic connection factory that can act as JRDataSource factory, or as a JDBC connection provider, or again as a more sophisticated connection provider usable in conjunction with a custom query language.

IReportConnection is an abstract class, but the only abstract method is getDescription, making the implementation of a derived class very easy.

As explained previously, there are three main ways to fill a report:

- Using a JRDataSource. (The query inside the report will be ignored.)

- Using a JDBC connection. (The query inside the report must be a SQL statement.)

- Avoiding specifying a JRDataSource or connection.

In the last case, you need to set a value for some special built-in parameters according to the language of the query stored inside the report in order to establish the required connection. For example, when a report is based on an XPath expression as a query, the report engine expects to find a valid document set for the parameter XML_DATA_DOCUMENT.

So, an IReportConnection implementation is able to indicate whether it is a JDBC connection provider, or a JRDataSource provider, or something different, in which case the getSpecialParameters and disposeSpecialParameters methods will be called before and after report execution, respectively.

To make this kind of connection more easily configurable, the graphic interface to edit it contains a table to set named parameters, as shown in Figure 9-56.

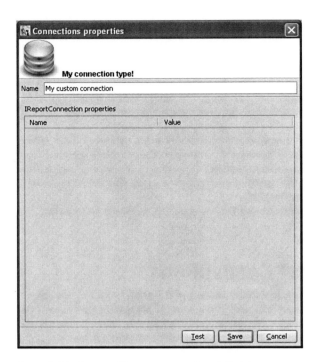

Figure 9-56. *Custom iReport connection definition*

These properties will be available to the IReportConnection class when the method

```
public void loadProperties(java.util.HashMap map)
```

is executed. When requested, the same properties are saved with the method save.

Several samples of working IReportConnection implementations are available in the package it/businesslogic/ireport/connection.

Let's see how to create and use a custom IReportConnection. The first step is to create a class that extends the abstract class it.businesslogic.ireport.IReportConnection. Listing 9-10 shows a simple implementation.

Listing 9-10. *Simple Implementation of a Custom IReportConnection*

```
import it.businesslogic.ireport.IReportConnection;
import java.util.Map;

public class MyIReportConnection extends IReportConnection {

    public String getDescription()
    {
        return "My connection type!";
    }

    public net.sf.jasperreports.engine.JRDataSource getJRDataSource() {
        return new net.sf.jasperreports.engine.JREmptyDataSource(5);
    }
}
```

```
public Map getSpecialParameters(Map map) throws
  net.sf.jasperreports.engine.JRException
{
    map.put("MY_TITLE", "Built-in title!");
    return map;
}

}
```

When used, this connection produces a JREmptyDataSource and sets the value of the parameter MY_TITLE (useful only if this parameter is declared in the report or if it is a built-in parameter of the query executer used to fill the report).

In order to see this connection type in the list of the available connection types when configuring a new datasource, you need a simple iReport plug-in. Chapter 17 will explain in depth how to create a plug-in. In this section, I will explain just a few concepts you need to activate the custom connection.

Listing 9-11 shows the code of a very simple plug-in.

Listing 9-11. *Plug-In for the Custom IReportConnection*

```
import it.businesslogic.ireport.plugin.IReportPlugin;

public class MyIReportConnectionPlugin extends IReportPlugin {
  public void call()
  {
      getMainFrame().addConnectionImplementation( "MyIReportConnection" );
  }
}
```

The only interesting operation here is the call to the method addConnectionImplementation, which is the way to activate a new IReportConnection implementation in iReport. In order to run the plug-in, you need a little descriptor, which is an XML file that must be placed in the classpath in a directory called ireport. The file must be named plugin.xml. Listing 9-12 shows the plugin.xml file required to execute the plug-in only once when iReport starts.

Listing 9-12. *The plugin.xml File for Executing the Example Plug-In*

```
<iReportPlugin
    name="My new connection"
    class="MyIReportConnectionPlugin"
    loadOnStartup="true"
    hide = "true"
    configurable = "false">

    <Description></Description>

</iReportPlugin>
```

Figure 9-57 shows the connection now available in the list of the connection types.

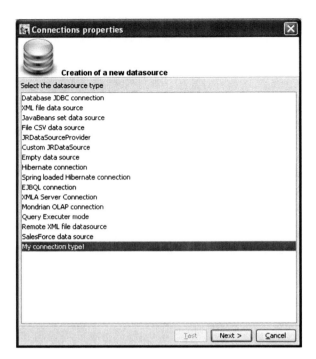

Figure 9-57. *The custom connection is available in the list of connection types.*

Finally, the abstract IReportConnection class provides a method to provide a personalized GUI to use when configuring the custom connection. The method, called getIReportConnectionEditor, should return an object of type IReportConnectionEditor. If your implementation does not override this method, the generic interface shown in Figure 9-57 is used instead.

All the connections and datasources available in iReport are implemented using this mechanism. If you are interested in implementing a new IReportConnection and providing a custom user interface to configure it, take a look at the source code of iReport, in particular the classes in the package it.businesslogic.ireport.connection and it.businesslogic.ireport.connection.gui.

CHAPTER 10

■ ■ ■

Internationalization

JasperReports 0.6.2 introduced some new features for report internationalization. *Internationalizing* a report means making all static text set at design time (such as labels and messages) adaptable to locale options used to build the report: the report engine will print the text using the most appropriate available translation. The text translations in the different languages supported by the report are stored in particular resource files collectively named the *Resource Bundle*.

This chapter moreover covers the built-in function msg( ) and how it's possible to "localize" very complex sentences created dynamically.

Using a Resource Bundle Base Name

When a report is internationalized, it's necessary to locate all locale-dependent text, such as labels and static strings. A key (a name) is associated with every text fragment and is used to recall these fragments. These keys and the relative text translation are written in special files (one per language), as shown in Listing 10-1.

Listing 10-1. *Resource File Sample*

```
Title_GeneralData=General Data
Title_Address=Address
Title_Name=Name
Title_Phone=Phone
```

All files containing this information have to be saved with the .properties file extension. The effective file name (i.e., the file name without the file extension and the language/country code, which you will see later in this section) represents the report *Resource Bundle Base Name* (e.g., the Resource Bundle Base Name for the resource file i18nReport.properties is i18nReport). At execution time, the report engine will look in the classpath for a file that has as a name the Resource Bundle Base Name plus the .properties extension (so for the previous example, it will look for a file named exactly i18nReport.properties). If this file is found, it will be the default resource from which the localized text is read. The Resource Bundle Base Name has to be specified in the i18n tab in the Report properties dialog box (see Chapter 3).

When you need to print a report using a specific locale, JasperReports looks for a file starting with the Resource Bundle Base Name string, followed by the language and country code relative to the requested locale. For example, i18nReport_it_IT.properties is a file that contains all locale strings to print in Italian; in contrast, i18nReport_en_US.properties contains the translations in American English. The language codes are the lowercase, two-letter codes defined by ISO-639 (a list of these codes is available at http://www.loc.gov/standards/iso639-2/php/English_list.php).

The country codes are the uppercase, two-letter codes defined by ISO-3166 (a list of these codes is available at `http://www.iso.ch/iso/en/prods-services/iso3166ma/02iso-3166-code-lists/list-en1.html`).

As you can gather, it's important to always create a default resource file that will contain all the strings in the most widely used language and a set of language-specific files for the other languages.

The default resource file does not have a language/country code after the Resource Bundle Base Name, and the contained values are used only if there is no resource file that matches the requested locale or if the key of a translated string is not present in that file.

The complete resource file name is composed as follows:

`<Resource Bundle Base Name>[_language code[_country code[_other code]]]`

Here are some examples of valid resource file names:

```
i18nReport_fr_CA_UNIX
i18nReport_fr_CA
i18nReport_fr
i18nReport_en_US
i18nReport_en
i18nReport
```

The "other" code (or alternative code), which is the rightmost one after the language and the country code (_UNIX in the first of the preceding examples) is usually not used for reports, but it is a way to identify very specific resource files.

iReport has the ability to manage resource files for report localization by itself. The only conditions are that the resource files be located in the same directory where the JRXML source file is located, and that the Resource Bundle Base Name is equal to the JRXML source file name (extension excluded).

To access the list of available resource files for a report, as shown in Figure 10-1, select Edit ➤ Internationalization ➤ Localization files.

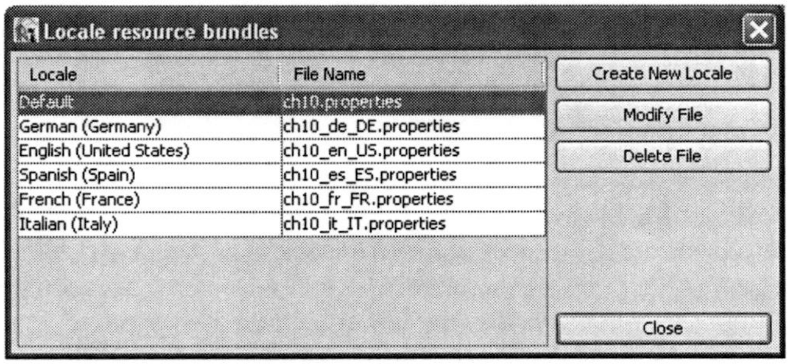

Figure 10-1. *Window to manage resource files*

From this window, you can create, modify, or remove all the resource files of a report.

To create a new locale file, it's necessary to duplicate the default file and specify the suffix (language/country code) to add after the Resource Bundle Base Name to form the new resource filename (see Figure 10-2). The suffix must follow the rules shown previously (for more details about language and country codes, and about resource file names in general, please refer to the Java documentation).

Figure 10-2. *Setting the suffix for a new resource file name*

The content of a selected file can be edited by clicking the Modify file button to bring up the window shown in Figure 10-3.

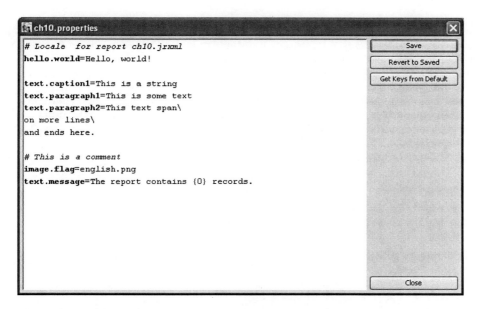

Figure 10-3. *Modifying a resource file*

To save a modified resource file, you have to click the Save button explicitly, because the file is never saved automatically.

Retrieving Localized Strings

There are two ways to retrieve the localized string for a particular key inside a JasperReports expression: you can use the built-in str("*key name*") function, or you can use the special syntax $R{*key name*}. Resource keys are not transformed into Java variables during report compilation as are fields, variables, and parameters, and can be arbitrary strings. So it is possible, for example, to use the dot character (.) inside these names, although it is better not to use the space character. Here is an example expression to retrieve a localized string:

$R{hello.world}

This expression will be converted to the text associated with the key hello.world using the most appropriate available translation for the selected locale.

Formatting Messages

JasperReports internationalization support is based on the support provided by Java. One of the most useful features is the msg function, which is used to dynamically build messages using arguments. In fact, msg uses strings as patterns. These patterns define where arguments, passed as parameters to the msg function, must be placed. The argument's position is expressed using numbers between braces, as in this example: "The report contains {0} records." The zero specifies where to place the value of the first argument passed to the msg function. The expression

```
msg($R{text.message}, $P{number})
```

uses the string referred to by the key text.message as the pattern for the call to msg. The second parameter is the first argument to be replaced in the pattern string. If text.message is the string "The report contains {0} records." and the value for the report parameter number is 100, the printed text becomes "The report contains 100 records."

The reason for using patterns instead of building messages like this by dividing them into substrings translated separately (for example, [The report contains] {0} [records]), is that sometimes the second approach is not possible. Localizers won't be able to create grammatically correct translations for all languages (e.g., for languages in which the verb appears at the end of the sentence).

It's possible to call the msg function in three ways (see Listing 10-2).

Listing 10-2. *The msg Function*

```
public String msg(String pattern, Object arg0)
public String msg(String pattern, Object arg0, Object arg1)
public String msg(String pattern, Object arg0, Object arg1, Object arg2)
```

The only difference between the three calls is the number of passed arguments.

Deploying Localized Reports

The necessary first step before deploying a localized report is to be sure that all .properties files containing the translated strings are present in the classpath.

JasperReports looks for resource files using the getBundle method of the ResourceBundle Java class. To learn more about how this class works, visit http://java.sun.com/docs/books/tutorial/i18n/, where you will find all the main concepts about how Java supports internationalization fully explained.

Running a Report Using a Specific Locale and Time Zone

If you wish to use a specific locale or to run a report using a particular time zone, go to Build ➤ Set report locale or Build ➤ Set time zone. You will see the current settings in the log window each time you run a report, as shown in Figure 10-4.

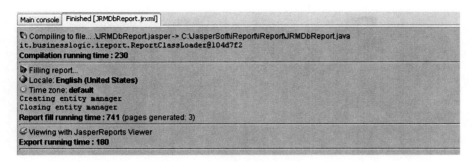

Figure 10-4. *Info displayed during the fill process*

CHAPTER 11

Scriptlets

A *scriptlet* is a Java class used to execute special elaborations during print generation. The script-let exposes a set of methods that are invoked by the reporting engine when some particular events, like the creation of a new page or the end of processing a detail row, occur.

In this chapter, you will see how to write a simple scriptlet and how to use it in a report. You will also see how iReport handles scriptlets and what tactics are useful when deploying a report using this kind of functionality.

Understanding the JRAbstractScriptlet Class

To implement a scriptlet, you have to extend the Java class net.sf.jasperreports.engine. JRAbstractScriptlet. This class exposes all abstract methods to handle the events that occur during report generation and provides data structures to access all variables, fields, and parameters present in the report.

The simplest scriptlet implementation is provided directly by JasperReports: it is the class JRDefaultScriptlet, shown in Listing 11-1, which extends the class JRAbstractScriptlet and implements all the required abstract methods with a void function body.

Listing 11-1. *JRDefaultScriptlet*

```
package net.sf.jasperreports.engine;

/**
 * @author Teodor Danciu (teodord@users.sourceforge.net)
 * @version $Id: JRDefaultScriptlet.java,v 1.3 2004/06/01 20:28:22 teodord Exp $
 */
public class JRDefaultScriptlet extends JRAbstractScriptlet
{
    public JRDefaultScriptlet() {    }

    public void beforeReportInit() throws JRScriptletException
    {
    }

    public void afterReportInit() throws JRScriptletException
    {
    }

    public void beforePageInit() throws JRScriptletException
    {
    }
```

```
        public void afterPageInit() throws JRScriptletException
        {
        }

        public void beforeColumnInit() throws JRScriptletException
        {
        }

        public void afterColumnInit() throws JRScriptletException
        {
        }

        public void beforeGroupInit(String groupName) throws JRScriptletException
        {
        }

        public void afterGroupInit(String groupName) throws JRScriptletException
        {
        }

        public void beforeDetailEval() throws JRScriptletException
        {
        }

        public void afterDetailEval() throws JRScriptletException
        {
        }
}
```

As you can see, the class is formed by a set of methods with a name composed using the keyword after or before followed by an event or action name (e.g., DetailEval and PageInit). These methods map all of the events that can be handled by a scriptlet, which are summarized in Table 11-1.

Table 11-1. *Report Events*

Event/Method	Description
Before Report Init	This is called before the report initialization (i.e., before all variables are initialized).
After Report Init	This is called after all variables are initialized.
Before Page Init	This is called when a new page is created, before all variables having reset type Page are initialized.
After Page Init	This is called when a new page is created and after all variables having reset type Page are initialized.
Before Column Init	This is called when a new column is created, before all variables having reset type Column are initialized; this event is not generated if the columns are filled horizontally.
After Column Init	This is called when a new column is created, after all variables having reset type Column are initialized; this event is not generated if the columns are filled horizontally.
Before Group x Init	This is called when a new group x is created, and before all variables having reset type Group and group name x are initialized.
After Group x Init	This is called when a new group x is created, and after all variables having reset type Group and group name x are initialized.

Event/Method	Description
Before Detail Eval	This is called before a detail band is printed and all variables are newly evaluated.
After Detail Eval	This is called after a detail band is printed and all variables are evaluated for the current record.

Inside the scriptlet, you can refer to all of the fields, variables, and parameters using the following maps (java.util.HashMap) defined as class attributes: fieldsMap, variablesMap, and parametersMap.

The groups (if present in the report) can be accessed through the attribute groups, an array of JRFillGroup.

Scriptlet Handling in iReport

If you need to create a scriptlet for a certain report, you can ask iReport to handle it for you transparently.

In this case, the class that implements the scriptlet will be completely handled by iReport. You can disable scriptlet usage from the Report properties dialog box (see Figure 11-1) or specify an external class (already compiled and present in the classpath). In the latter case, if the class is modified and recompiled, iReport would not be able to use this most recently compiled version, due to the Java class loader that caches the class in memory except when the class or the root package directory (but not a jar) is placed in the same directory as the report. This directory, in fact, is managed by iReport using a dynamic classloader that is able to reload classes present in this directory each time the report is executed.

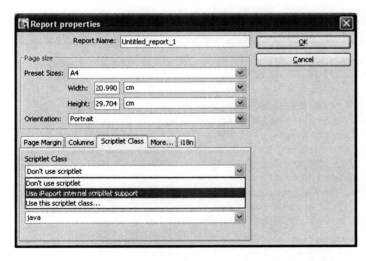

Figure 11-1. *Scriptlet Class tab on the Report properties dialog box*

If the scriptlet is handled internally by iReport, when the report is compiled, a new class with the same name as the report followed by the suffix Scriptlet.java is created. For example, if you have a report named "test," the generated scriptlet file will be named testScriptlet.java.

Scriptlets generated using iReport don't directly extend JRAbstractServlet. Instead, they extend a top-level class named IreportScriptlet, which is present in the it.businesslogic.ireport package. Besides the various methods for handling events, this new class provides some new features to work with data series (see Chapter 14); other features will be added in future versions of iReport. Please note that if you want to use the charting support provided by iReport, you have to use the internal support for scriptlets, too.

In iReport, a scriptlet can be modified by selecting Edit ➤ Scriptlet Editor. The scriptlet source file is handled independently from the main report source file, so you have to save it yourself by clicking the Save button every time you change it (see Figure 11-2).

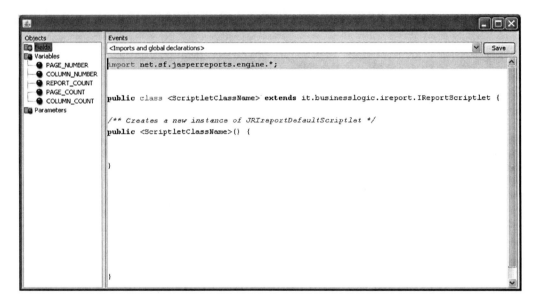

Figure 11-2. *The scriptlet editor*

The editor window shows all scriptlet methods/events in a combo box placed at the top of the form. On the left are all of the Java objects accessible from the scriptlet code. By double-clicking a desired object, you generate the code to access it.

It is possible to insert import directives, new methods, and class members for the scriptlet by selecting the item <imports and global declarations> from the combo box.

Many times accessor methods used in expressions are included in a scriptlet. Suppose, for example, that you need to print numbers using Roman numerals (I, II, III, IV, etc.). In this case, it is possible to add a method to the scriptlet to convert an integer number into a string that represents the number written in Roman numerals. It would look something like this:

```
public String numberToRoman(int myNumber)
```

The syntax to execute this conversion, calling the method inserted in the scriptlet, is as follows:

```
$P{REPORT_SCRIPTLET}.numberToRoman(< my number >)
```

JasperReports automatically casts the generic parameter REPORT_SCRIPTLET to your scriptlet class. When the report is compiled, a type check is performed to avoid errors (like a no such method error) at run time.

Deploying Reports That Use Scriptlets

When a report with a scriptlet is compiled, the scriptlet is compiled in the same directory where the generated JASPER file for this report will be stored. iReport adds this directory to the classpath by default. In this way, the scriptlet class will be directly visible from Java, and the report will be filled without problems.

However, when the report is deployed (e.g., in a web application), the scriptlet is often forgotten, and the reporting engine throws an error when filling the report. So, it is necessary in this case to put the scriptlet class in the application classpath. If the scriptlet extends the class IReportScriptlet, you have to add the class it.businesslogic.ireport.IReportScriptlet to the classpath, too (this class is released under the LGPL license).

CHAPTER 12

■■■

Templates

One of the most useful tools of iReport is the *Report Wizard*, which lets you create reports using *templates*, a kind of prebuilt model to use as a base for new reports. In this chapter, I will explain how to build custom templates and how to add them to those already available.

Template Structure Overview

A template is a normal JRXML file. When a new report is created using the Report Wizard, the JRXML file of the selected template is loaded and modified according to options you specify.

There are two types of templates: the *columnar* type and the *tabular* type. The former creates a group of lines for every single record composed of static text (a label) that displays the field names and a text field that displays the field value (see Figure 12-1).

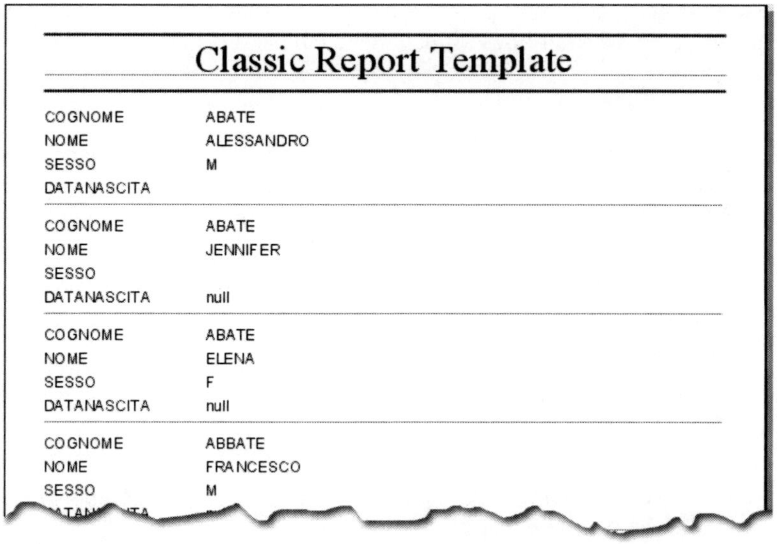

Figure 12-1. *Columnar template*

Alternatively, the tabular type shows all records in a table-like view (see Figure 12-2).

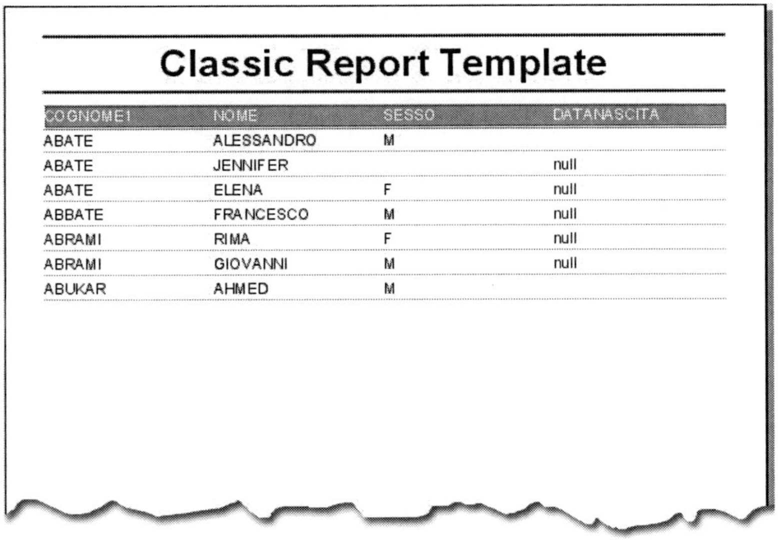

Figure 12-2. *Tabular template*

As I said, the templates are JRXML files (the extension used for them is simply .xml), and they are located in the templates directory. iReport recognizes from the name whether a file contains a columnar or a tabular template: if the file name ends with "T," it is a tabular template, and if it ends with "C," it is a columnar template.

Table 12-1 lists templates shipped with iReport.

Table 12-1. *Templates Shipped with iReport*

File	Report Type
classicC.xml	Columnar report
classicT.xml	Tabular report
classic_landscapeT.xml	Tabular report
graycC.xml	Columnar report
grayT.xml	Tabular report
gray_landscapeT.xml	Tabular report

The Report Wizard permits the creation of up to four groups (a group header and group footer are associated with each group). These groups will be created in the final file produced only if during the Report Wizard execution you specify grouping data by using one or more criteria. Using the Report Wizard, you can choose only one field name as criteria.

By opening the classicC.xml file, it is possible to see and understand how a template is structured, as shown in Figure 12-3. In this file, you will find four groups: Group1, Group2, Group3, and Group4, for which the title band (group header) and the group footer are visible.

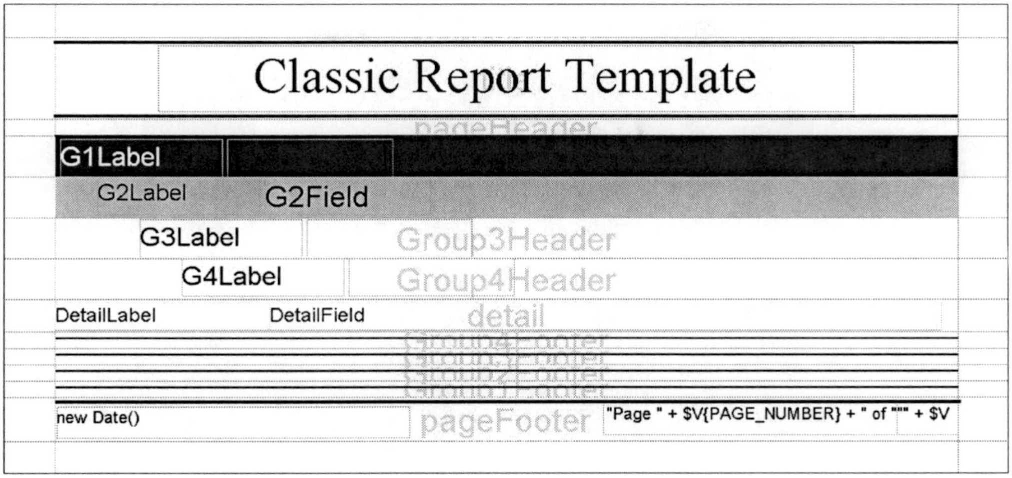

Figure 12-3. *The classicC.xml columnar template*

The column band is hidden (because for columnar reports this band is not useful), and in the detail band there are static text labels used as template labels for every future field, as shown earlier in Figure 12-1, and a text field containing the field value. The text (or the expression dealing with the text field) associated with the text elements has to follow simple wizard specifications; in particular, each group can contain as many graphic elements as you want and a Static Text element containing simply this text:

GnLabel

where *n* represents the group number in which the text element is placed, and a Text Field element containing the following special expression:

GnField

This element will contain the value used as the group expression.

The detail must contain at least a Static Text element with the expression

DetailLabel

and a Text Field element with the expression

DetailField

The Report Wizard replicates these two elements, creating as many static text/text field pairs as there are in the selected fields for the report.

All the other bands can contain whatever elements you desire; these bands will be reproduced as they are in the generated files starting from the template.

The design of a tabular report template is very similar. Figure 12-4 shows how the classicT.xml template appears in the design window.

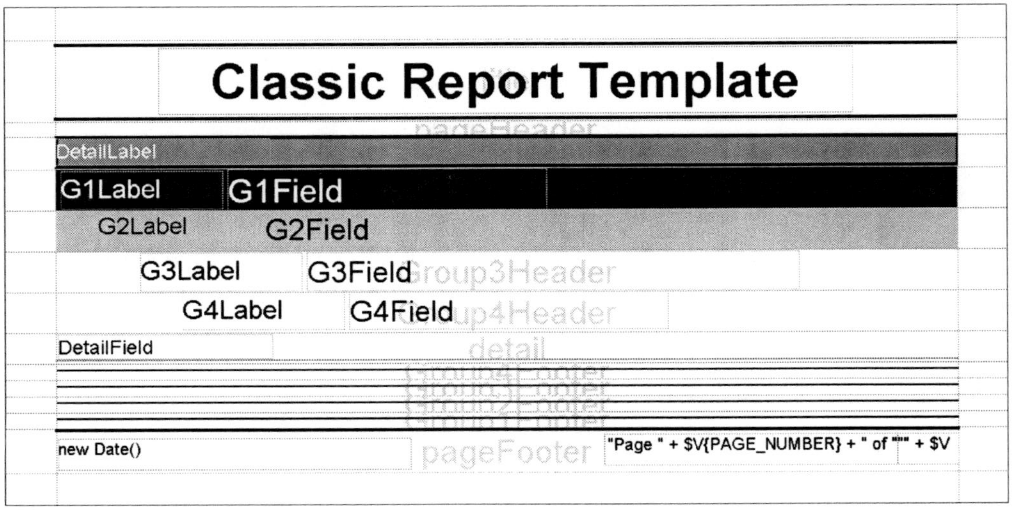

Figure 12-4. *The classicT.xml tabular report*

Once again, there are four groups. Preceding them is the column header, where it is necessary to insert a Static Text element to use as a model for column labels.

In the detail band, you will find the DetailField element, which will be used as a model for the column values.

The templates cannot be compiled: this is because expressions contained in the text fields are not valid Java expressions.

Using a Custom Template

So, let's see how to create and use a custom template. The shortest way is to open one of the already existing templates, choosing the one that is closest to what you want. At this point, you have to edit the report to your preferences by changing the existing element properties or adding and removing other elements. Figure 12-5 shows an example custom template.

In order to use a custom template, you have to put it in the templates directory. Remember to use the .xml file extension. As shown in Figure 12-5, the example template has been named testC.xml. You always have to add a "C" or a "T" as the last letter of the name before the extension.

If everything is configured correctly, when you execute the Report Wizard, you will see your new template in the templates list for either columnar reports or tabular reports. Figure 12-6 shows the example custom template displayed in the columnar reports list.

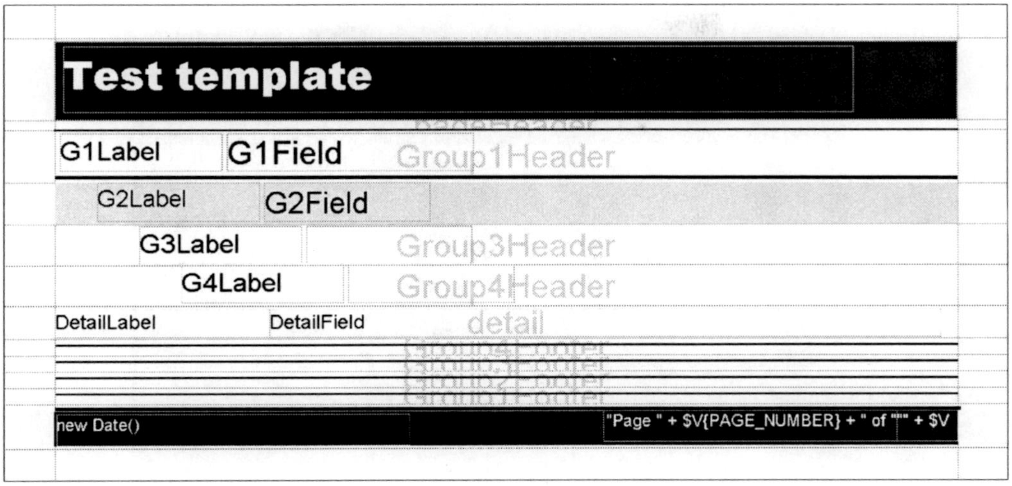

Figure 12-5. *A custom template*

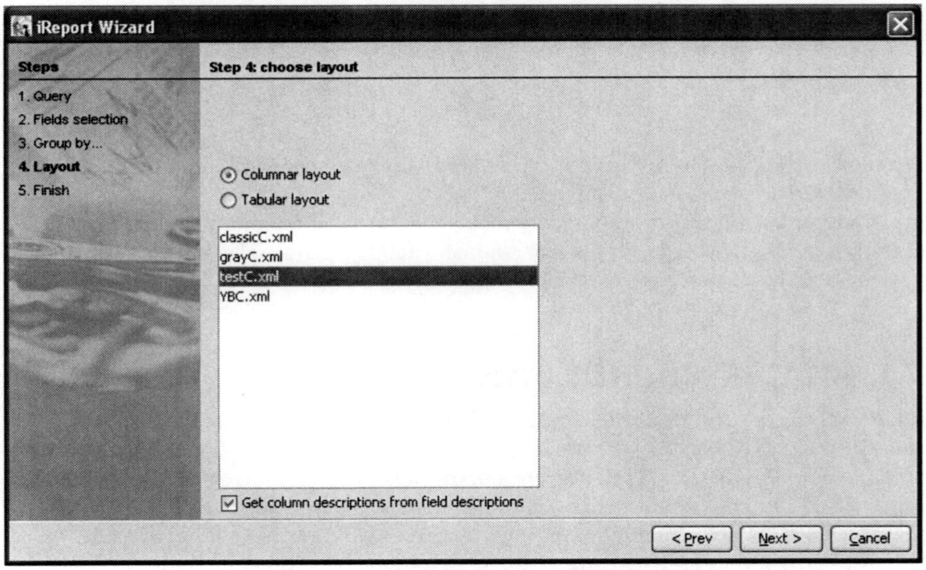

Figure 12-6. *The new template appears in the available template list.*

However, you may notice that the example custom template does not have a preview image available. It is possible to associate a preview image with a template by inserting into the templates directory an image in GIF format of maximum dimensions 150×150 pixels; the file must be named exactly as the template, except for the extension (in the case of this example, testC.gif).

Figure 12-7 shows the wizard window that displays the preview for the new template. The preview image is derived from a screenshot of a report created using the new template.

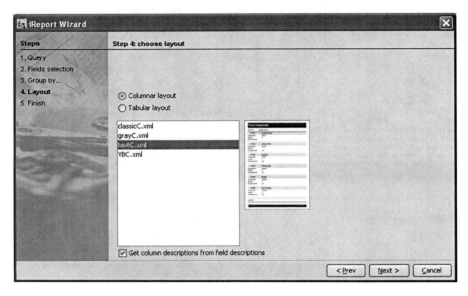

Figure 12-7. *The new template with a preview image*

When you place the image in the `templates` directory, you need to restart iReport in order to see the preview picture when executing the wizard.

The use of a template increases productivity relative to the development of reports that share a common graphic setting. If you develop a very sophisticated template and you want to share it with other users, send it as a patch to the iReport web site.

Putting Templates into JAR Files

Templates files are placed in the `templates` directory. This can be a problem when iReport can't access remote file systems (e.g., using Java Web Start to start iReport). From version 0.5.0, it's possible to include templates in JAR files. Each JAR file can contain one or more templates that are described in an XML file named `template.xml` placed in a directory named `ireport`. When the Report Wizard is executed, iReport looks for all files named `/ireport/templates.xml` available in the classpath.

To see how to provide a template using a JAR, let's look at an example that builds a JAR containing only one template named Classic Template Resource.

`template.xml` will be as follows:

```
<?xml version="1.0" encoding="UTF-8"?>
<iReportTemplateSet>
 <iReportTemplate name="Classic Template Resource" type="Columnar">
 <XmlFile>/it/businesslogic/ireport/templates/classic.xml</XmlFile>
 <IconFile>/it/businesslogic/ireport/templates/classic.gif</IconFile>
 </iReportTemplate>
</iReportTemplateSet>
```

This defines a set of templates. For each template, the name, type (columnar or tabular), JRXML file that implements the template, and icon (used as a preview image) can be defined.

The JRXML file and the icon are specified as Java resources using a path that starts with /.

The directory tree inside the JAR will be as follows:

```
template_sample.jar

|----ireport
|----it
|    |---businesslogic
|        |---ireport
|            |---templates
|----META-INF
```

template.xml will be included in the ireport directory, and all the other files (in this case classic.xml and classic.gif) will be placed in /it/businesslogic/ireport/templates.

By adding the created JAR to iReport classpath, it becomes possible to use templates without using the templates directory.

CHAPTER 13

■ ■ ■

Charts

As of iReport version 0.5.1, chart support in iReport has been completely rewritten to use new functionality within JasperReports. The previous implementation, based on manual creation of series via a scriptlet, is no longer supported.

To support this new functionality, JasperReports uses the latest version of *JFreeChart*, a powerful open source chart-generation library.

The new mechanism for creating charts is based on the *dataset* concept, not the *data series* concept of previous versions of iReport. This makes data management and visualization possible for more complex chart types such as Candlestick and High Low Open Close.

There are multiple advantages to the latest chart implementation for JasperReports. Support is native and perfectly integrated into the library, which means it is no longer necessary to use a scriptlet to create a graph. Also, there is a much wider variety of chart types available. Specifically, in addition to the aforementioned Candlestick and High Low Open Close charts, JasperReports now supports Area, Bar, Bar 3D, Bubble, Line, Pie, Pie 3D, Scatter Plot, Stacked Bar, Stacked Bar 3D, Time Series, XY Area, XY Bar, and XY Line charts. Three new charts were added to JasperReports 1.2.7: Meter, Thermometer, and MultiAxis, and the latter is a special chart used to aggregate multiple charts into a single one. And finally, another chart type has been added to JasperReports 1.3.1: the Stacked Area chart.

Creating a Simple Chart

In this section, you will learn how to use the Chart tool by building a report containing a Pie 3D chart step by step; then you will explore all the details regarding chart management.

In this example, use the datasource Northwind on HSQLDB.

Create a new empty document. Open the Report query dialog box by clicking this button:

and enter the following expression, as shown in Figure 13-1:

```
select SHIPCOUNTRY, COUNT(*) AS ORDERS_COUNT from ORDERS group by SHIPCOUNTRY
```

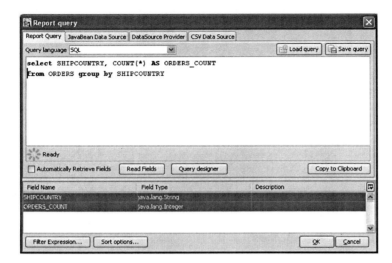

Figure 13-1. *Query of the report*

The idea is to produce a chart to display the sales in different countries. Confirm your query by clicking OK; iReport will register the query-selected fields. Place the fields in the detail band by dragging them from the objects library (see Figure 13-2).

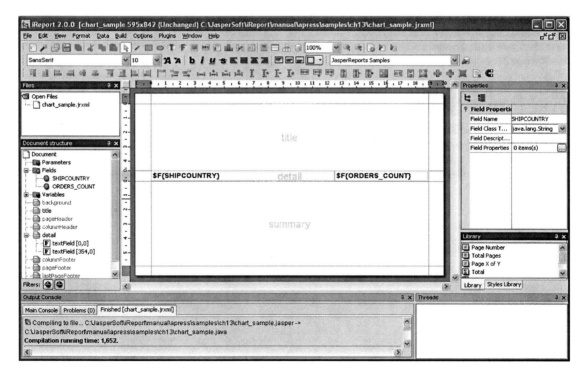

Figure 13-2. *The report with the SHIPCOUNTRY and ORDERS_COUNT fields*

Reset the bands exceeding the height (except for the summary and the detail bands).

Select the Chart tool and place a new chart in the summary band. From the charts window that appears, select the Pie 3D icon and click OK. Figure 13-3 shows what your report should now look like.

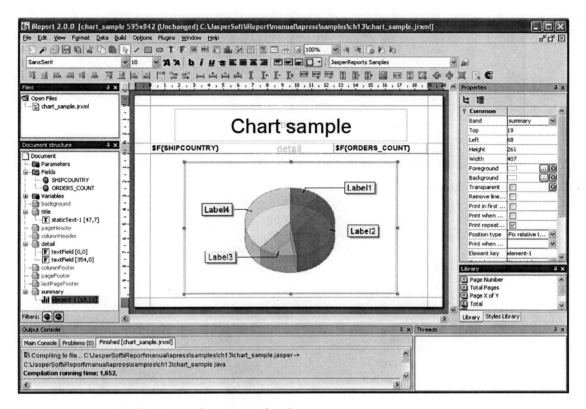

Figure 13-3. *Positioning the chart in the summary band*

At this point, configure the chart. Open the element properties window (double-click the Chart element) and in the Chart tab, click the Edit chart properties button (see Figure 13-4). You can access the same properties by right-clicking and selecting Chart Properties from the context menu, as shown in Figure 13-5.

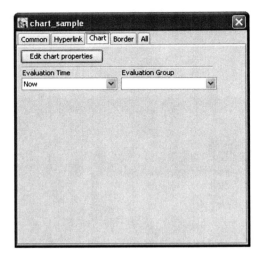

Figure 13-4. *Chart tab*

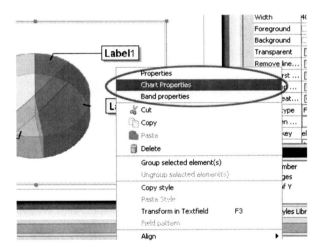

Figure 13-5. *Chart Properties context menu option*

The Chart Properties window, as shown in Figure 13-6, will appear.

This window contains two tabs: Chart Properties and Chart Data. The first tab contains a list of parameters that control the appearance of the graph, and the second determines the data associated with the graph.

Modify various visual properties of the graph. Set the Background Alpha and Foreground Alpha properties to 0.5 and Depth Factor property to 0.2.

Next, you will define the data associated with the graph. Switch to the Chart Data tab (see Figure 13-7).

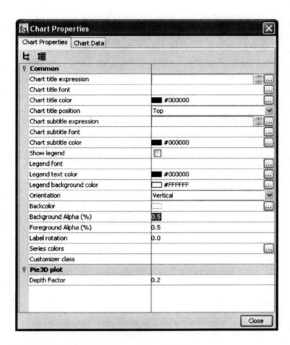

Figure 13-6. *Chart Properties window*

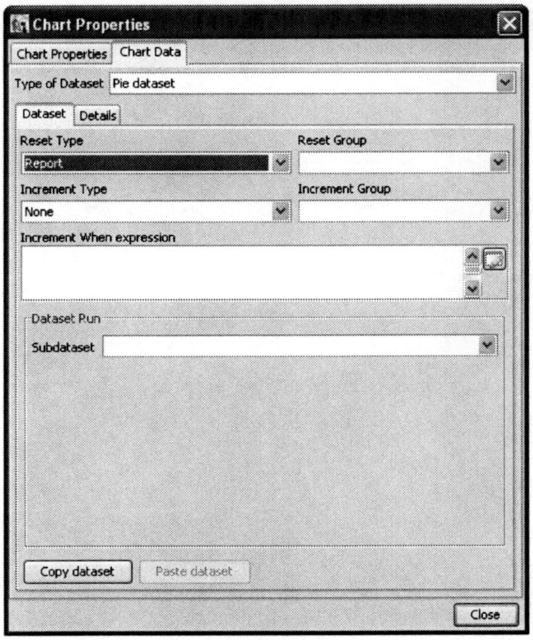

Figure 13-7. *Chart Data tab*

The Type of Dataset combo box allows you to specify the dataset types to generate the graph. Only one dataset type is available, except when generating an XY Bar chart.

In the Dataset tab, you can define the dataset within the context of the report. Specifically, Reset Type and Reset Group allow you to periodically reset the dataset. This is useful, for example, when summarizing data relative to a special grouping. Increment Type and Increment Group specify the events that determine when new values must be added to the dataset. This is useful, for example, for reprinting the subtotals for a special grouping.

The Increment When expression area allows you to add a flag to determine whether to add a record to the record set designed to feed the chart. This expression must return a Boolean value. iReport considers a blank string to mean "add all the records."

For the purposes of this example, set the Reset Type to Report since you don't want the data to be reset, and leave the Increment Type set to None so that each record will be appended to your dataset.

The Details tab allows you to enter an expression to associate with every single value in the datasource. For the Pie 3D chart type, three expressions can be entered: *key*, *value*, and *label* (see Figure 13-8).

The key expression allows you to uniquely identify a slice of the pie chart. If a key value is repeated, the label and value values previously associated with that key are overwritten. A key can never be null.

The value expression specifies the numeric value associated with the key.

The label expression allows you to specify a label for each slice of the pie chart. The expression is optional, and the default value is *key* = *value*, for example, A = 100, where A is the key of a particular slice and 100 is its value.

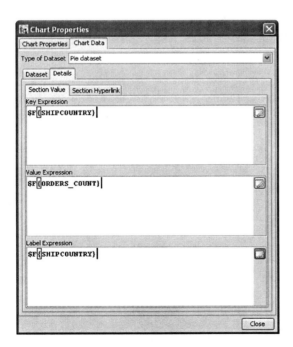

Figure 13-8. *Chart Data tab—Pie 3D chart dataset*

Confirm the modifications to the chart, save the file, and start the report by clicking the following button:

The result is visible in Figure 13-9.

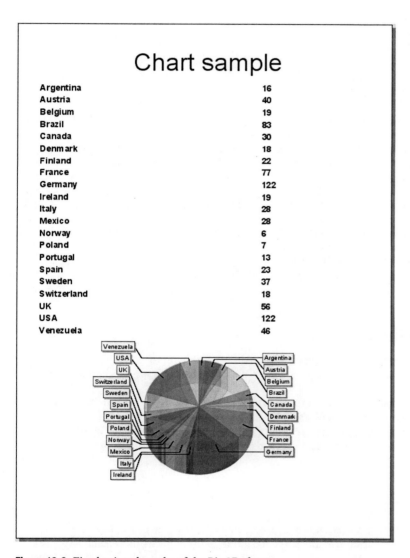

Figure 13-9. *Final printed results of the Pie 3D chart*

Using Datasets

The data represented within charts is collected when the report is generated and then stored within the associated dataset. The dataset types are as follows:

- Pie
- Category
- Time period
- Time series
- XY
- XYZ
- High low
- Value

Think of a dataset as a table. Each dataset has different columns (fields). When a new record is inserted into the dataset, values are added to the fields.

Figure 13-7, shown earlier, demonstrates the options that you can select in JasperReports to indicate when and how to acquire data for the dataset. Specifically, you can indicate whether and when the dataset should be emptied (through Reset Type and Reset Group settings), and when to append a new record to the dataset (through Increment Type and Increment Group settings). These four fields have the same effect as the corresponding fields used for report variables (see Chapter 6's discussion of variables).

Depending on the dataset type that you have selected, the Chart Data tab shows the fields within the specified dataset.

Detailed descriptions of the various field types and their functionality are available in *The Definitive Guide to JasperReports* by Teodor Daniciu, Lucian Chirita, Sanda Zaharia, and Ionut Nedelcu (Apress, 2007).

Value Hyperlinks

Some types of dataset provide a way to set a hyperlink to the value represented in the chart, enhancing the user experience by allowing the user to click the chart to open a web page or drill down the report.

The clickable area depends on the chart type. For pie charts, the hyperlink is tied to each slice of the pie; for the bar charts, the clickable areas are the bars themselves.

Adding hyperlinks to elements is described in Chapter 4; recall from that discussion that hyperlinks utilize expressions to include all the fields, variables, and parameters of the dataset used by a chart.

Properties of Charts

The appearance of a chart is managed by the element properties window shown in Figure 13-4. You can see and edit properties common to all charts and graphs within this window (such as the title and the visibility of the legend) as well as other properties specific to the chart or graph that is being created. Properties that differ among chart types are known as *plot properties.*

You can change chart title and chart subtitle expressions using the expression editor, which you can open by clicking the button marked by three dots (see Figure 13-10).

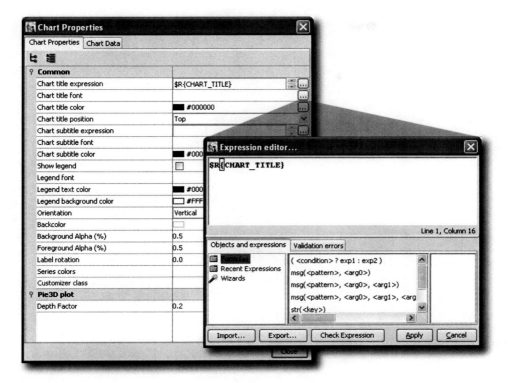

Figure 13-10. *Editing expressions through the expression editor*

Currently, JasperReports takes advantage of only a small portion of the capabilities of the JFreeChart library. To customize a graph, a class must be written that implements the following interface:

```
net.sf.jasperreports.engine.JRChartCustomizer
```

The only method available from this interface is the following:

```
public void customize(JFreeChart chart, JRChart jasperChart);
```

which takes a JFreeChart object and a JRChart object as its arguments. The first object is used to actually produce the image, while the second contains all the features you specify during the design phase that are relevant to the customize method.

CHAPTER 14

■ ■ ■

Subdatasets

Report generation is based on a single datasource (such as a query, a collection of JavaBeans, or an XML file). When you deal with a chart or a crosstab, this might not be sufficient, or it might simply be easier to retrieve the chart or crosstab data using a specific query or in general using another dataset. A *subdataset* is used to provide a secondary record set inside a report (performing an additional query using a new datasource). Currently, you can use a subdataset to fill only a chart or a crosstab. You can have an arbitrary number of subdatasets in a report.

A subdataset has its own fields, variables, and parameters and can have a query executed as needed. The dataset records can be grouped in one or more groups (like in a main report); these groups are used in subdataset variables.

A subdataset is linked to a chart or crosstab by means of a *dataset run*. The dataset run specifies all the information needed by the subdataset to retrieve and filter data and process the rows used to fill the chart or crosstab.

Creating a Subdataset

To create a new subdataset, right-click the object library and select Add ➤ Sub dataset from the context menu (see Figure 14-1).

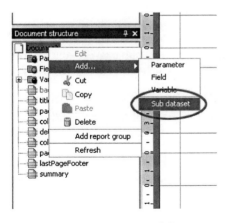

Figure 14-1. *Creating a new subdataset*

The SubDataset dialog box, shown in Figure 14-2, will appear.

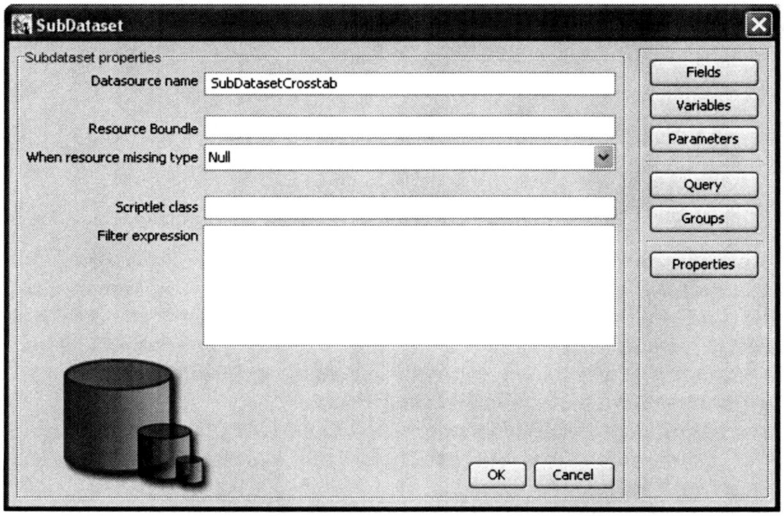

Figure 14-2. *SubDataset dialog box*

Here you simply have to set the subdataset name. Optionally, you may also specify a Resource Bundle with the appropriate When resource missing type setting for this subdataset (see Chapter 10 for more about Resource Bundles).

JasperReports permits the use of a scriptlet to perform special calculations on a subdataset's records in a way similar to that provided for the main report. If you need it, you can set the name of your scriptlet class when you create your new subdataset.

Finally, you can set a filter expression to select which records should be used by your subdataset. This expression must return a Boolean object. A blank filter expression is not considered by iReport, and the final result is that all the records are implicitly accepted.

Clicking the Create button in the SubDataset dialog box adds the new subdataset to the report. The buttons on the right then become enabled, and the Create button changes to an OK button, as shown in Figure 14-2.

You can see the new subdataset in the Document structure panel, shown in Figure 14-3, or in the SubDatasets dialog box, shown in Figure 14-4 (accessed by selecting Edit ➤ Subdatasets).

Caution You can't use subdataset objects (fields, variables, and parameters) in the main report.

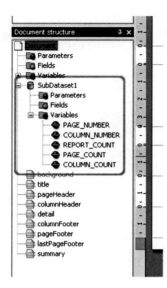

Figure 14-3. *The new subdataset in the document structure view*

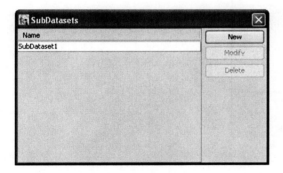

Figure 14-4. *SubDatasets dialog box*

Now you can add fields, variables, and parameters to your subdataset using the same logic as you would in the main report. The Query button in the SubDataset dialog box opens the Report query dialog box for specifying a query (as in the main report): you can use it to retrieve fields using a query or another kind of datasource (a JavaBean class, a JR datasource provider, etc.).

Creating Dataset Runs

As mentioned previously, you can use a subdataset in a chart or in a crosstab. To fill the subdataset, JasperReports needs some extra information, like what JDBC connection to use to perform the subdataset SQL query, or how to set the value of a specific subdataset parameter. All this information is provided using a dataset run. Figure 14-5 shows a dataset run for a chart.

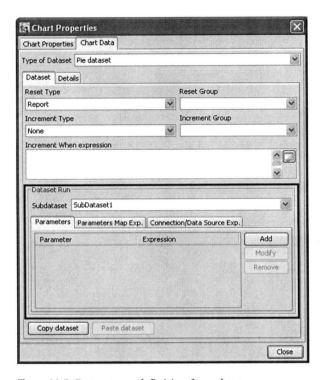

Figure 14-5. *Dataset run definition for a chart*

A dataset run works in a way similar to the process used to connect a subreport to a master report: you can set the value of the subdataset parameters using expressions containing main report objects (like fields, variables, and parameters), define a parameters map to set values for the subdataset parameters at runtime, and finally define the connection or datasource that will be used by the subdataset to get its data.

Working Through an Example Subdataset

The following step-by-step example shows how to use a subdataset to fill a chart. The main report will have only one record with the count of all orders (select count(*) as tot_orders from orders). Let's get started:

1. Create a new blank report, as shown in Figure 14-6.

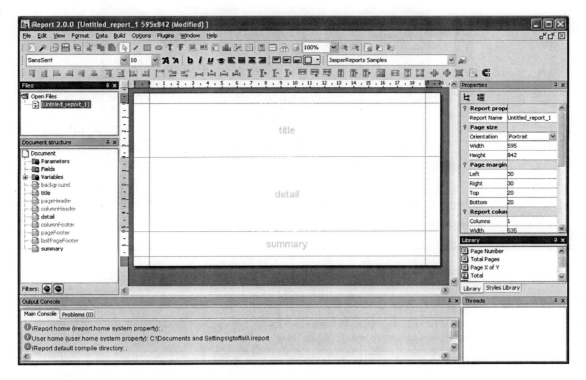

Figure 14-6. *Step 1—creating an empty report*

2. Open the Report query dialog box by clicking the following button:

and insert the following query:

select count(*) as tot_orders from orders

Your screen should resemble Figure 14-7.

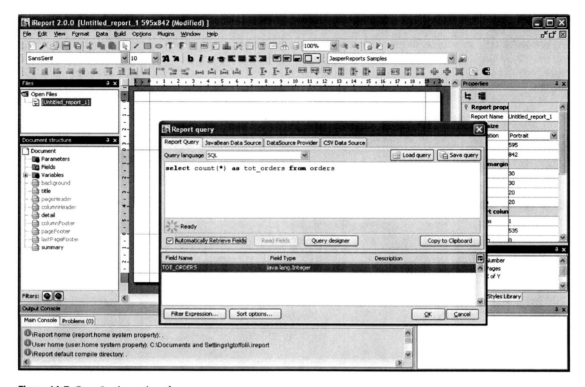

Figure 14-7. *Step 2—inserting the query*

3. Drag the field TOT_ORDERS from the Library tab into the detail band and add some labels like the ones shown in Figure 14-8.

4. At this point, create the subdataset: select Add ➤ Sub dataset from the library context menu, name the new subdataset SubDataset1 (see Figure 14-9), and click the Create button.

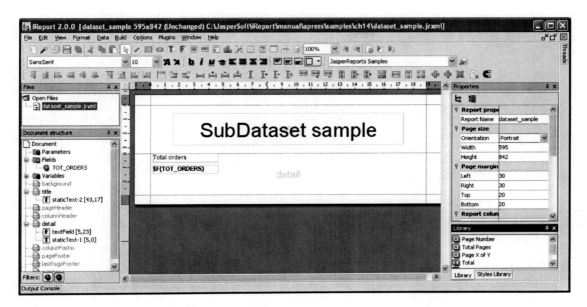

Figure 14-8. *Step 3—adding the field TOT_ORDERS*

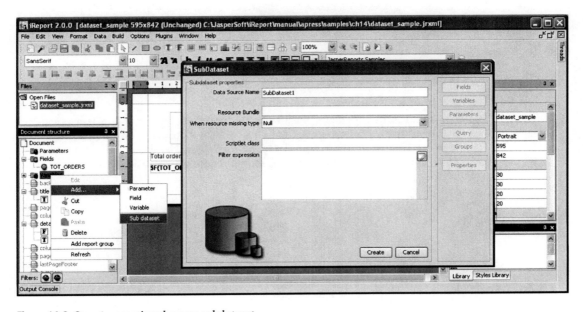

Figure 14-9. *Step 4—creating the new subdataset*

5. Click the Query button in the Subdataset dialog box and enter the following query as shown in Figure 14-10:

```
select SHIPCOUNTRY, COUNT(*) country_orders from ORDERS group by SHIPCOUNTRY
```

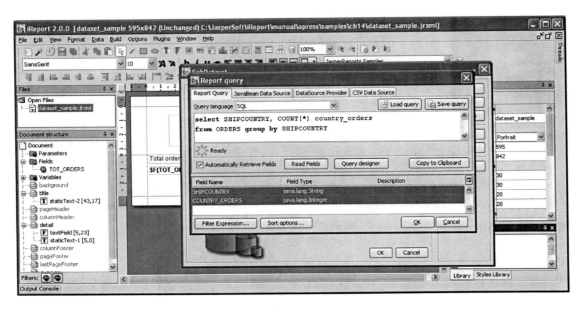

Figure 14-10. *Step 5—defining the subdataset query*

6. Add a Pie 3D chart to the report (see Figure 14-11).

7. Open the Chart Properties dialog box to edit the chart data, and enter SubDataset1 in the Subdataset field, as shown in Figure 14-12. Your subdataset has no parameters to set. Go to the Connection/Data Source Exp. tab and choose Use connection expression from the combo box. You will use the master report connection to fill the subdataset ($P{REPORT_CONNECTION}).

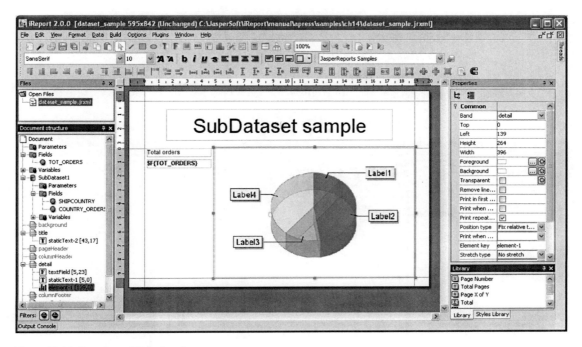

Figure 14-11. *Step 6—adding the chart*

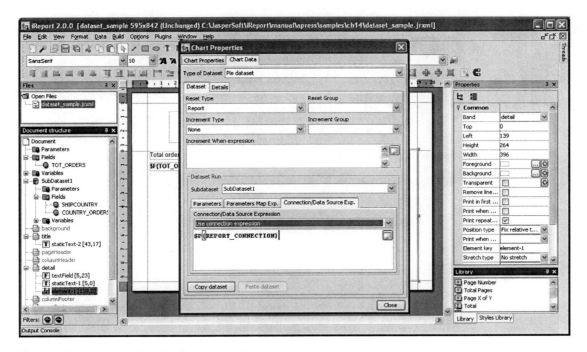

Figure 14-12. *Step 7—setting the chart properties*

8. Now you have to set details for the chart dataset. Go to the Details tab, shown in Figure 14-13, and enter these values:

- *Key expression*: $F{SHIPCOUNTRY}
- *Value expression*: $F{COUNTRY_ORDERS}
- *Label expression*: $F{SHIPCOUNTRY}

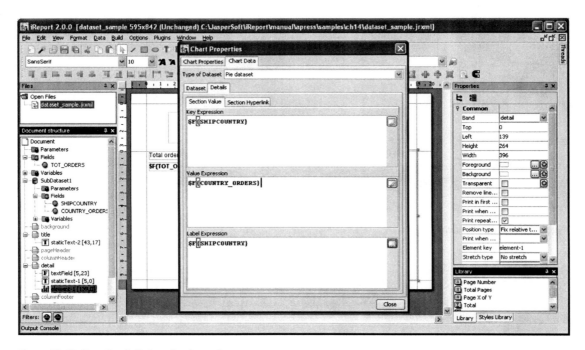

Figure 14-13. *Step 8—defining the chart data*

9. Save the report, as shown in Figure 14-14.

10. Now run the report. Figure 14-15 shows the final chart.

Figure 14-14. *Step 9—saving the report*

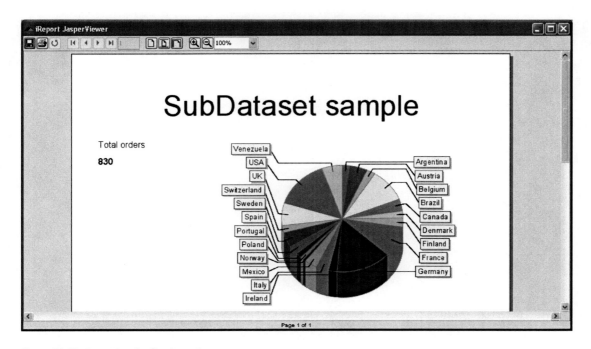

Figure 14-15. *Step 10—the final result*

CHAPTER 15

■ ■ ■

Crosstabs

A *crosstab* is a kind of table where the number of rows and columns is not known at design time, like a table that shows the sales of some products (rows) during different years (columns):

Fruit/Year	2004	2005	2006	...
Strawberry				
Wild cherry				
Big banana				
...				

Crosstabs are present in JasperReports version 1.1.0 and later, and they are supported by iReport starting from the same version (1.1.0).

JasperReports' crosstab implementation allows the grouping of columns and rows, the calculation of totals, and the customization of every cell. For each row or column group, you have a detail row/column and an optional total row/column. Data to fill the crosstab can come from the main report dataset or from a subdataset. Thanks to an intuitive wizard, iReport makes it easy to create and use this powerful reporting component.

Using the Crosstab Wizard

To understand how a crosstab works, I will walk you through creating one using the Crosstab Wizard. This wizard is automatically activated when you add a Crosstab element to a report.

Start with a blank report containing this query:

```
select * from orders
```

You will put the crosstab at the end of the report, in the summary band. To do so, click the Crosstab tool on the toolbar and draw your Crosstab element in the summary band. The first screen of the Crosstab Wizard appears.

In the first step, you have to choose the dataset to fill the crosstab. Specify the dataset of the main report (in this case, untitled_report_1, as shown in Figure 15-1). Click Next to go to the next step.

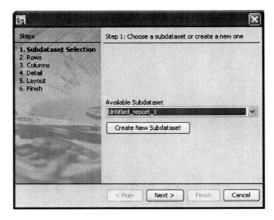

Figure 15-1. *Crosstab Wizard step 1—dataset selection*

In the second screen, you have to define at least one row group. For the purposes of this example, you will choose to group all records by SHIPCOUNTRY, as shown in Figure 15-2. This means that each row in the crosstab will refer to a specific country. Unlike what happens in the main report, JasperReports will sort the data for you (this function can be disabled if data is presorted to speed up the fill process). Using the Crosstab Wizard, it is possible to define up to two row groups. This is a limitation of the wizard only; you can define as many row and column groups as you need from the Crosstab properties dialog box (I'll talk more about this dialog box later in the "Modifying Rows and Columns" section.) Click Next to move to the third step.

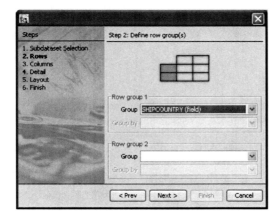

Figure 15-2. *Crosstab wizard step 2—specifying row groups*

As with the rows, from the third screen you can define up to two column groups. For this example, you will use only one column group, grouping the data by the SHIPPEDDATE field, as shown in Figure 15-3. More specifically, you will use a function that returns only the year of the date, thus grouping the orders by year.

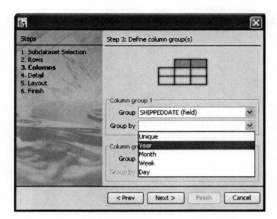

Figure 15-3. *Crosstab wizard step 3—specifying column groups*

As you can see in Figure 15-3, whenever you have a time field (time stamp, date, etc.), you can use a time-based aggregation function (such as Year, Month, Week, or Day), or treat it as a plain value (in which case you can use the Unique aggregation function to group records having the same value). Click Next to move to the next step.

It's time to define the detail data. Normally, the detail is the result of an aggregation function like the count of orders by country by year, or the sum of freight for the same combination (country/ year). You will choose to print the number of orders placed by specifying ORDERID (field) in the Detail Field combo box and Count in the Function combo box (see Figure 15-4). Once again, click Next to continue.

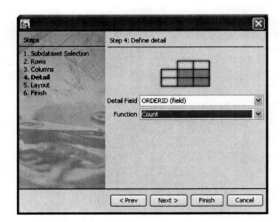

Figure 15-4. *Crosstab wizard step 4—defining the detail data*

In the last step, you can set a few options for the crosstab layout. You can indicate whether you want to see grid lines or not, and whether you want to include the totals for rows and columns. For this example, select all checkbox options, as shown in Figure 15-5, and click Finish.

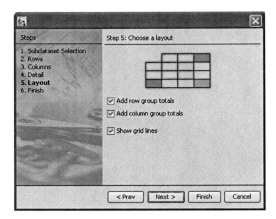

Figure 15-5. *Crosstab wizard step 5—defining the crosstab layout*

Note that when a crosstab is added to the report, a new tab is created in the design window. This tab is the crosstab designer for the new Crosstab element.

Click the crosstab-1 tab. As shown in Figure 15-6, two additional panels are now displayed on the right of the design window: the crosstab structure pane displays a tree that shows the crosstab cells and helps you in selecting elements, and the crosstab objects pane provides a list that displays the set of measures and crosstab parameters that can be dragged and dropped into the crosstab.

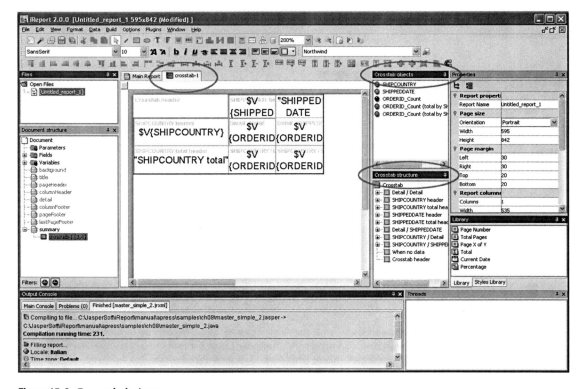

Figure 15-6. *Crosstab designer*

When you click the Run button on the toolbar, the report is filled. Figure 15-7 shows the generated report.

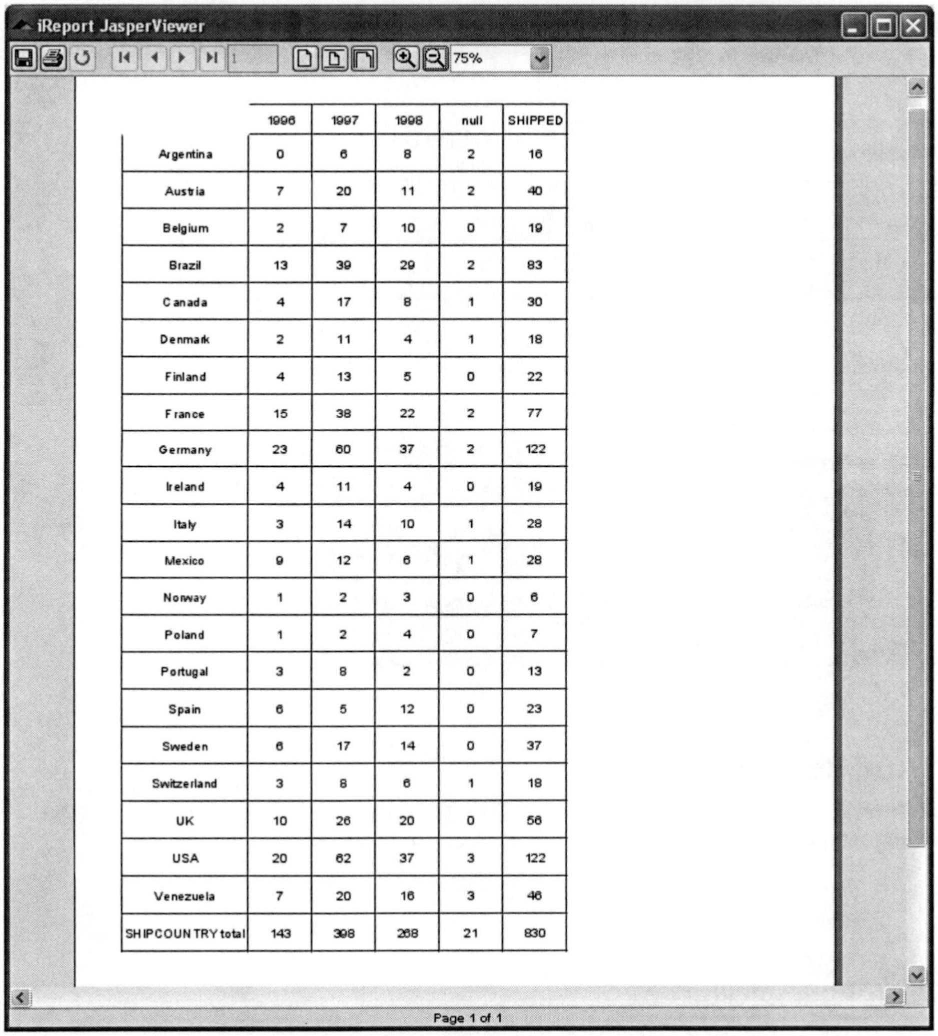

	1996	1997	1998	null	SHIPPED
Argentina	0	6	8	2	16
Austria	7	20	11	2	40
Belgium	2	7	10	0	19
Brazil	13	39	29	2	83
Canada	4	17	8	1	30
Denmark	2	11	4	1	18
Finland	4	13	5	0	22
France	15	38	22	2	77
Germany	23	60	37	2	122
Ireland	4	11	4	0	19
Italy	3	14	10	1	28
Mexico	9	12	6	1	28
Norway	1	2	3	0	6
Poland	1	2	4	0	7
Portugal	3	8	2	0	13
Spain	6	5	12	0	23
Sweden	6	17	14	0	37
Switzerland	3	8	6	1	18
UK	10	26	20	0	56
USA	20	62	37	3	122
Venezuela	7	20	16	3	46
SHIPCOUNTRY total	143	398	268	21	830

Figure 15-7. *The example crosstab in the generated report*

The last column contains the total for each row, across all columns. The last row contains the total for each column, across all rows. Finally, the last cell (in the corner on the bottom right) contains the combined total for all orders (830).

Working with Columns, Rows, and Cells

A crosstab must have at least one row group and one column group. Each row or column group can have an optional total row/column.

The rows and columns are defined by these groups. The following is a basic crosstab with one column group and one row group:

Crosstab header cell	Column group 1 header	Column group 1 total header
Row group 1 header	Detail	Column group 1 total
Row group 1 total header	Row group 1 total	Row group 1 total/ Column group 1 total

When another row group is added, the crosstab appears as follows:

Crosstab header cell		Column group 1 header	Column group 1 total header
Row group 1 header	Row group 2 header	Detail	Column group 1 total
	Row group 2 total header	Row group 2 total	Row group 2 total/ Column group 1 total
Row group 1 total header		Row group 1 total	Row group 1 total/ Column group 1 total

Modifying Rows and Columns

A row or column group can be modified using the Crosstab properties dialog box (right-click the crosstab designer and select Crosstab Properties as shown in Figure 15-8).

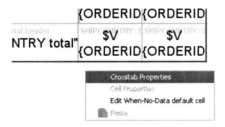

Figure 15-8. *Context menu that opens the Crosstab properties dialog box*

Click the Row and column groups tab (see Figure 15-9). Here you can see the row and column groups you have defined.

Figure 15-9. *Row and column group lists*

To add a row group, click the Add button under the Row groups area to bring up the dialog box shown in Figure 15-10.

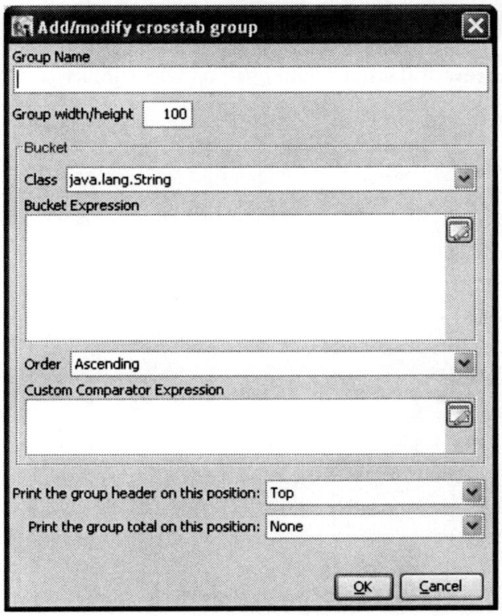

Figure 15-10. *Creating a row group*

All groups must have a unique name. When you add or modify a row group, you can set the width of the row group header:

ROW GROUP WIDTH	Column group 1 header	Column group 1 total header
Row group 1 header	Detail	Column group 1 total
Row group 1 total header	Row group 1 total	Row group 1 total/ Column group 1 total

The *bucket* is the grouping criteria. It is defined by an expression class (the Java type of the bucket expression), an expression, an order (ascending or descending), and an optional comparator class used to compare bucket expressions.

In a bucket expression, you can use all fields, variables, and parameters from the main report; however, if you choose to fill the crosstab with a subdataset, the subdataset's fields, variables, and parameters must be used instead.

A header cell can grow depending on the number of rows it spans. You can choose how elements in the header should be positioned:

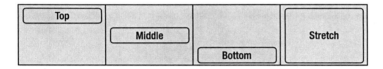

Finally, you can choose whether to print the total row and where. The options are as follows:

- *None*: No total row is printed.
- *Start*: The total row is printed before the detail row.
- *End*: The total row is printed after the detail row.

The creation of a column group is pretty similar. This time you can define the column height instead of the row width:

COLUMN GROUP HEIGHT	Column group 1 header	Column group 1 total header
Row group 1 header	Detail	Column group 1 total
Row group 1 total header	Row group 1 total	Row group 1 total/ Column group 1 total

The bucket works as it does in the row group, and the positions for the header cell contents are similar. But in this case, the details can change the width of the header, not the height:

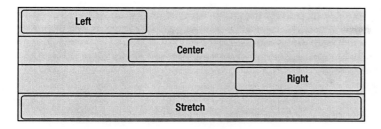

Once again, you can choose whether to print the total column and where. The options are as follows:

- *None*: No total column is printed.
- *Start*: The total column is printed before the detail column.
- *End*: The total column is printed after the detail column.

The width and height of columns and rows can easily be changed in the crosstab designer by using the cursor and dragging the grid lines (see Figure 15-11).

Crosstab header	COLUMN header	COLUMN total header
ROW header	Detail / Detail	Detail / COLUMN
ROW total header	ROW / Detail	ROW / COLUMN

Figure 15-11. *Resizing rows and columns through the grid lines of a crosstab*

When a row or column is added to a crosstab, a special variable is created that refers to the value of the bucket expression. It has the same name as the new group. You can identify this bucket variable in the crosstab objects pane (see Figure 15-12) by looking for entries with a green dot beside them.

Figure 15-12. *Crosstab objects pane*

iReport simply creates the new header cells for the group, without adding any extra elements to the crosstab. You have to fill the cells as you like, the most common way is by dragging and dropping the bucket measure into the new cell from the crosstab objects list.

Figure 15-13 shows a crosstab before the addition of a new group, and Figure 15-14 shows the crosstab after the group has been added.

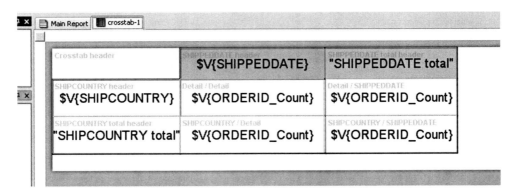

Figure 15-13. *Crosstab before the addition of a new group*

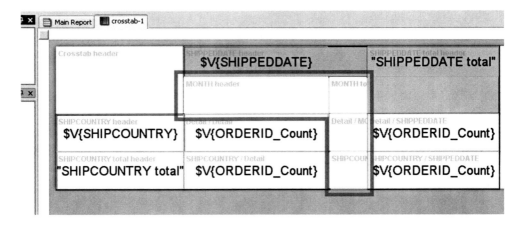

Figure 15-14. *Crosstab after the addition of a new group*

In Figure 15-14, you can see how four new cells were added to the crosstab with the addition of a new, nested column group: the group header cell, the group total header cell, the SHIPCOUNTRY totals cell, and the total across all of SHIPCOUNTRY.

You can change the nesting order of your group with the Up and Down buttons in the Crosstab properties dialog box, shown in Figure 15-15.

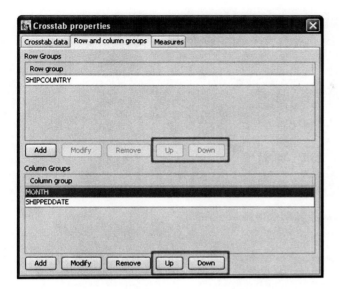

Figure 15-15. *Move groups using the Up and Down buttons.*

Figure 15-16 shows the crosstab from Figure 15-14 after the MONTH group has been moved up.

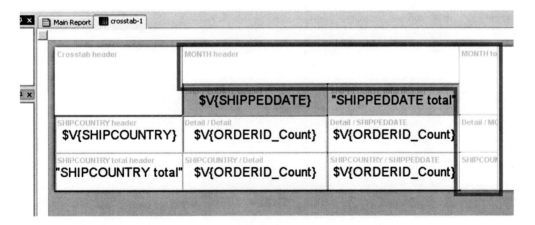

Figure 15-16. *The effect of moving up the MONTH group*

Modifying Cells

Each intersection between a row and a column defines a cell. You have header cells, total cells, a detail cell, and an optional when-no-data cell. Cells can contain a set of elements like text fields, static texts, rectangles, images . . . but they can't contain a subreport, a chart, or another crosstab. Figure 15-17 shows a crosstab with some colored cells and several text fields.

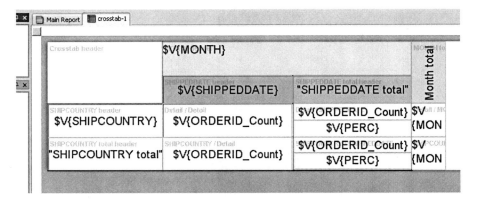

Figure 15-17. *MONTH header and total cells filled with some elements*

You can modify the background color and borders of each single cell: right-click the cell you want to change to bring up the context menu and choose Cell Properties to open the Modify cell dialog box, shown in Figure 15-18. From this dialog box you can modify the look of the cell.

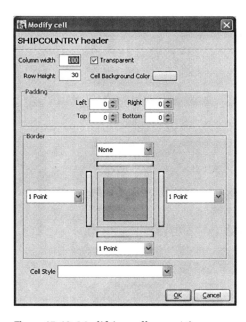

Figure 15-18. *Modifying cell properties*

Modifying Special Cells

If the crosstab does not contain any data, you can choose to print something else instead. For example, you could include a message. To do this, you must edit the when-no-data cell. View this cell by right-clicking the crosstab and checking the When-No-Data default cell check box (see

Figure 15-19). This will enable a distinct editing mode in which you can interact only with the contents of the when-no-data cell.

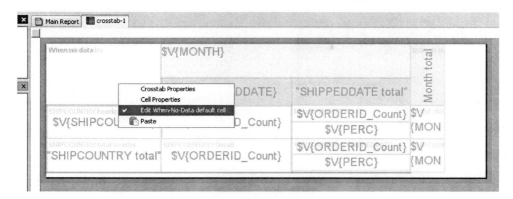

Figure 15-19. *Activating when-no-data cell editing*

The when-no-data cell has the same size as the crosstab. It is printed instead of the crosstab when no data is present. An orange frame shows the cell bounds and signals that you are editing this cell. Populate the cell by adding one or more elements.

In a crosstab, all elements refer to a cell. If an element is outside or partly outside a cell, it is incorrectly positioned, and JasperReports will throw an error when compiling the report. iReport signals this incorrect condition by drawing a red frame around the element.

Understanding Measures

Expressions for elements in a crosstab such as print when expressions and text field expressions can contain only *measures*. In this context, you cannot use fields, variables, or parameters directly: you always have to use a measure.

A measure is an object similar to a variable. To create a measure, open the Crosstab properties dialog box (right-click the crosstab designer and select Crosstab properties) and go to the Measures tab (see Figure 15-20).

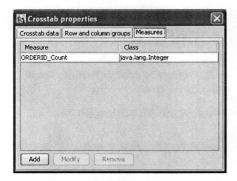

Figure 15-20. *Measures tab*

Click the Add button to create a new measure. The Add/modify measure dialog box will appear (see Figure 15-21). Here, you have to set at least the name, the class type, and the expression for the measure.

Figure 15-21. *Modifying measure properties in the Add/modify measure dialog box*

For the measure expression, you can use all the fields, variables, and parameters of the subdataset used to fill the report (or all fields, variables, and parameters coming from the main report if no subdataset is used to fill the crosstab), and all crosstab parameters (defined in the element properties dialog box when the crosstab element is selected on the Main Report tab).

A measure can store the actual value coming from your source (by specifying a calculation type of Nothing) or a calculated value like the count, the sum, and so on.

For each measure, you can provide a custom incrementer class (a class that extends the interface net.sf.jasperreports.engine.fill.JRIncrementerFactory) to implement special increment functions.

The Percentage of option lets you choose to represent the value as a percentage of the final value of this variable (the grand total).

You can provide a special class to calculate the percentage value. This time the class must implement net.sf.jasperreports.crosstabs.fill.JRPercentageCalculator.

Modifying Crosstab Element Properties

Double-clicking a crosstab in the main design window opens the element properties dialog box. Click the tab labeled Crosstab, shown in Figure 15-22, to see the properties specific to the crosstab.

Following is a brief rundown of some of the options in this dialog box:

Repeat column headers: If selected, the column headers will be printed again when the crosstab spans additional pages.

Repeat row headers: If selected, the row headers will be printed again when the crosstab spans additional pages.

Column Break Offset: This specifies the space between two pieces of a crosstab when the crosstab exceeds the page width (see Figure 15-23).

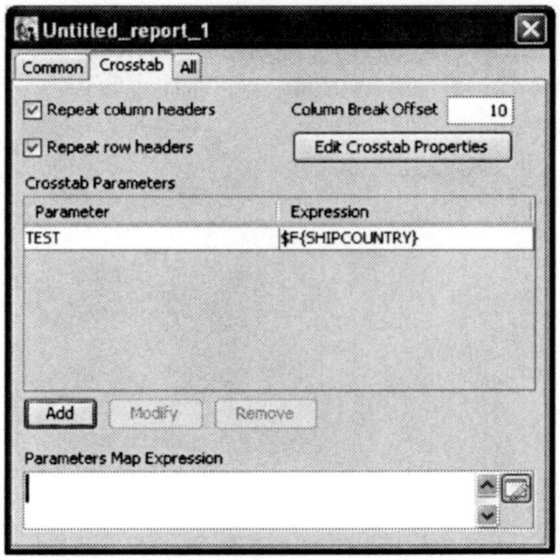

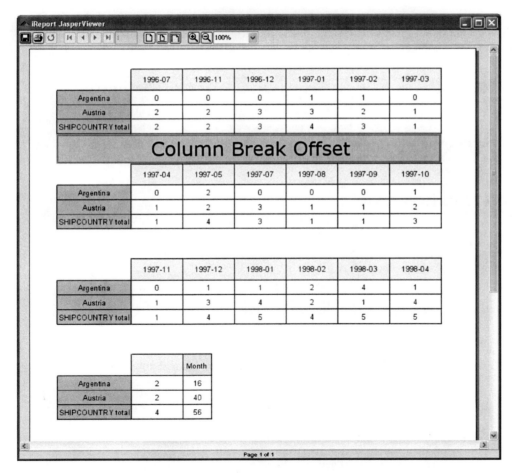

Figure 15-22. *Crosstab element properties*

Figure 15-23. *Column break offset*

Also in the element properties dialog, you can create a crosstab parameter and set a default expression for it using the Crosstab Parameters table. To add a parameter, click the Add button. The Add/modify crosstab parameter dialog box, shown in Figure 15-24, will appear.

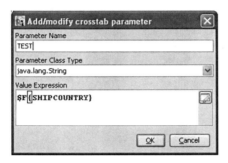

Figure 15-24. *Add/modify crosstab parameter dialog box*

You have to set the name of the parameter (which must be unique in this crosstab), a class type, and an optional default expression, which may include any of the main report objects (fields, variables, and parameters).

■**Caution** To filter the dataset query, you must use the dataset run parameters defined in the Crosstab properties dialog box, not the crosstab parameters.

You can see the crosstab parameters in the crosstab objects pane, too: they are indicated by a red bullet. Figure 15-25 shows the TEST parameter in this pane.

Figure 15-25. *TEST parameter in the crosstab objects pane*

You can use a map to set the value of declared crosstab parameters at runtime. In this case, you'll need to provide a valid parameters map expression in the element properties dialog box.

Working with Crosstab Data

As mentioned previously, you can fill a crosstab using data from the main report or from a subdataset. In the latter case, you must specify the dataset run in the Crosstab data tab of the Crosstab properties dialog box (see Figure 15-26).

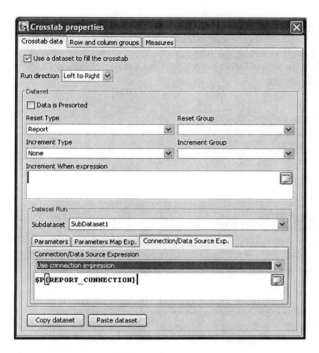

Figure 15-26. *Crosstab data tab*

The increment when expression is a flag to determine whether to add a record to the record set designed to feed the chart. This expression must return a Boolean value. iReport considers a blank string to mean "add all the records."

If your data is presorted, you can select the Data is Presorted check box option to speed up the filling process.

The Reset Type/Reset Group and Increment Type/Increment Group options can be used to define when the collected data must reset and when to add a record to your dataset.

See Chapter 14 for details on how to set the dataset run properties.

Using Crosstab Total Variables

Crosstab total variables (see Figure 15-27) are built-in objects that you can use inside crosstab text field expressions to combine data at different aggregation levels (e.g., to calculate a percentage).

Figure 15-27. *Crosstab total variables appearing at the bottom of the crosstab objects list*

For each measure, JasperReports creates variables that store the total value of the measure by each row/column group.

The following example is a simple report that shows the number of orders shipped in several regions in several years. Figure 15-28 shows the simple crosstab for this example, and Figure 15-29 shows the printed results of this crosstab.

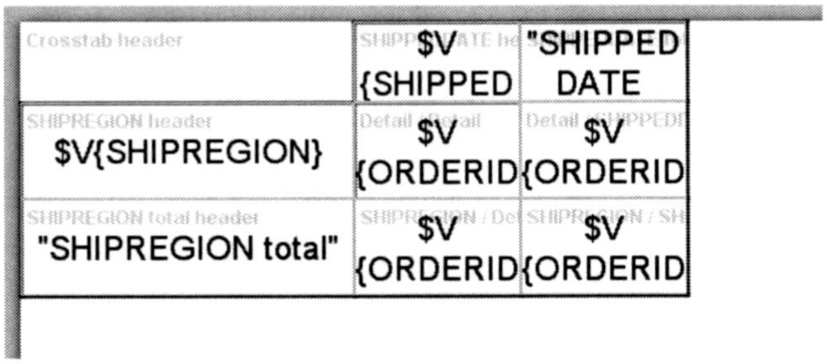

Figure 15-28. *Design of a simple crosstab*

	1996	1997	1998	null	SHIPPED
AK	2	4	4	0	10
BC	1	7	8	1	17
CA	0	3	1	0	4
Co. Cork	4	11	4	0	19

Figure 15-29. *Result of the crosstab shown in Figure 15-28*

To calculate the percentage of orders shipped in each region per year, add a text field with the following expression:

```
new Double(
    $V{ORDERID_Count}.doubleValue()
    /
    $V{ORDERID_Count_SHIPPEDDATE_ALL}.doubleValue()
)
```

in other words:

(Number of orders shipped in this region and in this year) / (All orders shipped in this region)

A percentage must be treated as a floating-point number. For this reason, extract the double scalar value from the ORDERID_Count and ORDERID_Count_SHIPPEDDATE_ALL objects even if there are objects of class type Integer (actually, a percentage derives from a number between 0 and 1 multiplied by 100).

To print the value of the expression as a percentage, set the value of the pattern text field attribute to #,##0.00 %.

Figure 15-30 shows the modified crosstab in the design window, and Figure 15-31 shows the final printed results.

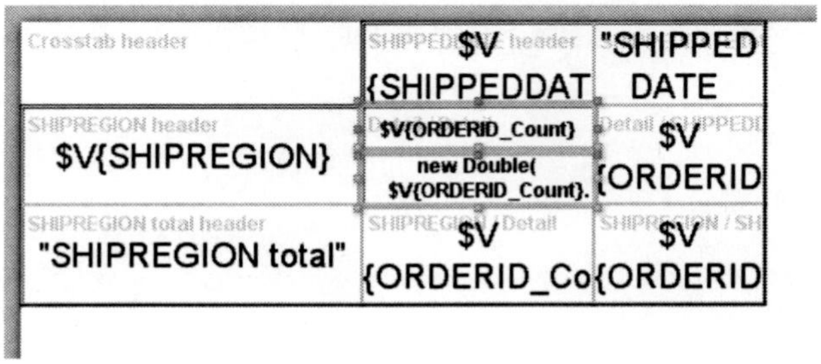

Figure 15-30. *Design of the example crosstab showing a percentage*

	1996	1997	1998	null	SHIPPED
AK	2 20,00 %	4 40,00 %	4 40,00 %	0 0,00 %	10
BC	1 5,88 %	7 41,18 %	8 47,06 %	1 5,88 %	17
CA	0 0,00 %	3 75,00 %	1 25,00 %	0 0,00 %	4
Co. Cork	4 21,05 %	11 57,89 %	4 21,05 %	0 0,00 %	19

Figure 15-31. *The final result of the modified crosstab*

■ ■ ■

CHAPTER 16

Other Interface Components

This chapter covers the various components of the iReport graphical interface that have not yet been discussed: the object library, the log window, and the list of active processes (see Figure 16-1), as well as rules and magnetic guidelines.

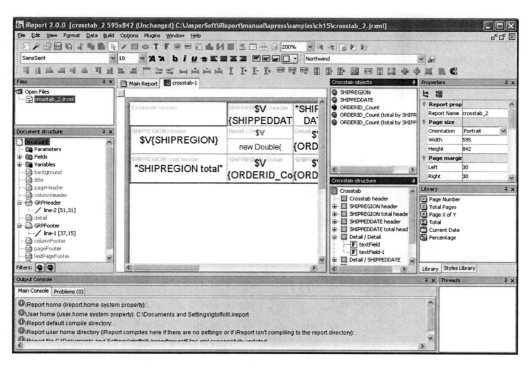

Figure 16-1. *Object library, log window, and thread list*

iReport uses FlexDock as its docking framework. All panes in the main window are dockable and can be dragged to a different position. Each pane can be iconified and optionally closed through the buttons shown in Figure 16-2.

Figure 16-2. *Iconify and close buttons*

When a pane is iconified, it appears on the left or right side of the window as a button, as shown in Figure 16-3.

Figure 16-3. *A set of iconified panes*

If a pane is hidden (closed), it can be reopened using the menu command View ➤ Docking panes, as shown in Figure 16-4.

Figure 16-4. *Show or hide panes through this menu*

Using the Document Structure Panel and the Object Library

The Document structure panel, which can be found on the right side of the main window, is composed of a tree containing the report's fields, parameters, variables, and other elements (see Figure 16-5). Any item within the tree can be selected and subsequently dragged into a band within the design window. When an object is dragged into the report, iReport creates a new Text Field element containing the expression representing the object chosen.

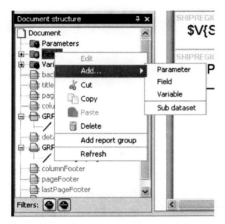

Figure 16-5. *Document structure panel*

Using the context menus and tree views, you can add, change, or delete fields, variables, or parameters and manage groups and subdatasets.

The object library, located on the right side of the main window, contains a set of tools useful to perform common tasks like displaying a subtotal or the current date or the page number (see Figure 16-6). All these tools can be used by just dragging and dropping them into in the desired band in the design window. For example, dragging the Page Number object into the report creates a text field containing the expression $V\{PAGE\_NUMBER\}$ and an evaluation time set to Now. Similarly, if you drag the Total Pages object into the report, iReport creates an object identical to the Page Number object, except the evaluation time will be set to Report.

Figure 16-6. *The object library*

Generally, the drag-and-drop functionalities provided by the Document structure panel and the object library are helpful for new users who want to understand how to visualize a field value in a report or how to calculate a subtotal. For more experienced users, these tools represent a very fast way to add and edit the various report objects without having to use the values window.

You've learned about the Page Number and Total Pages objects. Now let's take a closer look at the other objects in the object library.

Page X of Y Object

In JasperReports, it is not possible to create an expression that contains both the current page number and the total number of pages in the report. This problem can be resolved by using two text fields: the first containing the current page number, and the second containing the total (see Figure 16-7). iReport will create the two fields with their corresponding evaluation time.

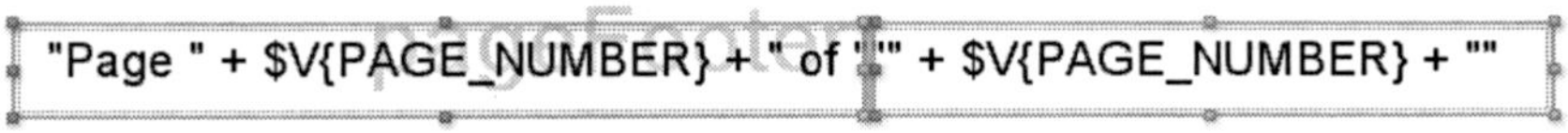

"Page " + $V{PAGE_NUMBER} + " of " + $V{PAGE_NUMBER} + ""

Figure 16-7. *Text fields created by the Page X of Y object*

Total Object

The Total object allows you to easily add elements that contain a total or subtotal derived from the sum of a field or variable. Depending on the band into which the object is dragged, iReport will determine what type of subtotal is required. For example, if the Total object is added to the group footer, iReport places the subtotal of the field's values relative to the associated group into the object. Likewise, if the Total object is dragged into the summary band, the calculated total is comprehensive.

As soon as the object is dragged into the report, the window shown in Figure 16-8 will appear, which allows you to select the exact values to summarize. These values can be based on a field, a variable, a parameter, or an expression (which can contain one or more of the aforementioned objects) in the report.

Figure 16-8. *Specifying values to sum for a Total object*

As always, if you want to customize an expression to extract a summarized value, invoke the text editor by double-clicking the object and opening the Text Field tab.

When you click the OK button, a new variable is created with type Sum, the reset type and reset group based on the band in which the object was dragged, and the correct Java type for the variable. This variable will be used to determine the value for the appropriate text field in the report.

Current Date Object

With this tool, you can easily add a text field showing a date. When you drag and drop the Current Date object into a report band, a window appears in which you can select the date format you want (see Figure 16-9). The selected format is then used as the pattern for the field.

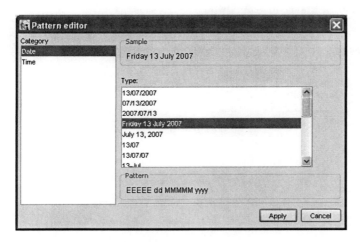

Figure 16-9. *Specifying a pattern for a Date object*

The text field expression is set to new java.util.Date(), and the text field evaluation time is set to Report, making several dates printed in this way as close as possible.

Percentage Object

The Percentage object helps the user create a text field containing a percentage.

When you drag and drop a Percentage object into a report band, the dialog box shown in Figure 16-10 appears. Here you specify the field whose percentage you want to calculate and the aggregation level on which to perform the percentage calculation.

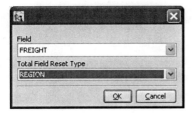

Figure 16-10. *Specifying a field and aggregation level for a Percentage object*

iReport creates a new variable to store the sum of the selected field. The reset type of this variable is set to the selected aggregation level (e.g., report, page, or a particular group). The text field expression generated is something like this:

```
new Double($F{Freight}.doubleValue() / $V{SUM_Freight_1}.doubleValue())
```

and the evaluation time is set to Auto to allow the evaluation of $F{Freight} and $V{SUM_Freight_1} at different aggregation times. Finally, the pattern of the text field is set to #,##0.00 %.

Understanding the Log Window

The lower portion of the iReport interface contains the log window. Since version 0.5.1, the log window has been organized into tabs, as shown in Figure 16-11.

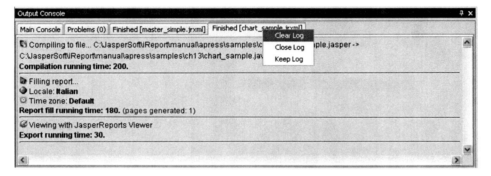

Figure 16-11. *Log window*

The main tab, called the Main Console tab, is always visible, and it shows messages indicating activity in iReport (when files are saved, for example). When a file is being compiled or a report is being printed, the subsequent processes are visible in a new tab. Terminated processes are made invisible at the beginning of a new process to avoid unnecessary accumulation of text in the tab. Nevertheless, it can be useful at times to keep a log open and start a new process in a new tab. You can keep a log open by selecting Keep Log from the context menu that appears when you right-click a log window tab's label. To close a previously "kept" log, select Close Log. To clear the contents of a log, select Clear Log.

Understanding the Thread List

When a file is compiled or a report is printing, iReport creates a new thread that completes the requested commands. Active threads and the activities they are performing appear in the box in the lower-right corner of the main iReport window (see Figure 16-12).

When a process is taking too long, you can kill it by highlighting the specific process and selecting Kill this thread from the context menu. This sends an interruption signal to the specified thread, but it is not guaranteed that the thread will be stopped immediately.

Figure 16-12. *Thread list*

Using Rules and Magnetic Guidelines

Rules are used to show the page dimensions and margins (see Figure 16-13).

Figure 16-13. *Rules*

You can create a *guideline* by clicking inside a rule. A guideline, painted with dotted blue lines, is a special line that can simplify the positioning of elements in a page. Guidelines are *magnetic*, which means that if an element is created or moved close to a guideline, its coordinates are "attracted" by the line. To test this effect, create four guidelines as illustrated in Figure 16-14: two horizontal and the other two vertical. Now draw a Rectangle element to fit inside the guidelines. You'll see that doing so becomes extremely easy due to the magnetic feature of the guidelines.

To remove a guideline, simply drag the guideline over the top-left corner of the design window.

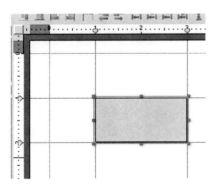

Figure 16-14. *Magnetic guidelines help drawing elements*

When an element is resized or moved, it is attracted not only by the guidelines, but also by all the other elements present in the report. This helps you to easily align several elements. However, sometimes it can be useful to disable the magnetic effect (e.g., when there are too many elements attracting the one you are trying to move). To disable all magnetic effects, just click the Magnet tool in the toolbar, shown here:

CHAPTER 17

Plug-Ins and Additional Tools

It is possible to extend iReport functionalities by means of *plug-ins*, external application modules designed to execute various tasks such as positioning elements using particular criteria or compiling a JASPER file and putting it in a BLOB database field.

Plug-ins are loaded when iReport starts and are accessible by selecting Plugins from the main menu bar (see Figure 17-1).

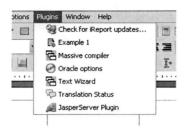

Figure 17-1. *Plugins menu*

By selecting Options ➤ Configure Plugins, as shown in Figure 17-2, you can access the plug-in list, shown in Figure 17-3, if you want to configure any of the plug-ins.

Figure 17-2. *Configure Plugins menu option*

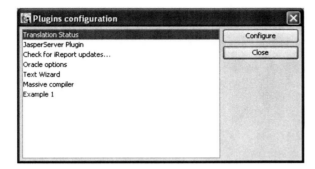

Figure 17-3. *Plugins configuration dialog box*

Each plug-in is created by extending the abstract class it.businesslogic.ireport.plugin. IReportPlugin and writing an XML file containing the plug-in deployment directives. The class (or the JAR that contains it) must be present in the classpath, and the XML file must be placed in the plugin directory in iReport's home directory. All XML files in this directory are processed to start up the corresponding plug-ins.

iReport comes with several plug-ins: Massive compiler, Text Wizard, Oracle options, Translation Status, Check for iReport updates, and Example 1, a simple plug-in provided as a sample.

Plug-In Configuration XML File Overview

The plug-in configuration XML file, used as the deployment descriptor, is really simple. Here is the DTD that describes its tags:

```
<?xml version="1.0" encoding="UTF-8"?>
  <!--
     Document    : iReportPlugin.dtd
     Created on  : 19 maggio 2004, 8.09
     Author      : Giulio Toffoli
     Description: This DTD defines the XML descriptor for an iReport plug-in.
  -->
  <!--
     iReportPlugin is the root element.
     ATTRIBUTES:
     name         The name of plug-in
     class        The class that extends
                          it.businesslogic.ireport.plugin.IReportPlugin
     loadOnStartup If true, the plug-in will be instanced on iReport startup
     hide         If true, this plug-in will be not visible on Plugin menu
  -->
  <!ELEMENT iReportPlugin (Author?,Description?, IconFile?)>
  <!ATTLIST iReportPlugin
        name NMTOKEN #REQUIRED
        class NMTOKEN #REQUIRED
        loadOnStartup (true | false) "false"
        hide (true | false) "false"
        configurable (true | false) "false">
```

```
<!ELEMENT Author (#PCDATA)>
<!ELEMENT Description (#PCDATA)>

<!--
    Icon file should be a file in the classpath i.e., com/my/plug/in/icon.gif
    Is used as optional icon for menu.
    Dim: 16x16
-->
<!ELEMENT IconFile (#PCDATA)>
```

The root element is iReportPlugin, and Table 17-1 lists its attributes.

Table 17-1. *iReportPlugin Attributes*

Attribute	Description
name	This is the plug-in name.
class	This is the Java class that implements the plug-in; it must be present in the classpath together with all required classes. If a JAR is needed to run the plug-in, you have to put it in iReport's lib directory.
loadOnStartup	iReport keeps in memory one and only one instance for each plug-in. By setting this attribute to true, you force iReport to instance the plug-in when iReport starts, without waiting for an invocation.
hide	By setting this to true, you can hide the plug-in (it will be hidden in all the menu entries related to the plug-in in question).
configurable	If set to true, iReport will enable the Configure button for this plug-in in the window shown in Figure 17-3.

If you want, you can specify an author name for a plug-in (using the tag Author, this information is currently not used or displayed by iReport), a small plug-in description (using the tag Description), and a 16×16-pixel icon that will be used for the menu (using the tag IconFile): since the icon file is loaded as a Java resource, the value for this tag must be a path in the classpath (e.g., /it/businesslogic/ireport/icons/menu/new.gif).

Following is the XML file used to activate the Example 1 plug-in shipped with iReport:

```
<iReportPlugin
    name="Example 1"
    class="it.businesslogic.ireport.plugin.examples.HelloWorld"
    loadOnStartup="false"
    hide = "false"
    configurable = "true">

    <IconFile>/it/businesslogic/ireport/icons/menu/new.gif</IconFile>

    <Description>
            This example shows how to create a very simple
            plugin for iReport.
    </Description>

</iReportPlugin>
```

To disable a plug-in, you have to remove its XML file from the `plugin` directory (or simply change its extension to something different from `.xml`). If the plug-in descriptor is contained in a JAR file (as discussed in the "Deploying a Plug-In As a JAR File" section later in this chapter), you need to remove that JAR from the classpath in order to disable the plug-in.

Working with the it.businesslogic.ireport.plugin.IReportPlugin Class

The most difficult part related to the creation of a plug-in is programming it. You have to create a new Java class that extends the abstract class `it.businesslogic.ireport.plugin.IReportPlugin`. This one contains two "entry points": the methods `configure` and `call`. The first is invoked only if the plug-in is labeled as "configurable" when you click the Configure button (shown earlier in Figure 17-3); the second is invoked when you select the plug-in name from the menu (shown earlier in Figure 17-1).

Here is the IReportPlugin class source code:

```java
package it.businesslogic.ireport.plugin;

import it.businesslogic.ireport.gui.MainFrame;

/**
 * This class must be extended by all iReport plug-ins.
 * To install a plug-in in iReport, put the plug-in XML in the plugin
 * directory of iReport.
 * See plug-in documentation on how to create a plug-in for iReport
 *
 * This is the first very simple interface to plug in. We hope it doesn't
 * change, but we can't say what it'll be in the future...
 *
 * @author  Administrator
 */
public abstract class IReportPlugin {

    MainFrame mainFrame = null;
    String name = "";

    /**
     * This method is called when the plug-in is selected from the Plugin menu
     */
    public abstract void call();

    /**
     * This method is called when the Configure button in the Plugins configuration
     * list is selected.
     * Configuration file of plug-in should be stored in
     * IREPORT_USER_HOME_DIR/plugins/
     */
    public void configure(){}
```

```
/**
 * Retrieve the plug-in name. Please note that the plug-in name must be
 * unique and should be used as a file name for the configuration file if
 * needed. This name can be different from the name specified in XML,
 * which is the name used for the menu item.
 */
public String getName(){
    return name;
}

/** Getter for property mainFrame.
 * @return Value of property mainFrame.
 *
 */
public it.businesslogic.ireport.gui.MainFrame getMainFrame() {
    return mainFrame;
}

/** Setter for property mainFrame.
 * @param mainFrame New value of property mainFrame.
 *
 */
public void setMainFrame(
                it.businesslogic.ireport.gui.MainFrame mf) {
    this.mainFrame = mf;
}
}
}
```

As you can see, the only real abstract method is call. In effect, the configure method is implemented (with a void body), because there is not much sense in forcing you to implement it if it is not used (that is, when the plug-in is not configurable).

It is a good idea to define a plug-in constructor without arguments and set a value for the class name attribute. As soon as the plug-in is instanced, iReport will call the plug-in method setMainFrame to fill the mainFrame attribute, which is a reference to the core class of iReport: through this class, you can access reports, you can compile, you can modify the iReport configuration, and so forth.

Now focus on the call method. I have already talked about the fact that iReport creates and keeps in memory only one instance of each plug-in; this means that the call method is not thread safe. This suggests that the class that extends IReportPlugin should be a kind of container for the real plug-in; the call method should be the only entry point to run the plug-in code. At this point, it's possible to describe two types of plug-ins: the ones that have a single persistent instance, which survives between two consecutive plug-in calls; and the ones that use multiple volatile instances, which burn and die when the plug-in code ends. In this case, the call method is implemented to create a new instance of the core plug-in class each time the plug-in is executed.

The following code represents a simplified example of how a plug-in with a persistent instance should work:

```
public class MyPlugin extends IReportPlugin {

    MyPluginFrame frame = null;

public MyPlugin()
{
    setName("my sample plugin");
}
```

```
    /**
     *  This method is called when the plug-in is selected from the Plugin menu
     */
public void call()
{
    if (frame == null)
    {
        frame = new MyPluginFrame();
    }

    if (!frame.isVisible()) frame.setVisible(true);
}

}
```

The example `MyPluginFrame` class is the core of this plug-in, and it is shown any time you select this plug-in from the menu. The Massive compiler plug-in also works this way. The plug-in window can be opened and closed many times, but `MyPluginFrame` is never deallocated, and it keeps its state untouched.

If you have to create a new instance of the plug-in core class each time the plug-in is executed, the `call` method must be converted something like this:

```
public class MyPlugin extends IReportPlugin {

public MyPlugin()
{
    setName("my sample plugin");
}

    /**
     *  This method is called when the plug-in is selected from the Plugin menu
     */
public void call()
{
    MyPluginFrame frame = new MyPluginFrame();
    frame.show();
}

}
```

In this case, when you start the plug-in, a new window of type `MyPluginFrame` will be opened.

To complete information related to plug-ins, let's look at a couple pieces of code that are useful for interacting with iReport.

This instruction returns a reference to the object `MainFrame`:

```
MainFrame mf = MainFrame.getMainInstance();
```

This call returns the active report window (`JReportFrame`), from which it is possible to retrieve the report object using the method `getReport`:

```
mf.getActiveReportFrame();
```

The development of new plug-ins is strongly supported. If you have suggestions on this topic or wish to have something on how to implement a new plug-in clarified, do not be afraid to contact me at giulio@jaspersoft.com.

Deploying a Plug-In As a JAR File

As mentioned earlier, plug-ins are installed in iReport by placing an XML file into the plugins directory. This can be a problem when iReport can't access the file system directly (e.g., using Java Web Start to start iReport). From version 0.5.0 on, it's possible to put all plug-in files into a JAR file. The XML file that will describe the plug-in must be called plugin.xml, and it must be placed in a directory named ireport.

Using the Massive Compiler Plug-In

The Massive compiler, shown in Figure 17-4, is a tool to compile a large set of JRXML source files at the same time. It was particularly useful up to the release of JasperReports 1.1.0, since at the time, to migrate to a new JasperReports version, you had to recompile all your JRXML files.

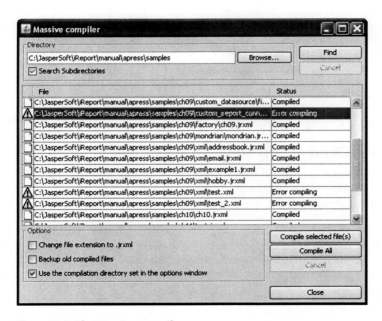

Figure 17-4. *The Massive compiler*

When this plug-in is started, a window to select the files to compile appears. Using the browse button, you have to input or select the directory in which the files to compile are stored (you can force the plug-in to search in subdirectories too by checking the Search Subdirectories check box option). Clicking the Find button will list all files found with a `.jrxml` or `.xml` extension. You only have to select the files to compile and click the Compile selected file(s) button.

If you want, you can replace files that still have the old `.xml` file extension with the new `.jrxml` extension. If a JASPER file already exists for a particular file, it is possible to create a backup copy of the old one before creating the new report.

If an error occurs while compiling a file, a warning icon is displayed to the left of the file name. When you double-click the offending file, you will see the details of the error (see Figure 17-5).

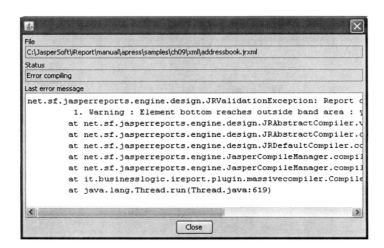

Figure 17-5. *Compilation error details*

Using the Text Wizard Plug-In

The Text Wizard plug-in was created to simplify the generation of text reports (reports based on characters). The aim was to allow building of tabular reports with labels and fields.

When you start this plug-in, it determines the width of the opened report and converts this width into characters. By clicking the Check for fields widths button, you refresh the list that contains the available report fields. To the right of the field names, there are two other columns. The first contains the maximum number of visible characters needed to show the entire content of the field (this information is retrieved using the `ResultSetMetaData` object returned by the JDBC driver). In the second column, you can manually change the maximum length of this field: all characters after this value will be cut off.

Clicking the Add Elements button adds labels and fields that will be placed in the report. The expression needed to truncate the contained value will be set in each text field, and it will look something like the following:

`( (($F{XYZ}!=null) && ($F{XYZ}.length() > 50)) ? $F{XYZ}.substring(0,50) : $F{XYZ})`

This expression checks for the length of the fields XYZ; if the length is greater than 50 characters, the expression returns a cut string.

Figure 17-6 shows the Text Wizard plug-in in action.

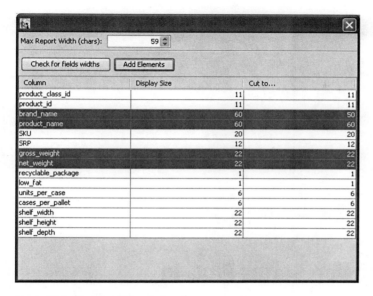

Figure 17-6. *The Text Wizard plug-in*

Using the Oracle Options Plug-In

The simple Oracle options plug-in permits you to specify the language and territory that must be used for the current Oracle connection (see Figure 17-7).

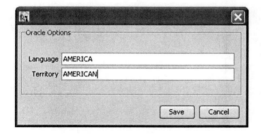

Figure 17-7. *Oracle options plug-in*

Using the Check for iReport Updates Plug-In

The Check for iReport updates plug-in checks whether updated versions of iReport are available. This plug-in is executed when iReport starts. You can disable it by selecting Options ➤ Configure Plugins, choosing Check for iReport updates, clicking the Configure button, and unchecking the Check for update on iReport startup option shown in Figure 17-8. In this window, you can configure the plug-in in order to use an HTTP Proxy when connecting to the Internet to check for updates.

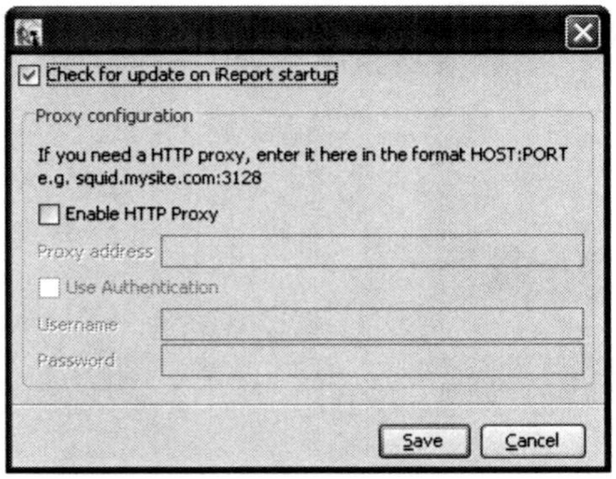
Check for update on iReport startup
Proxy configuration
If you need a HTTP proxy, enter it here in the format HOST:PORT
e.g. squid.mysite.com:3128
Enable HTTP Proxy
Proxy address
Use Authentication
Username
Password
Save
Cancel

Figure 17-8. *Configuration of Check for iReport updates plug-in*

Using the Translation Status Plug-In

The Translation Status plug-in provides translators with a quick view of the completion status of each translation file as well as a tool to help complete a translation.

When the plug-in is launched, the translation file list appears (see Figure 17-9). The table shows each language name (and optionally the country tied to each language), its completion status, and its file name (stored in the `it/businesslogic/ireport/locale` directory).

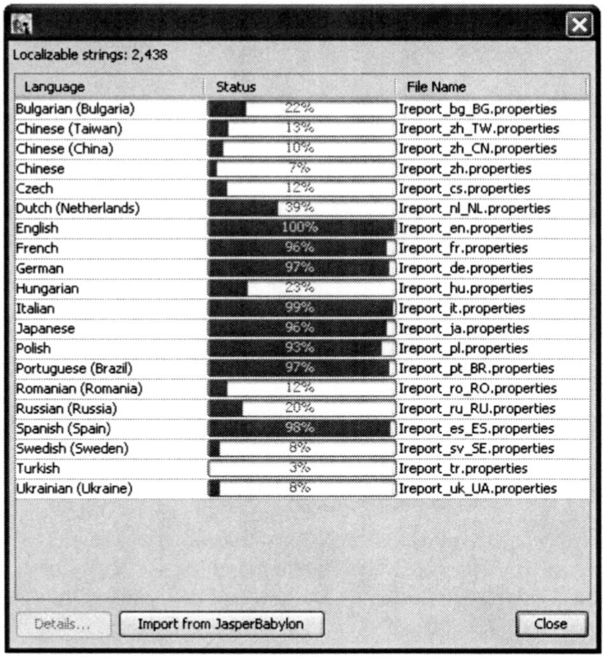
Localizable strings: 2,438
Language
Status
File Name
Bulgarian (Bulgaria) 22% Ireport_bg_BG.properties
Chinese (Taiwan) 13% Ireport_zh_TW.properties
Chinese (China) 10% Ireport_zh_CN.properties
Chinese 7% Ireport_zh.properties
Czech 12% Ireport_cs.properties
Dutch (Netherlands) 39% Ireport_nl_NL.properties
English 100% Ireport_en.properties
French 96% Ireport_fr.properties
German 97% Ireport_de.properties
Hungarian 23% Ireport_hu.properties
Italian 99% Ireport_it.properties
Japanese 96% Ireport_ja.properties
Polish 93% Ireport_pl.properties
Portuguese (Brazil) 97% Ireport_pt_BR.properties
Romanian (Romania) 12% Ireport_ro_RO.properties
Russian (Russia) 20% Ireport_ru_RU.properties
Spanish (Spain) 98% Ireport_es_ES.properties
Swedish (Sweden) 8% Ireport_sv_SE.properties
Turkish 3% Ireport_tr.properties
Ukrainian (Ukraine) 8% Ireport_uk_UA.properties
Details...
Import from JasperBabylon
Close

Figure 17-9. *Translation file list*

The percentage is based on the number of keys present in the file `ireport.properties`, which contains all the default strings. With each release, this file acquires even more keys that are not translated in languages other than Italian and English.

To see details of a language, double-click the language you desire or select it and click the Details button. This opens a new window showing all the keys present in `ireport.properties` and the related translation and default value in English (see Figure 17-10). Missing keywords are displayed in red.

From iReport 1.3.0 on, you can edit missing keywords and save them in a file stored in the following directory:

`<USER_HOME>/.ireport/classes/it/businesslogic/ireport/locale`

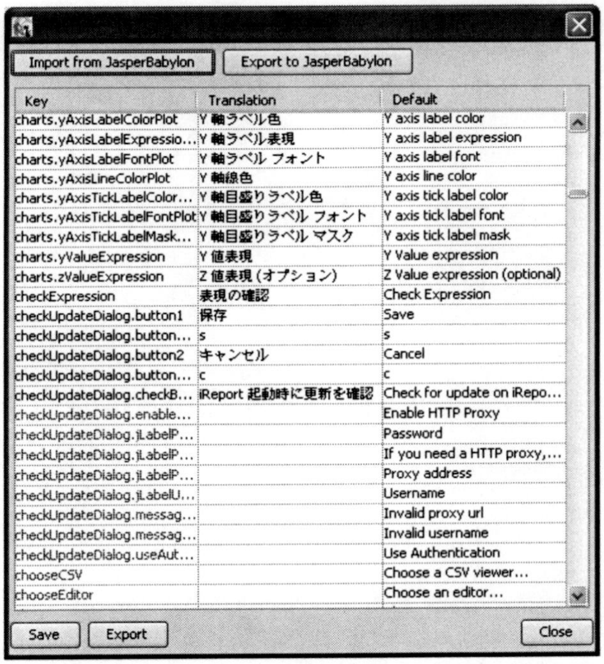

Figure 17-10. *Translation detail*

At startup, iReport will look for your favorite locale in this directory first.

Alternatively, you can click the Export button to generate a new file that stores all current translations and ends with all untranslated keywords starting with a # (which introduces a comment) and with the related default value ready to be translated. To use a locale file modified in this way, insert or replace it in the `it/businesslogic/ireport/locale` package. iReport will look for this package in the following directories:

- Paths defined in the classpath
- `<USER_HOME>/.ireport/classes`
- `<IREPORT_HOME>/classes`
- `<IREPORT_HOME>/lib/ireport.jar`

If you upgrade a current translation, or if you want to create a new translation for iReport, send your properties file to giulio@jaspersoft.com to make your translation available to all iReport users who speak your language, or sign up for JasperBabylon and become an official iReport contributor.

Working with JasperBabylon

All translatable strings of iReport are published on *JasperBabylon*, a web-based tool that makes the management of the Resource Bundle files easy (see Figure 17-11).

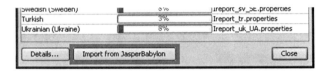

Figure 17-11. *Importing from JasperBabylon*

To list all the translations available, as shown in Figure 17-12, click the Import from JasperBabylon button.

Figure 17-12. *List of available translations imported from JasperBabylon*

iReport will connect to the JasperBabylon repository in order to get the translations list. If available, you can select your favorite language from this list and import it (you may still need to set which language iReport should use in the Options window).

JasperBabylon can be used to update an existing local translation, and if you are a registered contributor, you can send your translation to the JasperBabylon repository, making your translation available to others (note the Import from JasperBabylon and Export to JasperBabylon buttons in Figure 17-13). To do so, set your credentials in the Translation Status plug-in properties dialog box, shown in Figure 17-14 (click the Options ➤ Configure Plugins menu item, select the Translation Status item, and click Configure to bring up this dialog box).

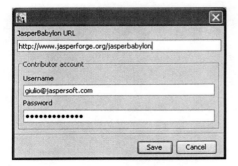

Key	Translation	Default
charts.categoryAxisTickLa...		Category axis tick label font
charts.categoryAxisTickLa...		Category axis tick label mask
charts.categoryExpression	Výraz pro kategorii	Category expression
charts.closeExpression	Zavři výraz	Close expression
charts.copyDataset	Kopírovat dataset	Copy dataset
charts.copyseries	Kopírovat sérii	Copy series
charts.dataRangeHigh		Data range high exp

Figure 17-13. *Import from JasperBabylon/Export to JasperBabylon buttons to update and share a translation*

JasperBabylon URL

http://www.jasperforge.org/jasperbabylon

Contributor account

Username

giulio@jaspersoft.com

Password

•••••••••••••

[Save] [Cancel]

Figure 17-14. *JasperBabylon credential to upload a new translation*

You can set your username and password from this window as well as the official URL of JasperBabylon: http://www.jasperforge.org/jasperbabylon. On this site, you can create an account, if you still don't have one.

■ ■ ■

CHAPTER 18

Solutions to Common Problems

In this chapter, you will learn how to solve some common problems related to using iReport and JasperReports; these are problems users frequently post about on the iReport forum and problems for which the JasperReports official documentation does not provide a clear solution.

Error Handling

iReport helps you understand real-time and compilation errors using the new Problems tab in the output console pane (see Figure 18-1).

	Description	JRXML location	Object
	Syntax error on token(s), misplace...	Line 112, Colum...	/jasperReport/detail[1]/band[1]/textField[1]/textFieldExpression[1]
	Syntax error on token ")", delete t...	Line 112, Colum...	/jasperReport/detail[1]/band[1]/textField[1]/textFieldExpression[1]
	Syntax error on token ";", delete t...	Line 177, Colum...	/jasperReport/detail[1]/band[1]/textField[5]/textFieldExpression[1]

Figure 18-1. *Problems tab of the output console pane*

Depending on the nature of the error, you can locate the source of the problem in two ways:

- *Clicking an error in the Problems tab*: This action will select in the design window the element that is the cause of the error (and optionally, the associated property is highlighted with a red exclamation mark in the property sheet).

- *Double-clicking an error in the Problems tab*: If the error is produced by an expression editable in some nested dialog box, the dialog box will pop up. In this case, iReport highlights the expression field where it has identified the problem.

Printing Large Reports Using Report Virtualizer

The only potential obstacle when creating a larger report in JasperReports is the amount of memory available. To help alleviate this "physical" limitation, JasperReports economizes on memory usage and employs other available media to save completed pages during the filling/printing of a report (typically the hard disk). Therefore, users can create reports with a very large number of pages without the risk of encountering "out of memory" exceptions.

To open the Report Virtualizer, select Build ➤ Use Report Virtualizer (see Figure 18-2). The Report Virtualizer is configurable in the iReport Options window in the Compiler tab (see Chapter 19).

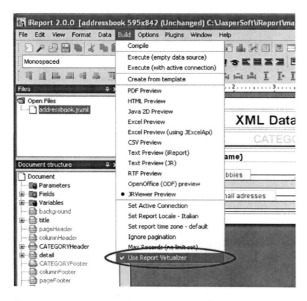

Figure 18-2. *Accessing the Report Virtualizer*

Printing a Percentage

In a report, often you will need to display the value of a field and the percentage of this value with respect to others. Consider the rows in the following table:

A	B	C
Bananas	10	20%
Oranges	25	50%
Strawberries	15	30%

In this case, the percentages inserted in column C represent the percentages respective to the values in column B calculated using the following formula:

$$C = (B \ / \ (\Sigma B)) * 100 \tag{1}$$

where ΣB equals the sum of all values in column B.

Although it looks like quite a simple way to calculate the percentage, formula (1) does not calculate correctly in JasperReports because the formula uses values that are not yet available at the time the formula is calculated. Specifically, the value ΣB is obtained only at the end of the report (or at the end of a group if the reset type is group) when all records have been processed. However, you do have available the value of B during the elaboration of the record for which you are calculating formula (1), otherwise known as an evaluation time of Now.

Up to JasperReports 1.2, there was no simple solution for this problem. The only way was to precalculate the totals needed to determine the percentages (in the previous example, the value ΣB). By precalculating the value and passing it to your report as a parameter, you could rewrite formula (1) as something like this:

```
new Double(($P{B}.doubleValue()*100)/$F{TOTAL_OF_B}.doubleValue())
```

where TOTAL_OF_B is the parameter name containing your precalculated value.

To solve the problem without performing external processing, you need to be using JasperReports 1.2 or later. These versions of JasperReports provide the Auto evaluation time setting for text fields. This setting is quite similar to Now, but it's smart enough to process an expression like

```
new Double( $F{B}.doubleValue() / $V{TOTAL_OF_B}.doubleValue() )
```

using the last available value of variable TOTAL_OF_B before it is reset. This enables printing of the percentage (note that the expression avoids multiplying the result by 100, because in this case it is better to use the percentage pattern to format the field).

In any case, this solution doesn't permit storing the percentage value in a variable to perform other calculations.

Counting Occurrences of a Group

Starting with JasperReports 1.0.0, you can count the occurrences of a particular group by creating a variable of calculation type Count, defining Group as the increment type, and then specifying the group to count. Here, you'll see how to perform the same calculation without selecting a specific increment type. The goal is a way to manage "custom" increment types.

Each group in JasperReports is associated with an expression. During report generation, as soon as the expression value changes, a new group occurrence starts. Sometimes you must count the number of groups (i.e., count how many times the value of the group expression changes). To do this, you need a variable: name it GRP_COUNT; the basic idea is to increment this variable if and only if the variable *group name*_COUNT is equal to 0. *group name*_COUNT is a built-in variable provided by JasperReports, and it contains the current number of processed records for the group defined by *group name*. Since the variable *group name*_COUNT for a certain group is equal to 0 only once, GRP_COUNT will contain the exact number of group occurrences.

The example in Figure 18-3 shows a simple report created using the query select * from customers order by country and the expression associated with the group COUNTRY is the field $F{COUNTRY}.

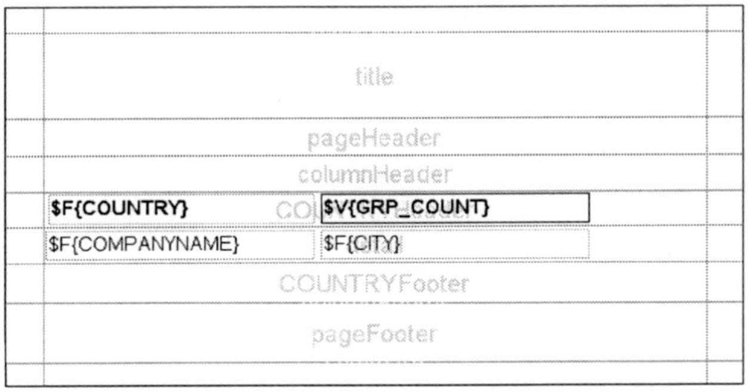

Figure 18-3. *Design of a report with a group counting variable*

You can declare the variable GRP_COUNT by specifying the following settings, as shown in Figure 18-4:

- *Variable Class Type*: java.lang.Integer

- *Calculation Type*: Count

- *Reset Type*: Report

- *Variable Expression*: ($V{COUNTRY_COUNT} != null && $V{COUNTRY_COUNT}.intValue() == 1) ? "" : null

- *Initial Value Expression*: new Integer(0)

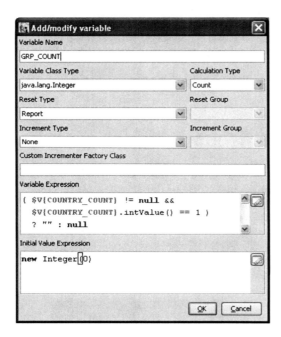

Figure 18-4. *Definition of the GRP_COUNT variable*

The expression says this: if you are evaluating the first record (the record number 0) for the current group instance, then return something that is not null; otherwise, return the null value. Since you choose Count as the calculation type, the variable GRP_COUNT will be incremented only when the expression value is not null—that is, when the first record of the current group is evaluated.

To display this value in a text field, you have to set the evaluation time of the element expression to Group and for the expression group specify the group for which you are counting occurrences, in this example, the COUNTRY group (see Figure 18-5).

In Figure 18-6, you can see the resulting printed report. The group instance number is displayed inside the black frames.

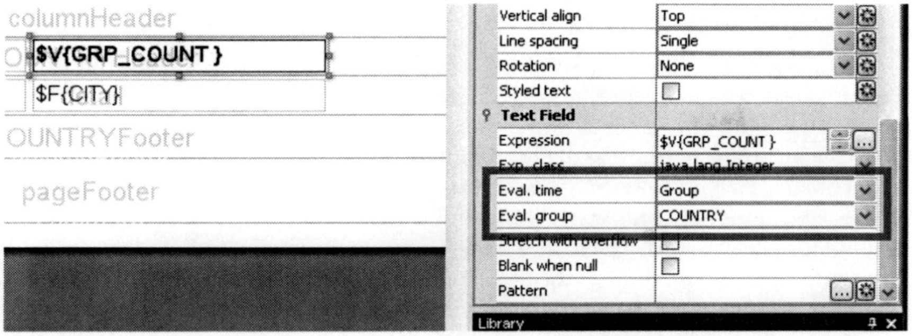

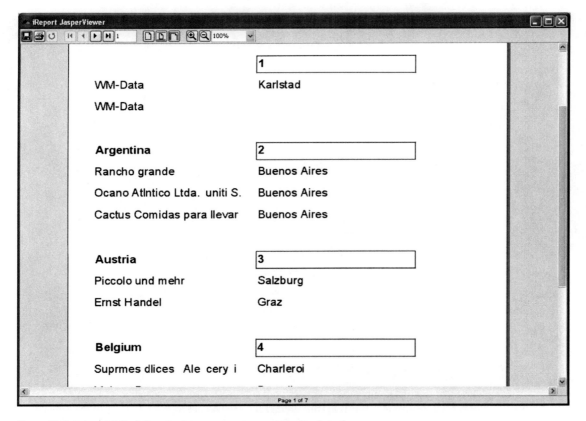

Figure 18-5. *Definition of the text field to display the GRP_COUNT variable*

Figure 18-6. *In each black frame, the group occurrence is displayed.*

If the Evaluation Time field is set to Report, the total number of group occurrences will be printed.

Splitting the Detail Band

Sometimes it is useful to split the detail band into more bands. For example, you might want to display a specific detail band instead of another when some conditions happen. These conditions must be tested by using the band's print when expression.

It is possible to have an arbitrary number of detail bands by creating new groups that use a group expression that changes in value on each record. You can use a primary key field of the record or a counter variable as an expression. This way, besides in the detail band, you will have a group header and group footer for each record, usable in the same way as the detail band.

In the report design shown in Figure 18-7, the detail band is hidden to leave space for the header bands of a couple of new groups for which the group expression is the same: the primary key of the record.

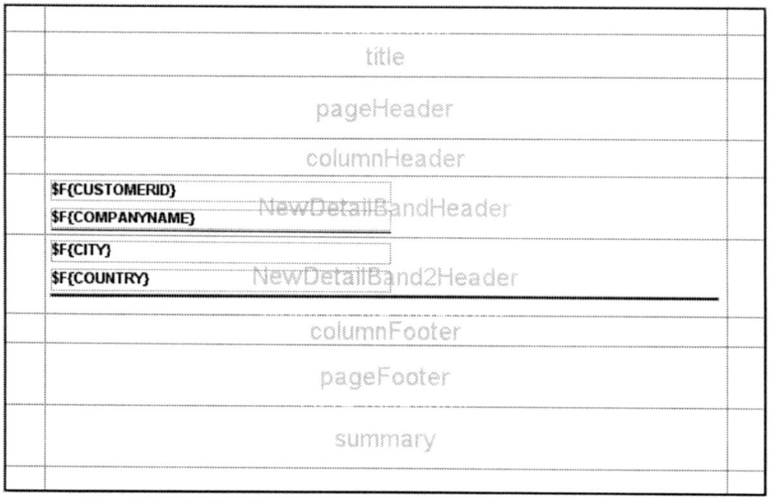

Figure 18-7. *A split detail band*

By selecting the Start on a New Page option for the first group, you can force a page break for each record. The page break is placed between sequential records, not between the two bands; if you need to split a record over more than a single page, you should use the Page Break element.

Inserting Additional Pages

The Page Break element provides a way to add a page break in a band, so that you can split a band into two pages. Unfortunately, this does not mean that you will get more space in which to design your report: the space available at design time is limited to the page height. In this section, you will see how to use subreports to have virtually an arbitrary number of pages available at design time. To start, you will split contents of the detail band into two pages: the first will display the code and name of a customer, and the second one will display that customer's address.

To complete the example, you will print each record on a new page so that you have two entire pages per record.

Let's go step by step. Start from the subreport: create a simple blank document with margins set to zero (you can easily remove the margins with Edit ➤ Remove Margins). Set to zero the height of all bands (title band and summary band excluded). In the report properties of this subreport (Edit ➤ Report Properties), select the Title on a new page option on the More tab and set the value of the When no data option to All sections, no detail (alternatively, you can set these options using the property sheet when the Document node in the Document structure panel is selected). All field values coming from the master report will be passed as parameters, so you have to declare all the necessary parameters. In this example, you only need these four parameters (see Figure 18-8):

- CUSTOMERID
- COMPANYNAME
- CITY
- REGION

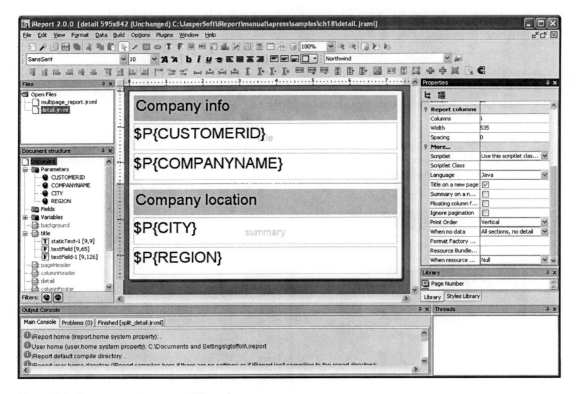

Figure 18-8. *Content on two pages: title and summary*

So insert into the report all the text fields you need. Please note that all elements inserted in the title band are printed on the first page, which consists of the detail band, and elements put in the summary band will be printed in the second page.

Now for the master report: create a blank report and add a group with $V\{REPORT\_COUNT\}$ as the group expression and the Start on a New Page group flag checked. This will result in a page break between each record. Add a Subreport element to the detail band (see Figure 18-9) without any connection or datasource (you have to set the Connection/Datasource property for the subreport to No connection or datasource). Since the subreport will always print two pages, this is how you'll divide the contents of the detail band.

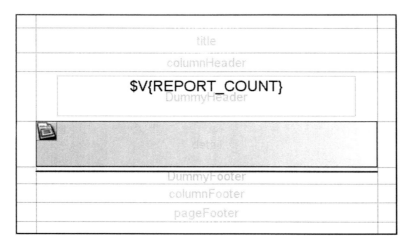

Figure 18-9. *The master report with subreport added*

You have to fill the subreport parameters with the right expressions in the master report (specifically, you have to fill the Subreport parameters table in the Subreport (Other) tab of the element properties window, as shown in Figure 18-10).

Figure 18-10. *Specifying the subreport parameters*

Compile both master and subreport and print the report. You should see pages like the ones shown in Figure 18-11.

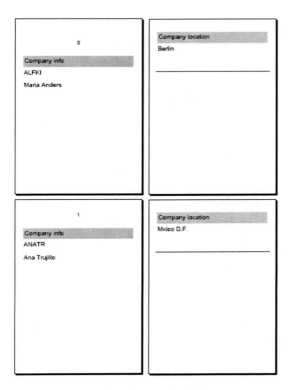

Figure 18-11. *Content split into several pages*

Retrieving Data Using Multiple Connections

Sometimes you need to retrieve data from more than a single database at the same time. To achieve this, the solution depends a lot on what you want. Usually, to execute multiple queries, subreports are used. Since you have to specify what connection a subreport must use, you can set a different connection expression for each subreport. You can pass alternative connections to use in your report as parameters.

If it is not possible to keep separated the data retrieved by different databases using subreports, you have to implement a lookup method, for example, using a static class or adding the method to the report scriptlet. This lookup method will be used to retrieve data from an arbitrary database.

The following example represents a simple lookup class to decode the name of a country given a country code. The method is passed an already opened JDBC connection and the code to decode as parameters.

```
public class LookUp {

    public static String decodeState(java.sql.Connection con, int code)
    {
        java.sql.Statement stmt = null;
        java.sql.ResultSet rs = null;

        try {
            stmt = con.createStatement();
```

```
            rs = stmt.executeQuery(
             "select STATE_NAME from STATES where code=" + code );

            if (rs.next())
            {
                return rs.getString(1);
            }

            return "#not found!";

        } catch (Exception ex)
        {
            return "#error";
        } finally {
            if (rs != null)
                try { rs.close(); }
                catch (Exception ex2) {}
            if (stmt != null)
                try { stmt.close(); }
                catch (Exception ex2) {}
        }
    }
}
```

Calling this method, passing as arguments different database connections, you can get a report filled using data coming from different databases.

Using Stored Procedures

In general, you can easily use stored procedures in JasperReports without any particular expedient. For example, the syntax to call a stored procedure depends on the particular DBMS. The following SQL statement executes a stored procedure called my_proc in a MySQL database:

```
call my_proc()
```

This approach of using a stored procedure to call a standard SQL query works well with databases like MySQL and Microsoft SQL Server (assuming that the procedure returns some kind of SELECT statement or a cursor). Unfortunately, it does not work with Oracle. This is because the Oracle JDBC driver does not return a result set when JasperReports invokes a query using the standard JDBC calls. In effect, Oracle requires some specific Java code to extract a result set from a stored procedure output parameter (which is normally declared as a cursor).

■**Note** Some skilled PL/SQL developers may be able to work around the problem using a query like the following in a report:

```
select a, b, c from table( cast( my_proc() ) )
```

my_proc must be defined as function with a return type defined as table of *myRecordType*, where *myRecordType* is the definition of a record type.

cast and table are two Oracle-specific functions. See the Oracle documentation for details on how to use them.

In any case, JasperReports is not able to handle output parameters apart from the result set that comes from the execution of the stored procedure.

Behind the scenes, JasperReports uses the PreparedStatement class (a standard Java interface to execute a SQL statement). This class provides a way to set values for input parameters that can be required by the statement itself; this mechanism works fine with common SQL queries and stored procedure calls as well. This class can be transparently used to execute a stored procedure on many DBMSs. JasperReports expects the statement execution to return a result set, and this strictly depends on the specific JDBC driver implementation.

There are other cases in which the result set is not what you are interested in, and you may need to get all the output parameter values coming from the stored procedure. This complicates the problem a bit: the query in a report is supposed to be used to generate a result set, nothing more.

Keeping in mind the need to get a result set out of the query execution, a possible approach is to delegate the execution of the stored procedure to the hosting application (the application that is using JasperReports) and run the report against some kind of temporary table filled dynamically by the stored procedure itself. This solution is actually a bit "expensive" in terms of implementation and requires the creation/fill/cleanup of a temporary table, all of which can address some performance issues; anyway, the basic idea is to use a temporary table to store the data required by the report. A stored procedure, executed autonomously by the host application, should extract the desired data and fill the temporary table that will be queried by the report with a regular SELECT statement. At the end of the report execution, when the final print is done, the host application is responsible for cleaning up the temporary table (or dropping it as necessary).

A better solution is to provide more "intelligence" for JasperReports query executers. This can be done by plugging in a custom query executer to deal with the stored procedures. This approach is extremely powerful and represents the best way to modify the default behavior of JasperReports when it must execute a query and manage the result in a specific (perhaps system-dependent) way. For instance, if you plan to use Oracle stored procedures, you can save a lot of time adopting the freely available implementation of a query executer for PL/SQL by Barry Klawans, described in the next section. (An in-depth exploration of query executers appears in Chapter 9.)

PL/SQL Query Executer

JasperReports 1.2.0 introduced the concept of the custom query executer. This mechanism provides a way to use a custom interpreter for a specific report query language. Barry Klawans from JasperSoft has released an implementation of a PL/SQL query executer on JasperForge.org. The project URL is http://jasperforge.org/sf/projects/oraclestoredprocedures.

This query executer defines the new language simply called plsql to distinguish it from sql. (Recall that in iReport, the query language used in a report is specified at the top of the Report query dialog box.) Although it is specifically for Oracle, it comes with the source code, so it can be easily modified to fit similar needs.

Following are the step-by-step instructions to use this new language in iReport after you download the ZIP archive containing all the required files (a sample and the source code are included). This package is not part of JasperReports because it requires the Oracle JDBC drivers in order to be compiled and to work.

1. Select Options ➤ Query executers in the main menu bar.

2. In the resulting dialog box, click New.

3. Set the language to plsql and the factory class to org.jasperforge.jaspersoft.demo. PlSqlQueryExecuterFactory.

4. Download and build the project OracleStoredProcedures.

5. Copy the build/classes directory to your iReport directory.

6. In iReport, select Data ➤ Connections/Data Sources.

7. In the resulting dialog box, click New.

8. From the list of datasource types, select Query Executer mode. Set the name to PlSql and click Save.

9. Add the Oracle JDBC driver to iReport's lib directory. (The Oracle 9 version is in the lib directory of this project, in classes12.jar.)

Now you can create a report that uses an Oracle stored procedure:

1. Create a new report.

2. Add a parameter to your report called "cursor" with the type java.sql.ResultSet. Be sure that the Use as a Prompt option is not selected.

3. Set the datasource to the PlSql source defined earlier.

4. Select Data ➤ Report Query.

5. Enter plsql in the Query language field—it won't appear in the list of languages, but you can type it into the field.

6. Set the query to {call your_procedure($P{cursor}, $F{some_field})}. The important thing is that the cursor parameter must be wherever the Oracle REF_CURSOR is in the parameters list.

In order to use this query executer on a server, or in general, outside iReport, you need to set the JasperReports property

```
net.sf.jasperreports.query.executer.factory.plsql
```

to this value:

```
org.jasperforge.jaspersoft.demo.PlSqlQueryExecuterFactory
```

This can be done programmatically (see *The Definitive Guide to JasperReports* by Teodor Daniciu, Lucian Chirita, Sanda Zaharia, and Ionut Nedelcu [Apress, 2007]) or by simply inserting in the classpath the file jasperreports.properties (shipped with this OracleStoredProcedures package). It simply contains the following line (a single line without spaces):

```
net.sf.jasperreports.query.executer.factory.plsql=➥
              org.jasperforge.jaspersoft.demo.PlSqlQueryExecuterFactory
```

iReport Options

This chapter focuses on the many iReport configuration options.

When options are applied, they are saved in a file named config.xml, stored in the directory <USER_HOME>/.ireport.

Select Options ➤ Settings to open the Options window, where you define iReport configuration options. Let's take a closer look at this window, starting with the general options.

Configuring General Options

In the General tab of the Options window, shown in Figure 19-1, it's possible to set options relative to the editor interface (such as the language or the look and feel).

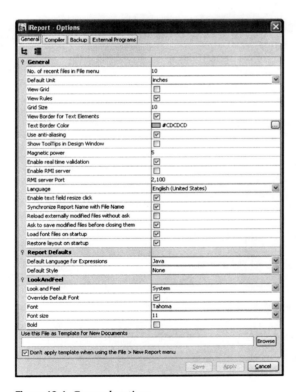

Figure 19-1. *General options*

Most of the options present should be self-explanatory.

The Default Unit setting is not yet used in all iReport frames (this will be fixed in the future). The same applies to the Grid Size setting.

The Synchronize Report Name with File Name option means that the report name and the file name are set to the same value when saving the file.

If you specify a JRXML file in the Use this File as Template for New documents field, it will be used as the "blank document" when clicking the New button in the toolbar.

The iReport UI and Non-Latin Languages

iReport tries to set Tahoma as the default font for the UI. For non-Latin languages, this could be a problem because Tahoma defines only a restricted set of characters.

There are two ways to avoid changes to default UI fonts:

- Uncheck the Override Default Font option, shown in Figure 19-2 (or select a good font like Dialog).

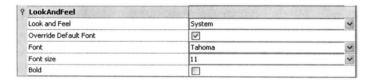

Figure 19-2. *Font settings of the General tab*

- Select a look and feel different from Metal.

Configuring Compiler Options

Compilation options are set in the Compiler tab of the Options window (see Figure 19-3).

The Default compilation directory option defines the directory where JASPER files are compiled.

A report can be compiled using different compilers. The default JasperReports compiler is the JDT compiler (used by the Eclipse IDE). If you use this compiler and you have problems executing your report, add the jdt-compiler.jar file to your application classpath.

iReport works using the tools.jar compiler. To use it, you have to put the tools.jar file provided by your JDK into the lib directory.

The BeanShell compiler is no longer officially supported by JasperReports; use it only if you really need it.

The Jikes compiler uses the jikes command to compile reports.

■**Caution** If the language you choose to use for expressions is Groovy, a special compiler for Groovy will be used instead of the default compiler.

Figure 19-3. *Compiler options*

Configuring Report Virtualizer

In the Compiler tab, you can also configure the Report Virtualizer, which optimizes the application for the generation of larger reports. Currently, three different implementations of the Report Virtualizer are available:

File Virtualizer: Stores completed pages on the hard disk rather than storing each page in memory

Single Swap/File Virtualizer: Works like the File Virtualizer, but keeps all pages stored on the hard disk in a single file

GZIP In-Memory Virtualizer: Keeps all pages in memory but uses a compression algorithm to reduce the memory used by completed pages

The configurable options for the Report Virtualizer include the directory to use for temporary file storage and the maximum number of pages to keep in memory (for file-based virtualizers).

Caution For very large reports, the number of files generated will be much higher. Please ensure that your file system has enough free disk space to accommodate these files.

For JasperReports versions 1.0.3 and above, the files produced by the Report Virtualizer are deleted when the JRPrint object containing the printed report is closed and deleted from the JVM.

Configuring Backup Options

iReport provides different policies to keep a backup version of a modified file. If you want to take advantage of iReport backup options, select the best one for you on the Backup tab, shown in Figure 19-4.

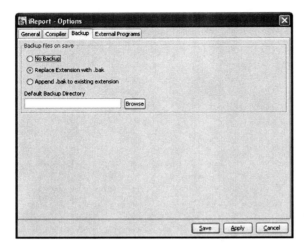

Figure 19-4. *Backup options*

Configuring External Programs

Use the External Programs tab, shown in Figure 19-5, to set external viewers for each file format. You can select a preview with the Build menu.

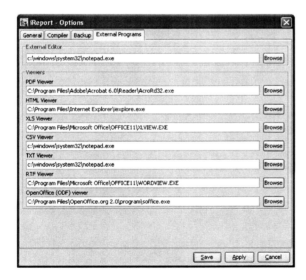

Figure 19-5. *External programs options*

Extending the Classpath

By selecting Options ➤ Classpath, you can extend the iReport classpath (see Figure 19-6). Be aware that adding too many entries can slow down iReport.

Figure 19-6. *Extending the iReport classpath*

Configuring Export Options

If necessary, you can test and use most of the options provided by JasperReports for exporters (Options ➤ Export Options). Not all displayed options, shown in Figure 19-7, are usable in iReport.

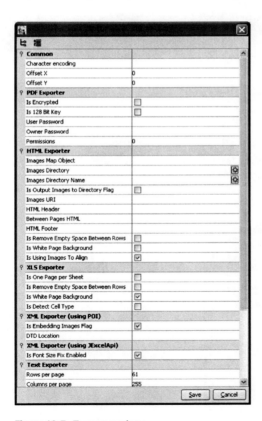

Figure 19-7. *Export options*

Creating Custom Expressions (Formulas)

All expressions in iReport can be edited using the expression editor (see Figure 19-8). To edit the list of ready-to-use expressions available in the Formula folder, select Options ➤ Formulas. From the window that appears, you can add, remove, and modify expressions, as well as change the order of the expressions in the list (see Figure 19-9). These expressions or formulas are not validated, so you are free to add meta expressions to the list such as the following:

```
( <boolean expression>) ? <expression on true> : <expression on false>
```

This particular expression can't work as is, but it can help you to remember the syntax of a typical conditional structure.

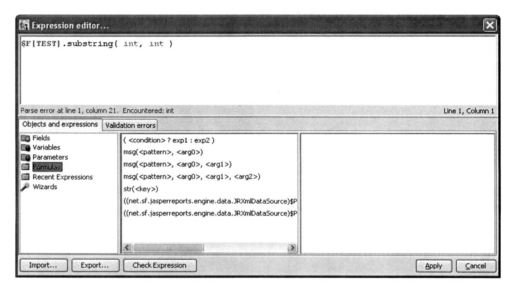

Figure 19-8. *Expression editor*

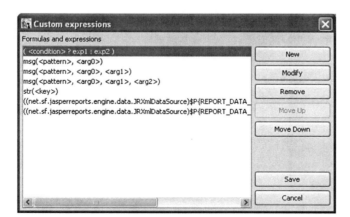

Figure 19-9. *Formulas list*

■ ■ ■

GNU General Public License

IReport is distributed based on the terms outlined in the GNU General Public License. Other license types are available if necessary.

The GNU General Public License

Version 2, June 1991

Copyright © 1989, 1991 Free Software Foundation, Inc., 675 Mass Ave, Cambridge, MA 02139, USA.

Everyone is permitted to copy and distribute verbatim copies of this license document, but changing it is not allowed.

Preamble

The licenses for most software are designed to take away your freedom to share and change it. By contrast, the GNU General Public License is intended to guarantee your freedom to share and change free software—to make sure the software is free for all its users. This General Public License applies to most of the Free Software Foundation's software and to any other program whose authors commit to using it. (Some other Free Software Foundation software is covered by the GNU Library General Public License instead.) You can apply it to your programs, too.

When we speak of free software, we are referring to freedom, not price. Our General Public Licenses are designed to make sure that you have the freedom to distribute copies of free software (and charge for this service if you wish), that you receive source code or can get it if you want it, that you can change the software or use pieces of it in new free programs; and that you know you can do these things.

To protect your rights, we need to make restrictions that forbid anyone to deny you these rights or to ask you to surrender the rights. These restrictions translate to certain responsibilities for you if you distribute copies of the software, or if you modify it.

For example, if you distribute copies of such a program, whether gratis or for a fee, you must give the recipients all the rights that you have. You must make sure that they, too, receive or can get the source code. And you must show them these terms so they know their rights.

We protect your rights with two steps: (1) copyright the software, and (2) offer you this license which gives you legal permission to copy, distribute and/or modify the software.

Also, for each author's protection and ours, we want to make certain that everyone understands that there is no warranty for this free software. If the software is modified by someone else and passed on, we want its recipients to know that what they have is not the original, so that any problems introduced by others will not reflect on the original authors' reputations.

Finally, any free program is threatened constantly by software patents. We wish to avoid the danger that redistributors of a free program will individually obtain patent licenses, in effect making the program proprietary. To prevent this, we have made it clear that any patent must be licensed for everyone's free use or not licensed at all.

The precise terms and conditions for copying, distribution and modification follow.

Terms and Conditions for Copying, Distribution, and Modification

This License applies to any program or other work which contains a notice placed by the copyright holder saying it may be distributed under the terms of this General Public License. The "Program", below, refers to any such program or work, and a "work based on the Program" means either the Program or any derivative work under copyright law: that is to say, a work containing the Program or a portion of it, either verbatim or with modifications and/or translated into another language. (Hereinafter, translation is included without limitation in the term "modification".) Each licensee is addressed as "you".

Activities other than copying, distribution and modification are not covered by this License; they are outside its scope. The act of running the Program is not restricted, and the output from the Program is covered only if its contents constitute a work based on the Program (independent of having been made by running the Program). Whether that is true depends on what the Program does.

You may copy and distribute verbatim copies of the Program's source code as you receive it, in any medium, provided that you conspicuously and appropriately publish on each copy an appropriate copyright notice and disclaimer of warranty; keep intact all the notices that refer to this License and to the absence of any warranty; and give any other recipients of the Program a copy of this License along with the Program.

You may charge a fee for the physical act of transferring a copy, and you may at your option offer warranty protection in exchange for a fee.

You may modify your copy or copies of the Program or any portion of it, thus forming a work based on the Program, and copy and distribute such modifications or work under the terms of Section 1 above, provided that you also meet all of these conditions:

You must cause the modified files to carry prominent notices stating that you changed the files and the date of any change.

You must cause any work that you distribute or publish, that in whole or in part contains or is derived from the Program or any part thereof, to be licensed as a whole at no charge to all third parties under the terms of this License.

If the modified program normally reads commands interactively when run, you must cause it, when started running for such interactive use in the most ordinary way, to print or display an announcement including an appropriate copyright notice and a notice that there is no warranty (or else, saying that you provide a warranty) and that users may redistribute the program under these conditions, and telling the user how to view a copy of this License. (Exception: if the Program itself is interactive but does not normally print such an announcement, your work based on the Program is not required to print an announcement.)

These requirements apply to the modified work as a whole. If identifiable sections of that work are not derived from the Program, and can be reasonably considered independent and separate works in themselves, then this License, and its terms, do not apply to those sections when you distribute them as separate works. But when you distribute the same sections as part of a whole which is a work based on the Program, the distribution of the whole must be on the terms of this License, whose permissions for other licensees extend to the entire whole, and thus to each and every part regardless of who wrote it.

Thus, it is not the intent of this section to claim rights or contest your rights to work written entirely by you; rather, the intent is to exercise the right to control the distribution of derivative or collective works based on the Program.

In addition, mere aggregation of another work not based on the Program with the Program (or with a work based on the Program) on a volume of a storage or distribution medium does not bring the other work under the scope of this License.

You may copy and distribute the Program (or a work based on it, under Section 2) in object code or executable form under the terms of Sections 1 and 2 above provided that you also do one of the following:

Accompany it with the complete corresponding machine-readable source code, which must be distributed under the terms of Sections 1 and 2 above on a medium customarily used for software interchange; or,

Accompany it with a written offer, valid for at least three years, to give any third party, for a charge no more than your cost of physically performing source distribution, a complete machine-readable copy of the corresponding source code, to be distributed under the terms of Sections 1 and 2 above on a medium customarily used for software interchange; or,

Accompany it with the information you received as to the offer to distribute corresponding source code. (This alternative is allowed only for noncommercial distribution and only if you received the program in object code or executable form with such an offer, in accord with Subsection b above.)

The source code for a work means the preferred form of the work for making modifications to it. For an executable work, complete source code means all the source code for all modules it contains, plus any associated interface definition files, plus the scripts used to control compilation and installation of the executable. However, as a special exception, the source code distributed need not include anything that is normally distributed (in either source or binary form) with the major components (compiler, kernel, and so on) of the operating system on which the executable runs, unless that component itself accompanies the executable.

If distribution of executable or object code is made by offering access to copy from a designated place, then offering equivalent access to copy the source code from the same place counts as distribution of the source code, even though third parties are not compelled to copy the source along with the object code.

You may not copy, modify, sublicense, or distribute the Program except as expressly provided under this License. Any attempt otherwise to copy, modify, sublicense or distribute the Program is void, and will automatically terminate your rights under this License. However, parties who have received copies, or rights, from you under this License will not have their licenses terminated so long as such parties remain in full compliance.

You are not required to accept this License, since you have not signed it. However, nothing else grants you permission to modify or distribute the Program or its derivative works. These actions are prohibited by law if you do not accept this License. Therefore, by modifying or distributing the Program (or any work based on the Program), you indicate your acceptance of this License to do so, and all its terms and conditions for copying, distributing or modifying the Program or works based on it.

Each time you redistribute the Program (or any work based on the Program), the recipient automatically receives a license from the original licensor to copy, distribute or modify the Program subject to these terms and conditions. You may not impose any further restrictions on the recipients' exercise of the rights granted herein. You are not responsible for enforcing compliance by third parties to this License.

If, as a consequence of a court judgment or allegation of patent infringement or for any other reason (not limited to patent issues), conditions are imposed on you (whether by court order, agreement or otherwise) that contradict the conditions of this License, they do not excuse you from the conditions of this License. If you cannot distribute so as to satisfy simultaneously your obligations under this License and any other pertinent obligations, then as a consequence you may not distribute the Program at all. For example, if a patent license would not permit royalty-free redistribution of the Program by all those who receive copies directly or indirectly through you, then the only way you could satisfy both it and this License would be to refrain entirely from distribution of the Program.

If any portion of this section is held invalid or unenforceable under any particular circumstance, the balance of the section is intended to apply and the section as a whole is intended to apply in other circumstances.

It is not the purpose of this section to induce you to infringe any patents or other property right claims or to contest validity of any such claims; this section has the sole purpose of protecting the integrity of the free software distribution system, which is implemented by public license practices. Many people have made generous contributions to the wide range of software distributed through that system in reliance on consistent application of that system; it is up to the author/donor to decide if he or she is willing to distribute software through any other system and a licensee cannot impose that choice.

This section is intended to make thoroughly clear what is believed to be a consequence of the rest of this License.

If the distribution and/or use of the Program is restricted in certain countries either by patents or by copyrighted interfaces, the original copyright holder who places the Program under this License may add an explicit geographical distribution limitation excluding those countries, so that distribution is permitted only in or among countries not thus excluded. In such case, this License incorporates the limitation as if written in the body of this License.

The Free Software Foundation may publish revised and/or new versions of the General Public License from time to time. Such new versions will be similar in spirit to the present version, but may differ in detail to address new problems or concerns.

Each version is given a distinguishing version number. If the Program specifies a version number of this License which applies to it and "any later version", you have the option of following the terms and conditions either of that version or of any later version published by the Free Software Foundation. If the Program does not specify a version number of this License, you may choose any version ever published by the Free Software Foundation.

If you wish to incorporate parts of the Program into other free programs whose distribution conditions are different, write to the author to ask for permission. For software which is copyrighted by the Free Software Foundation, write to the Free Software Foundation; we sometimes make exceptions for this. Our decision will be guided by the two goals of preserving the free status of all derivatives of our free software and of promoting the sharing and reuse of software generally.

NO WARRANTY

BECAUSE THE PROGRAM IS LICENSED FREE OF CHARGE, THERE IS NO WARRANTY FOR THE PROGRAM, TO THE EXTENT PERMITTED BY APPLICABLE LAW. EXCEPT WHEN OTHERWISE STATED IN WRITING THE COPYRIGHT HOLDERS AND/OR OTHER PARTIES PROVIDE THE PROGRAM "AS IS" WITHOUT WARRANTY OF ANY KIND, EITHER EXPRESSED OR IMPLIED, INCLUDING, BUT NOT LIMITED TO, THE IMPLIED WARRANTIES OF MERCHANTABILITY AND FITNESS FOR A PARTICULAR PURPOSE. THE ENTIRE RISK AS TO THE QUALITY AND PERFORMANCE OF THE PROGRAM IS WITH YOU. SHOULD THE PROGRAM PROVE DEFECTIVE, YOU ASSUME THE COST OF ALL NECESSARY SERVICING, REPAIR OR CORRECTION.

IN NO EVENT UNLESS REQUIRED BY APPLICABLE LAW OR AGREED TO IN WRITING WILL ANY COPYRIGHT HOLDER, OR ANY OTHER PARTY WHO MAY MODIFY AND/OR REDISTRIBUTE THE PROGRAM AS PERMITTED ABOVE, BE LIABLE TO YOU FOR DAMAGES, INCLUDING ANY GENERAL, SPECIAL, INCIDENTAL OR CONSEQUENTIAL DAMAGES ARISING OUT OF THE USE

OR INABILITY TO USE THE PROGRAM (INCLUDING BUT NOT LIMITED TO LOSS OF DATA OR DATA BEING RENDERED INACCURATE OR LOSSES SUSTAINED BY YOU OR THIRD PARTIES OR A FAILURE OF THE PROGRAM TO OPERATE WITH ANY OTHER PROGRAMS), EVEN IF SUCH HOLDER OR OTHER PARTY HAS BEEN ADVISED OF THE POSSIBILITY OF SUCH DAMAGES.
END OF TERMS AND CONDITIONS

Appendix: How to Apply These Terms to Your New Programs

If you develop a new program, and you want it to be of the greatest possible use to the public, the best way to achieve this is to make it free software which everyone can redistribute and change under these terms.

To do so, attach the following notices to the program. It is safest to attach them to the start of each source file to most effectively convey the exclusion of warranty; and each file should have at least the "copyright" line and a pointer to where the full notice is found.

> (one line to give the program's name and a brief idea of what it does.) Copyright (C) 19yy (name of author)

> This program is free software; you can redistribute it and/or modify it under the terms of the GNU General Public License as published by the Free Software Foundation; either version 2 of the License, or (at your option) any later version.

> This program is distributed in the hope that it will be useful, but WITHOUT ANY WARRANTY; without even the implied warranty of MERCHANTABILITY or FITNESS FOR A PARTICULAR PURPOSE. See the GNU General Public License for more details.

> You should have received a copy of the GNU General Public License along with this program; if not, write to the Free Software Foundation, Inc., 675 Mass Ave, Cambridge, MA 02139, USA.

Also add information on how to contact you by electronic and paper mail.

If the program is interactive, make it output a short notice like this when it starts in an interactive mode:

> Gnomovision version 69, Copyright (C) 19yy name of author Gnomovision comes with ABSOLUTELY NO WARRANTY; for details type 'show w'. This is free software, and you are welcome to redistribute it under certain conditions; type 'show c' for details.

The hypothetical commands 'show w' and 'show c' should show the appropriate parts of the General Public License. Of course, the commands you use may be called something other than 'show w' and 'show c'; they could even be mouse-clicks or menu items—whatever suits your program.

You should also get your employer (if you work as a programmer) or your school, if any, to sign a "copyright disclaimer" for the program, if necessary. Here is a sample; alter the names:

> Yoyodyne, Inc., hereby disclaims all copyright interest in the program 'Gnomovision' (which makes passes at compilers) written by James Hacker.

> (signature of Ty Coon), 1 April 1989

> Ty Coon, President of Vice

This General Public License does not permit incorporating your program into proprietary programs. If your program is a subroutine library, you may consider it more useful to permit linking proprietary applications with the library. If this is what you want to do, use the GNU Library General Public License instead of this License.

DTD Definitions

jaspereport.dtd (v.1.3.4)

```
<?xml version="1.0" encoding="UTF-8"?>
<!ELEMENT jasperReport (property*, import*, reportFont*, style*, subDataset*,
parameter*, queryString?, field*, sortField*, variable*, filterExpression?,
group*, background?, title?, pageHeader?, columnHeader?, detail?, columnFooter?,
pageFooter?, lastPageFooter?, summary?)>
<!ATTLIST jasperReport
    name CDATA #REQUIRED
    language CDATA "java"
    columnCount NMTOKEN "1"
    printOrder (Vertical | Horizontal) "Vertical"
    pageWidth NMTOKEN "595"
    pageHeight NMTOKEN "842"
    orientation (Portrait | Landscape) "Portrait"
    whenNoDataType (NoPages | BlankPage | AllSectionsNoDetail) "NoPages"
    columnWidth NMTOKEN "555"
    columnSpacing NMTOKEN "0"
    leftMargin NMTOKEN "20"
    rightMargin NMTOKEN "20"
    topMargin NMTOKEN "30"
    bottomMargin NMTOKEN "30"
    isTitleNewPage (true | false) "false"
    isSummaryNewPage (true | false) "false"
    isFloatColumnFooter (true | false) "false"
    scriptletClass CDATA #IMPLIED
    resourceBundle CDATA #IMPLIED
    whenResourceMissingType (Null | Empty | Key | Error) "Null"
    isIgnorePagination (true | false) "false"
    formatFactoryClass CDATA #IMPLIED
>

<!ELEMENT property EMPTY>
<!ATTLIST property
    name CDATA #REQUIRED
    value CDATA #IMPLIED
>

<!ELEMENT import EMPTY>
<!ATTLIST import
    value CDATA #REQUIRED
>
```

```
<!ELEMENT reportFont EMPTY>
<!ATTLIST reportFont
    name CDATA #REQUIRED
    isDefault (true | false) "false"
    fontName CDATA #IMPLIED
    size NMTOKEN #IMPLIED
    isBold (true | false) #IMPLIED
    isItalic (true | false) #IMPLIED
    isUnderline (true | false) #IMPLIED
    isStrikeThrough (true | false) #IMPLIED
    pdfFontName CDATA #IMPLIED
    pdfEncoding CDATA #IMPLIED
    isPdfEmbedded (true | false) #IMPLIED
>

<!ELEMENT style (conditionalStyle*)>
<!ATTLIST style
    name CDATA #IMPLIED
    isDefault (true | false) "false"
    style CDATA #IMPLIED
    mode (Opaque | Transparent) #IMPLIED
    forecolor CDATA #IMPLIED
    backcolor CDATA #IMPLIED
    pen (None | Thin | 1Point | 2Point | 4Point | Dotted) #IMPLIED
    fill (Solid) #IMPLIED
    radius NMTOKEN #IMPLIED
    scaleImage (Clip | FillFrame | RetainShape) #IMPLIED
    hAlign (Left | Center | Right | Justified) #IMPLIED
    vAlign (Top | Middle | Bottom) #IMPLIED
    border (None | Thin | 1Point | 2Point | 4Point | Dotted) #IMPLIED
    borderColor CDATA #IMPLIED
    padding NMTOKEN #IMPLIED
    topBorder (None | Thin | 1Point | 2Point | 4Point | Dotted) #IMPLIED
    topBorderColor CDATA #IMPLIED
    topPadding NMTOKEN #IMPLIED
    leftBorder (None | Thin | 1Point | 2Point | 4Point | Dotted) #IMPLIED
    leftBorderColor CDATA #IMPLIED
    leftPadding NMTOKEN #IMPLIED
    bottomBorder (None | Thin | 1Point | 2Point | 4Point | Dotted) #IMPLIED
    bottomBorderColor CDATA #IMPLIED
    bottomPadding NMTOKEN #IMPLIED
    rightBorder (None | Thin | 1Point | 2Point | 4Point | Dotted) #IMPLIED
    rightBorderColor CDATA #IMPLIED
    rightPadding NMTOKEN #IMPLIED
    rotation (None | Left | Right | UpsideDown) #IMPLIED
    lineSpacing (Single | 1_1_2 | Double) #IMPLIED
    isStyledText (true | false) #IMPLIED
    fontName CDATA #IMPLIED
    fontSize NMTOKEN #IMPLIED
    isBold (true | false) #IMPLIED
    isItalic (true | false) #IMPLIED
    isUnderline (true | false) #IMPLIED
    isStrikeThrough (true | false) #IMPLIED
    pdfFontName CDATA #IMPLIED
    pdfEncoding CDATA #IMPLIED
    isPdfEmbedded (true | false) #IMPLIED
```

```
      pattern CDATA #IMPLIED
      isBlankWhenNull (true | false) #IMPLIED
>


<!ELEMENT conditionalStyle (conditionExpression?, style)>

<!ELEMENT conditionExpression (#PCDATA)>

<!ELEMENT subDataset (property*, parameter*, queryString?, field*, sortField*,
variable*, filterExpression?, group*)>
<!ATTLIST subDataset
      name CDATA #REQUIRED
      scriptletClass CDATA #IMPLIED
      resourceBundle CDATA #IMPLIED
      whenResourceMissingType (Null | Empty | Key | Error) "Null"
>

<!ELEMENT parameter (property*, parameterDescription?, defaultValueExpression?)>
<!ATTLIST parameter
      name CDATA #REQUIRED
      class CDATA "java.lang.String"
      isForPrompting (true | false) "true"
>
<!ELEMENT parameterDescription (#PCDATA)>
<!ELEMENT defaultValueExpression (#PCDATA)>

<!ELEMENT queryString (#PCDATA)>
<!ATTLIST queryString
      language CDATA "sql"
>

<!ELEMENT field (property*, fieldDescription?)>
<!ATTLIST field
      name CDATA #REQUIRED
      class CDATA "java.lang.String"
>
<!ELEMENT fieldDescription (#PCDATA)>

<!ELEMENT sortField EMPTY>
<!ATTLIST sortField
      name CDATA #REQUIRED
      order (Ascending | Descending) "Ascending"
>

<!ELEMENT variable (variableExpression?, initialValueExpression?)>
<!ATTLIST variable
      name CDATA #REQUIRED
      class CDATA "java.lang.String"
      resetType (None | Report | Page | Column | Group) "Report"
      resetGroup CDATA #IMPLIED
      incrementType (None | Report | Page | Column | Group) "None"
      incrementGroup CDATA #IMPLIED
      calculation (Nothing | Count | DistinctCount | Sum | Average | Lowest |
      Highest | StandardDeviation | Variance | System | First) "Nothing"
      incrementerFactoryClass CDATA #IMPLIED
>
```

```
<!ELEMENT variableExpression (#PCDATA)>
<!ELEMENT initialValueExpression (#PCDATA)>

<!ELEMENT filterExpression (#PCDATA)>

<!ELEMENT group (groupExpression?, groupHeader?, groupFooter?)>
<!ATTLIST group
    name CDATA #REQUIRED
    isStartNewColumn (true | false) "false"
    isStartNewPage (true | false) "false"
    isResetPageNumber (true | false) "false"
    isReprintHeaderOnEachPage (true | false) "false"
    minHeightToStartNewPage NMTOKEN "0"
>
<!ELEMENT groupExpression (#PCDATA)>
<!ELEMENT groupHeader (band?)>
<!ELEMENT groupFooter (band?)>

<!ELEMENT background (band?)>
<!ELEMENT title (band?)>
<!ELEMENT pageHeader (band?)>
<!ELEMENT columnHeader (band?)>
<!ELEMENT detail (band?)>
<!ELEMENT columnFooter (band?)>
<!ELEMENT pageFooter (band?)>
<!ELEMENT lastPageFooter (band?)>
<!ELEMENT summary (band?)>

<!ELEMENT band (printWhenExpression?, (break | line | rectangle | ellipse |
image | staticText | textField | subreport | pieChart | pie3DChart | barChart |
bar3DChart | xyBarChart | stackedBarChart | stackedBar3DChart| lineChart |
xyLineChart | areaChart | xyAreaChart | scatterChart | bubbleChart |
timeSeriesChart | highLowChart | candlestickChart | meterChart | thermometerChart |
multiAxisChart | stackedAreaChart | elementGroup | crosstab | frame)*)>
<!ATTLIST band
    height NMTOKEN "0"
    isSplitAllowed (true | false) "true"
>

<!ELEMENT break (reportElement)>
<!ATTLIST break
    type (Page | Column) "Page"
>

<!ELEMENT line (reportElement, graphicElement?)>
<!ATTLIST line
    direction (TopDown | BottomUp) "TopDown"
>

<!ELEMENT reportElement (printWhenExpression?)>
<!ATTLIST reportElement
    key CDATA #IMPLIED
    style CDATA #IMPLIED
    positionType (Float | FixRelativeToTop |
        FixRelativeToBottom) "FixRelativeToTop"
```

```
        stretchType (NoStretch | RelativeToTallestObject |
            RelativeToBandHeight) "NoStretch"
        isPrintRepeatedValues (true | false) "true"
        mode (Opaque | Transparent) #IMPLIED
        x NMTOKEN #REQUIRED
        y NMTOKEN #REQUIRED
        width NMTOKEN #REQUIRED
        height NMTOKEN #REQUIRED
        isRemoveLineWhenBlank (true | false) "false"
        isPrintInFirstWholeBand (true | false) "false"
        isPrintWhenDetailOverflows (true | false) "false"
        printWhenGroupChanges CDATA #IMPLIED
        forecolor CDATA #IMPLIED
        backcolor CDATA #IMPLIED
>
<!ELEMENT printWhenExpression (#PCDATA)>

<!ELEMENT graphicElement EMPTY>
<!ATTLIST graphicElement
        stretchType (NoStretch | RelativeToTallestObject |
            RelativeToBandHeight) #IMPLIED
        pen (None | Thin | 1Point | 2Point | 4Point | Dotted) #IMPLIED
        fill (Solid) #IMPLIED
>

<!ELEMENT rectangle (reportElement, graphicElement?)>
<!ATTLIST rectangle
        radius NMTOKEN #IMPLIED
>

<!ELEMENT ellipse (reportElement, graphicElement?)>

<!ELEMENT image (reportElement, box?, graphicElement?, imageExpression?,
anchorNameExpression?, hyperlinkReferenceExpression?,
hyperlinkAnchorExpression?, hyperlinkPageExpression?,
hyperlinkTooltipExpression?, hyperlinkParameter*)>
<!ATTLIST image
        scaleImage (Clip | FillFrame | RetainShape) #IMPLIED
        hAlign (Left | Center | Right) #IMPLIED
        vAlign (Top | Middle | Bottom) #IMPLIED
        isUsingCache (true | false) #IMPLIED
        isLazy (true | false) "false"
        onErrorType (Error | Blank | Icon) "Error"
        evaluationTime (Now | Report | Page | Column | Group | Band | Auto) "Now"
        evaluationGroup CDATA #IMPLIED
        hyperlinkType CDATA "None"
        hyperlinkTarget (Self | Blank) "Self"
        bookmarkLevel NMTOKEN "0"
>
<!ELEMENT imageExpression (#PCDATA)>
<!ATTLIST imageExpression
        class (java.lang.String | java.io.File | java.net.URL |
        java.io.InputStream | java.awt.Image |
        net.sf.jasperreports.engine.JRRenderable) "java.lang.String"
>
```

```
<!ELEMENT box EMPTY>
<!ATTLIST box
    border (None | Thin | 1Point | 2Point | 4Point | Dotted) #IMPLIED
    borderColor CDATA #IMPLIED
    padding NMTOKEN #IMPLIED
    topBorder (None | Thin | 1Point | 2Point | 4Point | Dotted) #IMPLIED
    topBorderColor CDATA #IMPLIED
    topPadding NMTOKEN #IMPLIED
    leftBorder (None | Thin | 1Point | 2Point | 4Point | Dotted) #IMPLIED
    leftBorderColor CDATA #IMPLIED
    leftPadding NMTOKEN #IMPLIED
    bottomBorder (None | Thin | 1Point | 2Point | 4Point | Dotted) #IMPLIED
    bottomBorderColor CDATA #IMPLIED
    bottomPadding NMTOKEN #IMPLIED
    rightBorder (None | Thin | 1Point | 2Point | 4Point | Dotted) #IMPLIED
    rightBorderColor CDATA #IMPLIED
    rightPadding NMTOKEN #IMPLIED
>

<!ELEMENT anchorNameExpression (#PCDATA)>
<!ELEMENT hyperlinkReferenceExpression (#PCDATA)>
<!ELEMENT hyperlinkAnchorExpression (#PCDATA)>
<!ELEMENT hyperlinkPageExpression (#PCDATA)>
<!ELEMENT hyperlinkTooltipExpression (#PCDATA)>

<!ELEMENT hyperlinkParameter (hyperlinkParameterExpression)>
<!ATTLIST hyperlinkParameter
    name CDATA #REQUIRED
>

<!ELEMENT hyperlinkParameterExpression (#PCDATA)>
<!ATTLIST hyperlinkParameterExpression
    class CDATA "java.lang.String"
>


<!ELEMENT staticText (reportElement, box?, textElement?, text?)>
<!ELEMENT text (#PCDATA)>

<!ELEMENT textElement (font?)>
<!ATTLIST textElement
    textAlignment (Left | Center | Right | Justified) #IMPLIED
    verticalAlignment (Top | Middle | Bottom) #IMPLIED
    rotation (None | Left | Right | UpsideDown) #IMPLIED
    lineSpacing (Single | 1_1_2 | Double) #IMPLIED
    isStyledText (true | false) #IMPLIED
>

<!ELEMENT font EMPTY>
<!ATTLIST font
    reportFont CDATA #IMPLIED
    fontName CDATA #IMPLIED
    size NMTOKEN #IMPLIED
    isBold (true | false) #IMPLIED
    isItalic (true | false) #IMPLIED
```

```
        isUnderline (true | false) #IMPLIED
        isStrikeThrough (true | false) #IMPLIED
        pdfFontName CDATA #IMPLIED
        pdfEncoding CDATA #IMPLIED
        isPdfEmbedded (true | false) #IMPLIED
>


<!ELEMENT textField (reportElement, box?, textElement?, textFieldExpression?,
anchorNameExpression?, hyperlinkReferenceExpression?,
hyperlinkAnchorExpression?, hyperlinkPageExpression?,
hyperlinkTooltipExpression?, hyperlinkParameter*)>
<!ATTLIST textField
        isStretchWithOverflow (true | false) "false"
        evaluationTime (Now | Report | Page | Column | Group | Band | Auto) "Now"
        evaluationGroup CDATA #IMPLIED
        pattern CDATA #IMPLIED
        isBlankWhenNull (true | false) #IMPLIED
        hyperlinkType CDATA "None"
        hyperlinkTarget (Self | Blank) "Self"
        bookmarkLevel NMTOKEN "0"
>
<!ELEMENT textFieldExpression (#PCDATA)>
<!ATTLIST textFieldExpression
        class (java.lang.Boolean | java.lang.Byte | java.util.Date |
        java.sql.Timestamp | java.sql.Time | java.lang.Double | java.lang.Float |
        java.lang.Integer | java.lang.Long | java.lang.Short |
        java.math.BigDecimal | java.lang.Number |
        java.lang.String) "java.lang.String"
>


<!ELEMENT subreport (reportElement, parametersMapExpression?,
subreportParameter*, (connectionExpression | dataSourceExpression)?,
returnValue*, subreportExpression?)>
<!ATTLIST subreport
        isUsingCache (true | false) #IMPLIED
>
<!ELEMENT parametersMapExpression (#PCDATA)>
<!ELEMENT subreportParameter (subreportParameterExpression?)>
<!ATTLIST subreportParameter
        name CDATA #REQUIRED
>
<!ELEMENT subreportParameterExpression (#PCDATA)>

<!ELEMENT returnValue EMPTY>
<!ATTLIST returnValue
        subreportVariable CDATA #IMPLIED
        toVariable CDATA #IMPLIED
        calculation (Nothing | Count | DistinctCount | Sum | Average | Lowest |
        Highest | StandardDeviation | Variance | First) "Nothing"
        incrementerFactoryClass CDATA #IMPLIED
>

<!ELEMENT connectionExpression (#PCDATA)>
<!ELEMENT dataSourceExpression (#PCDATA)>
<!ELEMENT subreportExpression (#PCDATA)>
```

```
<!ATTLIST subreportExpression
    class (java.lang.String | java.io.File | java.net.URL |
    java.io.InputStream | net.sf.jasperreports.engine.JasperReport |
    dori.jasper.engine.JasperReport) "java.lang.String"
>

<!ELEMENT elementGroup (break | line | rectangle | ellipse | image |
staticText | textField | subreport | pieChart | pie3DChart | barChart |
bar3DChart | xyBarChart | stackedBarChart | stackedBar3DChart| lineChart |
xyLineChart | areaChart | xyAreaChart | scatterChart | bubbleChart |
timeSeriesChart | highLowChart | candlestickChart | meterChart |
thermometerChart | multiAxisChart | stackedAreaChart | elementGroup |
crosstab | frame)*>

<!ELEMENT chart (reportElement, box?, chartTitle?, chartSubtitle?, chartLegend?,
anchorNameExpression?, hyperlinkReferenceExpression?,
hyperlinkAnchorExpression?, hyperlinkPageExpression?,
hyperlinkTooltipExpression?, hyperlinkParameter*)>
<!ATTLIST chart
    isShowLegend (true | false) "true"
    evaluationTime (Now | Report | Page | Column | Group | Band) "Now"
    evaluationGroup CDATA #IMPLIED
    hyperlinkType CDATA "None"
    hyperlinkTarget (Self | Blank) "Self"
    bookmarkLevel NMTOKEN "0"
    customizerClass CDATA #IMPLIED
>
<!ELEMENT chartTitle (font?, titleExpression?)>
<!ATTLIST chartTitle
    position (Top | Bottom | Left | Right) "Top"
    color CDATA #IMPLIED
>
<!ELEMENT titleExpression (#PCDATA)>
<!ELEMENT chartSubtitle (font?, subtitleExpression?)>
<!ATTLIST chartSubtitle
    color CDATA #IMPLIED
>
<!ELEMENT subtitleExpression (#PCDATA)>
<!ELEMENT chartLegend (font?)>
<!ATTLIST chartLegend
    textColor CDATA #IMPLIED
    backgroundColor CDATA #IMPLIED
>

<!ELEMENT pieChart (chart, pieDataset, piePlot)>
<!ELEMENT pieDataset (dataset?, keyExpression?, valueExpression?,
labelExpression?, sectionHyperlink?)>
<!ELEMENT keyExpression (#PCDATA)>
<!ELEMENT valueExpression (#PCDATA)>
<!ELEMENT labelExpression (#PCDATA)>

<!ELEMENT sectionHyperlink (hyperlinkReferenceExpression?,
hyperlinkAnchorExpression?, hyperlinkPageExpression?,
hyperlinkTooltipExpression?, hyperlinkParameter*)>
<!ATTLIST sectionHyperlink
    hyperlinkType CDATA "None"
```

```
        hyperlinkTarget (Self | Blank) "Self"
>


<!ELEMENT piePlot (plot)>

<!ELEMENT dataset (incrementWhenExpression?, datasetRun?)>
<!ATTLIST dataset
    resetType (None | Report | Page | Column | Group) "Report"
    resetGroup CDATA #IMPLIED
    incrementType (None | Report | Page | Column | Group) "None"
    incrementGroup CDATA #IMPLIED
>


<!ELEMENT incrementWhenExpression (#PCDATA)>

<!ELEMENT datasetRun (parametersMapExpression?, datasetParameter*,
(connectionExpression | dataSourceExpression)?)>
<!ATTLIST datasetRun
    subDataset CDATA #REQUIRED
>


<!ELEMENT datasetParameter (datasetParameterExpression?)>
<!ATTLIST datasetParameter
    name CDATA #REQUIRED
>


<!ELEMENT datasetParameterExpression (#PCDATA)>

<!ELEMENT plot (seriesColor*) >
<!ATTLIST plot
    backcolor CDATA #IMPLIED
    orientation (Horizontal | Vertical) "Vertical"
    backgroundAlpha NMTOKEN "1"
    foregroundAlpha NMTOKEN "1"
    labelRotation CDATA "0.0"
>


<!ELEMENT seriesColor EMPTY>
<!ATTLIST seriesColor
    seriesOrder CDATA #REQUIRED
    color CDATA #REQUIRED
>


<!ELEMENT pie3DChart (chart, pieDataset, pie3DPlot)>
<!ELEMENT pie3DPlot (plot)>
<!ATTLIST pie3DPlot
    depthFactor CDATA "0.2"
>


<!ELEMENT barChart (chart, categoryDataset, barPlot)>
<!ELEMENT categoryDataset (dataset?, categorySeries*)>
<!ELEMENT categorySeries (seriesExpression?, categoryExpression?,
valueExpression?, labelExpression?, itemHyperlink?)>
<!ELEMENT seriesExpression (#PCDATA)>
<!ELEMENT categoryExpression (#PCDATA)>
```

```
<!ELEMENT itemHyperlink (hyperlinkReferenceExpression?,
hyperlinkAnchorExpression?, hyperlinkPageExpression?,
hyperlinkTooltipExpression?, hyperlinkParameter*)>
<!ATTLIST itemHyperlink
    hyperlinkType CDATA "None"
    hyperlinkTarget (Self | Blank) "Self"
>

<!ELEMENT barPlot (plot, categoryAxisLabelExpression?, categoryAxisFormat?,
valueAxisLabelExpression?, valueAxisFormat?)>
<!ATTLIST barPlot
    isShowLabels (true | false ) "false"
    isShowTickMarks (true | false) "true"
    isShowTickLabels (true | false) "true"
>
<!ELEMENT categoryAxisLabelExpression (#PCDATA)>
<!ELEMENT valueAxisLabelExpression (#PCDATA)>
<!ELEMENT categoryAxisFormat (axisFormat)>
<!ELEMENT valueAxisFormat (axisFormat)>

<!ELEMENT axisFormat (labelFont?, tickLabelFont?)>
<!ATTLIST axisFormat
    labelColor CDATA #IMPLIED
    tickLabelColor CDATA #IMPLIED
    tickLabelMask CDATA #IMPLIED
    axisLineColor CDATA #IMPLIED
>
<!ELEMENT labelFont (font?)>
<!ELEMENT tickLabelFont (font?)>

<!ELEMENT bar3DChart (chart, categoryDataset, bar3DPlot)>
<!ELEMENT bar3DPlot (plot, categoryAxisLabelExpression?, categoryAxisFormat?,
valueAxisLabelExpression?, valueAxisFormat?)>
<!ATTLIST bar3DPlot
    isShowLabels (true | false ) "false"
    xOffset CDATA #IMPLIED
    yOffset CDATA #IMPLIED
>

<!ELEMENT xyBarChart (chart, (timePeriodDataset | timeSeriesDataset |
xyDataset ), barPlot)>

<!ELEMENT timePeriodDataset (dataset?, timePeriodSeries*)>
<!ELEMENT timePeriodSeries (seriesExpression?, startDateExpression?,
endDateExpression?, valueExpression?, labelExpression?, itemHyperlink?)>
<!ELEMENT startDateExpression (#PCDATA)>
<!ELEMENT endDateExpression (#PCDATA)>

<!ELEMENT stackedBarChart (chart, categoryDataset, barPlot)>
<!ELEMENT stackedAreaChart (chart, categoryDataset, areaPlot)>

<!ELEMENT stackedBar3DChart (chart, categoryDataset, bar3DPlot)>

<!ELEMENT lineChart (chart, categoryDataset, linePlot)>
<!ELEMENT linePlot (plot, categoryAxisLabelExpression?, categoryAxisFormat?,
valueAxisLabelExpression?, valueAxisFormat?)>
```

```
<!ATTLIST linePlot
    isShowLines (true | false) "true"
    isShowShapes (true | false) "true"
>

<!ELEMENT xyLineChart (chart, xyDataset, linePlot)>
<!ELEMENT xyDataset (dataset?, xySeries*)>
<!ELEMENT xySeries (seriesExpression?, xValueExpression?, yValueExpression?,
labelExpression?, itemHyperlink?)>
<!ELEMENT xValueExpression (#PCDATA)>
<!ELEMENT yValueExpression (#PCDATA)>

<!ELEMENT areaChart (chart, categoryDataset, areaPlot)>
<!ELEMENT areaPlot (plot, categoryAxisLabelExpression?, categoryAxisFormat?,
valueAxisLabelExpression?, valueAxisFormat?)>

<!ELEMENT xyAreaChart (chart, xyDataset, areaPlot)>

<!ELEMENT scatterChart (chart, xyDataset, scatterPlot)>
<!ELEMENT scatterPlot (plot, xAxisLabelExpression?, xAxisFormat?,
yAxisLabelExpression?, yAxisFormat?)>
<!ATTLIST scatterPlot
    isShowLines (true | false) "true"
    isShowShapes (true | false) "true"
>
<!ELEMENT xAxisLabelExpression (#PCDATA)>
<!ELEMENT yAxisLabelExpression (#PCDATA)>
<!ELEMENT xAxisFormat (axisFormat)>
<!ELEMENT yAxisFormat (axisFormat)>

<!ELEMENT bubbleChart (chart, xyzDataset, bubblePlot)>
<!ELEMENT xyzDataset (dataset?, xyzSeries*)>
<!ELEMENT xyzSeries (seriesExpression?, xValueExpression?, yValueExpression?,
zValueExpression?, itemHyperlink?)>
<!ELEMENT bubblePlot (plot, xAxisLabelExpression?, xAxisFormat?,
yAxisLabelExpression?, yAxisFormat?)>
<!ATTLIST bubblePlot
    scaleType (BothAxes | DomainAxis | RangeAxis) "RangeAxis"
>
<!ELEMENT zValueExpression (#PCDATA)>

<!ELEMENT timeSeriesDataset (dataset?, timeSeries*)>
<!ATTLIST timeSeriesDataset
    timePeriod (Year | Quarter | Month | Week | Day | Hour | Minute | Second |
    Milisecond ) "Day"
>
<!ELEMENT timeSeries (seriesExpression?, timePeriodExpression?,
valueExpression?, labelExpression?, itemHyperlink?)>
<!ELEMENT timePeriodExpression (#PCDATA)>

<!ELEMENT timeSeriesChart (chart, timeSeriesDataset, timeSeriesPlot)>
<!ELEMENT timeSeriesPlot (plot, timeAxisLabelExpression?, timeAxisFormat?,
valueAxisLabelExpression?, valueAxisFormat?)>
<!ATTLIST timeSeriesPlot
    isShowLines (true | false) "true"
    isShowShapes (true | false) "true"
>
```

```
<!ELEMENT timeAxisLabelExpression (#PCDATA)>
<!ELEMENT timeAxisFormat (axisFormat)>

<!ELEMENT highLowChart (chart, highLowDataset, highLowPlot)>
<!ELEMENT highLowDataset (dataset?, seriesExpression?, dateExpression?,
highExpression?, lowExpression?, openExpression?, closeExpression?,
volumeExpression?, itemHyperlink?)>
<!ELEMENT highLowPlot (plot, timeAxisLabelExpression?, timeAxisFormat?,
valueAxisLabelExpression?, valueAxisFormat?)>
<!ATTLIST highLowPlot
    isShowCloseTicks (true | false) "true"
    isShowOpenTicks (true | false) "true"
>
<!ELEMENT dateExpression (#PCDATA)>
<!ELEMENT highExpression (#PCDATA)>
<!ELEMENT lowExpression (#PCDATA)>
<!ELEMENT openExpression (#PCDATA)>
<!ELEMENT closeExpression (#PCDATA)>
<!ELEMENT volumeExpression (#PCDATA)>

<!ELEMENT candlestickChart (chart, highLowDataset, candlestickPlot)>
<!ELEMENT candlestickPlot (plot, timeAxisLabelExpression?, timeAxisFormat?,
valueAxisLabelExpression?, valueAxisFormat?)>
<!ATTLIST candlestickPlot
    isShowVolume (true | false) "true"
>

<!ELEMENT meterChart (chart, valueDataset, meterPlot)>
<!ELEMENT valueDataset (dataset?, valueExpression )>
<!ELEMENT meterPlot (plot, valueDisplay?, dataRange, meterInterval*)>
<!ATTLIST meterPlot
    shape (chord | circle | pie) "pie"
    angle CDATA "180"
    units CDATA #IMPLIED
    tickInterval CDATA "10.0"
    meterColor CDATA #IMPLIED
    needleColor CDATA #IMPLIED
    tickColor CDATA #IMPLIED
>

<!ELEMENT valueDisplay (font?)>
<!ATTLIST valueDisplay
    color CDATA #IMPLIED
    mask CDATA #IMPLIED
>

<!ELEMENT dataRange (lowExpression, highExpression)>

<!ELEMENT meterInterval (dataRange)>
<!ATTLIST meterInterval
    label CDATA #IMPLIED
    color CDATA #IMPLIED
    alpha CDATA "1.0"
>
```

```
<!ELEMENT thermometerChart (chart, valueDataset, thermometerPlot)>
<!ELEMENT thermometerPlot (plot, valueDisplay?, dataRange, lowRange?,
mediumRange?, highRange?)>
<!ATTLIST thermometerPlot
    valueLocation ( none | left | right | bulb ) "bulb"
    isShowValueLines ( true | false) "false"
    mercuryColor CDATA #IMPLIED
>


<!ELEMENT lowRange (dataRange)>
<!ELEMENT mediumRange (dataRange)>
<!ELEMENT highRange (dataRange)>


<!ELEMENT multiAxisChart (chart, multiAxisPlot)>
<!ELEMENT multiAxisPlot (plot, axis+)>
<!ELEMENT axis (barChart | bar3DChart | xyBarChart | stackedBarChart |
stackedBar3DChart| lineChart | xyLineChart | areaChart | xyAreaChart |
scatterChart | bubbleChart | timeSeriesChart | highLowChart | candlestickChart
| stackedAreaChart)>
<!ATTLIST axis
    position (leftOrTop | rightOrBottom) "leftOrTop"
>


<!ELEMENT crosstab (reportElement, crosstabParameter*, parametersMapExpression?,
crosstabDataset?, crosstabHeaderCell?, rowGroup*, columnGroup*, measure*,
crosstabCell*, whenNoDataCell?)>
<!ATTLIST crosstab
    isRepeatColumnHeaders (true | false) "true"
    isRepeatRowHeaders (true | false) "true"
    columnBreakOffset NMTOKEN "10"
    runDirection (LTR | RTL) "LTR"
>


<!ELEMENT crosstabParameter (parameterValueExpression?)>
<!ATTLIST crosstabParameter
    name CDATA #REQUIRED
    class CDATA "java.lang.String"
>


<!ELEMENT parameterValueExpression (#PCDATA)>

<!ELEMENT crosstabDataset (dataset?)>
<!ATTLIST crosstabDataset
    isDataPreSorted (true | false) "false"
>


<!ELEMENT crosstabHeaderCell (cellContents)>

<!ELEMENT rowGroup (bucket, crosstabRowHeader?, crosstabTotalRowHeader?)>
<!ATTLIST rowGroup
    name CDATA #REQUIRED
    width NMTOKEN #REQUIRED
    totalPosition (Start | End | None) "None"
    headerPosition (Top | Middle | Bottom | Stretch) "Top"
>
```

```
<!ELEMENT crosstabRowHeader (cellContents?)>

<!ELEMENT crosstabTotalRowHeader (cellContents?)>

<!ELEMENT columnGroup (bucket, crosstabColumnHeader?,
crosstabTotalColumnHeader?)>
<!ATTLIST columnGroup
    name CDATA #REQUIRED
    height NMTOKEN #REQUIRED
    totalPosition (Start | End | None) "None"
    headerPosition (Left | Center | Right | Stretch) "Left"
>

<!ELEMENT crosstabColumnHeader (cellContents?)>

<!ELEMENT crosstabTotalColumnHeader (cellContents?)>

<!ELEMENT bucket (bucketExpression?, comparatorExpression?)>
<!ATTLIST bucket
    order (Ascending | Descending) "Ascending"
>

<!ELEMENT bucketExpression (#PCDATA)>
<!ATTLIST bucketExpression
    class CDATA #REQUIRED
>

<!ELEMENT comparatorExpression (#PCDATA)>

<!ELEMENT measure (measureExpression?)>
<!ATTLIST measure
    name CDATA #REQUIRED
    class CDATA #IMPLIED
    calculation (Nothing | Count | DistinctCount | Sum | Average | Lowest |
    Highest | StandardDeviation | Variance | First) "Nothing"
    incrementerFactoryClass CDATA #IMPLIED
    percentageOf (None | GrandTotal) "None"
    percentageCalculatorClass CDATA #IMPLIED
>

<!ELEMENT measureExpression (#PCDATA)>

<!ELEMENT crosstabCell (cellContents?)>
<!ATTLIST crosstabCell
    width NMTOKEN #IMPLIED
    height NMTOKEN #IMPLIED
    rowTotalGroup CDATA #IMPLIED
    columnTotalGroup CDATA #IMPLIED
>

<!ELEMENT cellContents (box?, (line | rectangle | ellipse | image |
staticText | textField | elementGroup | frame)*)>
<!ATTLIST cellContents
    backcolor CDATA #IMPLIED
    mode (Opaque | Transparent) #IMPLIED
    style CDATA #IMPLIED
>
```

```
<!ELEMENT whenNoDataCell (cellContents)>

<!ELEMENT frame (reportElement, box?, (break | line | rectangle | ellipse |
image | staticText | textField | subreport | pieChart | pie3DChart | barChart |
bar3DChart | xyBarChart | stackedBarChart | stackedBar3DChart| lineChart |
xyLineChart | areaChart | xyAreaChart | scatterChart | bubbleChart |
timeSeriesChart | highLowChart | candlestickChart | meterChart |
thermometerChart | multiAxisChart | stackedAreaChart | elementGroup |
crosstab | frame)*)>
```

iReportProperties.dtd

```
<?xml version="1.0" encoding="UTF-8"?>
<!ELEMENT iReportProperties (iReportConnection*, iReportProperty*)>

<!ELEMENT iReportProperty (#PCDATA)>
<!ATTLIST iReportProperty
    name NMTOKEN #REQUIRED
>

<!ELEMENT iReportConnection (connectionParameter*)>
<!ATTLIST iReportConnection
    name NMTOKEN #REQUIRED
    connectionClass NMTOKEN "it.businesslogic.ireport.connection.JDBCConnection"
>

<!ELEMENT connectionParameter (#PCDATA)>
<!ATTLIST connectionParameter
    name NMTOKEN #REQUIRED
>
```

iReportPlugin.dtd

```
<?xml version="1.0" encoding="UTF-8"?>

<!--
Document : iReportPlugin.dtd
Created on : 19 maggio 2004, 8.09
Author : Giulio Toffoli
Description: This DTD defines the XML descriptor for an iReport plugin.
-->

<!--
iReportPlugin is the root element.
ATTRIBUTES:
name The name of plugin
class The class that extends
it.businesslogic.ireport.plugin.IReportPlugin
loadOnStartup If true, the plugin will be instanced on iReport startup
hide If true, this plugin will not be visible on plugin menu
-->
```

```
<!ELEMENT iReportPlugin (Author?,Description?, IconFile?)>
<!ATTLIST iReportPlugin
        name NMTOKEN #REQUIRED
        class NMTOKEN #REQUIRED
        loadOnStartup (true | false) "false"
        hide (true | false) "false"
        configurable (true | false) "false"
>

<!ELEMENT Author (#PCDATA)>
<!ELEMENT Description (#PCDATA)>

<!--
Icon file should be a file in the classpath i.e. com/my/plug/in/icon.gif
Is used as optional icon for menu.
Dim: 16x16
-->
<!ELEMENT IconFile (#PCDATA)>
```

iReportFilesList.dtd

```
<?xml version="1.0" encoding="UTF-8"?>
<!ELEMENT iReportFilesList (iReportFile*)>
<!ELEMENT iReportFile (#PCDATA)>
```

APPENDIX C

■ ■ ■

iReport and JasperReports Versions

Table C-1 gives an overview of the versions of JasperReports used within the different versions of iReport.

Table C-1. *iReport Versions and Corresponding JasperReports Versions*

iReport Version	JasperReports Version
iReport 0.2.0	JasperReports 0.4.6
iReport 0.2.1	JasperReports 0.4.6
iReport 0.2.2	JasperReports 0.5.0
iReport 0.2.3	JasperReports 0.5.2
iReport 0.3.0	JasperReports 0.5.2
iReport 0.3.1	JasperReports 0.5.3
iReport 0.4.0	JasperReports 0.6.1
iReport 0.4.1	JasperReports 0.6.4
iReport 0.5.0	JasperReports 0.6.7
iReport 0.5.1	JasperReports 1.0.0
iReport 0.5.2	JasperReports 1.1.0 (not fully supported)
iReport 1.1.0	JasperReports 1.1.1
iReport 1.2.0	JasperReports 1.2.0
IReport 1.2.1	JasperReports 1.2.1

You can usually use iReport with a greater version of JasperReports by replacing `jaspereports.jar` in the `lib` directory.

Starting from version 1.2.0, iReport and JasperReports use the same version number.

Index

A

addConnectionImplementation() method, 189
afterColumnInit() method, 198
afterDetailEval() method, 199
afterGroupInit() method, 198
afterPageInit() method, 198
afterReportInit() method, 198
ancestor keyword, 141
anchors, 70
ANSI character set, 75
Ant, build.xml file and, 14
application development, GNU General Public
    License and, 297
Application Identifier setting, for barcodes, 69
Area charts, 211
Arrow tool, 42
attributes of attributes, syntax for, 138
Author tag, 263
Average calculation type, 95

B

Background setting, 51, 54
backgrounds, 27
backups of files, 289
bands (document sections), 25–27, 29, 50
    displaying list of, 97
    inserting elements into, 42
    modifying, 97
    resizing, 99
    splitting into pages, 280
Bar 3D charts, 211
Bar charts, 211
Bar Height setting, for barcodes, 69
Bar Wide setting, for barcodes, 69
Barcode Expression setting, 69
barcodes, 68
base name, 39
basic elements, 41, 50
BeanShell compiler (deprecated), 288
beforeColumnInit() method, 198
beforeDetailEval() method, 199
beforeGroupInit() method, 198
beforePageInit() method, 198

beforeReportInit() method, 198
Blank when null setting, 63
borders, 58
breaks (page/column), 69, 98
Bubble charts, 211
bucket expression, 240
build.xml file, 2, 14

C

calculation types, for variables, 95
Candlestick charts, 211
canvas objects, 55
case sensitivity, parameter names and, 111
CAST function (Oracle), 284
cells, crosstabs and, 243
character encodings, 39, 75
Chart tool, 211
charts, 211–219
    creating, 211
    properties of, 218
    subdatasets for, 221–231
Check for iReport updates plug-in, 269
Checksum setting, for barcodes, 69
children groups, 104
Cincom MDX query executer, XML/A
    connections and, 168
.class files, 15
class members, adding to scriptlets, 200
ClassCastException, 111
classes, JasperReports version compatibility
    and, 20
classes.jar file, 4
classicC.xml template, 204
classicT.xml template, 204
classic_landscapeT.xml template, 204
ClassNotFound exception, 4, 8
ClassNotFoundError exception, 132
close() method, 181
column breaks, 69
column footers, 27
column headers, 26, 246
Column variable reset type, 96
columnar templates, 11, 203

You've Read the Book, Now Work With the Experts

Save 10% on Any JasperSoft Training or Subscription

The Definitive Guide to JasperReports and The Definitive Guide to iReport are the best source of information for the JasperSoft market-leading reporting and business intelligence solutions.

Now that you've read the book, it's time to work with the experts. This coupon is worth 10% off any JasperSoft training class or product subscription, up to a US$250 value. Save on:

JasperSoft Training
Accelerate your implementation and reduce overall project costs through professionally delivered JasperSoft training. JasperSoft provides onsite and online courses at convenient hours and affordable prices. All classes are taught by trained and experienced instructors. JasperSoft classes include:

- Introduction to JasperReports
- Introduction to JasperServer

JasperSoft Subscriptions
JasperSoft is the market leader in open source business intelligence. JasperSoft open source business intelligence solutions are deployed worldwide for a range of users, applications, and industries. JasperSoft subscriptions include:

- JasperSoft BI Suite
- JasperAnalysis Professional
- JasperServer Professional
- JasperReports Developer Edition

To get 10% off today, please visit:

jaspersoft.com/experts

This offer cannot be combined with other discounts, has a maximum value of US$250, and cannot be applied retroactively.

LaVergne, TN USA
02 June 2010
184757LV00005B/144/P